# MEDIEVAL FURNITURE

# MEDIEVAL FURNITURE

## Plans and Instructions
## for Historical Reproductions

Daniel Diehl and Mark Donnelly

STACKPOLE
BOOKS

Published by
STACKPOLE BOOKS
5067 Ritter Road
Mechanicsburg, PA 17055
www.stackpolebooks.com

Printed in the United States of America

10 9 8 7 6 5 4 3 2 1

FIRST EDITION

*Cover design by Caroline Stover*
*Cover photo reproduced by kind permission of the Dean and Chapter of York Minster*

**Library of Congress Cataloging-in-Publication Data**

Diehl, Daniel.
    Medieval furniture: plans and instructions for historical reproductions / Daniel Diehl
and Mark Donnelly.—1st ed.
        p.    cm.
    Includes bibliographical references and index.
    ISBN 0–8117–2854–4
    1. Furniture—Drawings.  2. Furniture—Reproduction.  3. Furniture, Medieval.
I. Donnelly, Mark.  II. Title.
TT196.D56    1999
749.2'02—dc21
                                                                    99–17160
                                                                      CIP

To Jerry "Pop" Diehl.
Thanks for thirty years in the woodshop, a half century of patience,
and the courage to keep going.

# CONTENTS

# ACKNOWLEDGMENTS

The authors gratefully acknowledge the help of all who helped make this book a reality. Particular thanks are due to those who allowed us access to their marvelous furniture collections, many of which have never been photographed before. Thanks to His Grace the Duke of Rutland and the management of Haddon Hall, the Right Honorable Harry Orde-Powlett, the Dean and Chapter of York Minster, the Dean and Chapter of Hereford Cathedral, the Dean and Chapter of Winchester Cathedral, English Heritage, the Metropolitan Museum of Art and the Cloisters, Warwick Castle and Madame Tussaud's, and the University of Oxford. Special thanks are due to Mr. John Leask for his generosity in providing information for the chapter on woodcarving, Andy Elkerton of the Mary Rose Trust for his endless cooperation, the Ryedale Folk Museum for the rules of the game of Merrills, and Mr. Dave Greenhaigh and Mr. Chris Blythman for information and photographs on medieval locksets. We gratefully acknowledge the support of Kyle Weaver, our editor at Stackpole Books, for his patience and a continuing belief in the importance of our work.

Without the generous help and assistance of these people, the production of this book would not have been possible.

# INTRODUCTION

This book follows our previous work, *Constructing Medieval Furniture*, by a year and a half. Although we and Stackpole Books (to our delight) were thoroughly convinced of the need for such a book, the overwhelming popular response was both unexpected and gratifying.

Not only has the general public embraced our previous work, but we have found that it has become a permanent part of the libraries of such august institutions as the Metropolitan Museum, the Victoria and Albert Museum, and numerous theatrical houses and film production companies. This response has reinforced our belief that these rare and fine pieces of our physical past need to be carefully documented, ensuring that the work and techniques of medieval craftsmen are preserved for future generations to appreciate and emulate.

In *Constructing Medieval Furniture* we presented detailed histories and plans for sixteen pieces of furniture built between the early fourteenth and the mid-sixteenth centuries. In this new volume we present an entirely new selection of furniture and accessories dating from the thirteenth through the early seventeenth centuries, and from an even larger geographic area. Many of the pieces of furniture presented here have never been previously cataloged and some, like the thirteenth-century Church Pew, were erroneously listed many decades ago. We have attempted to present our readers with a wide variety of types and styles of furniture. Although there is not enough room in this book to take an in-depth look at the inventory of a complete household's furniture from any one historical era, we hope that we have presented a tantalizing look into the lives of a variety of people from a wide range

of time periods. By combining the pieces of furniture presented in this book with those contained in *Constructing Medieval Furniture*, we can begin to build up a fairly well-rounded picture of the material world of the Middle Ages. To augment the furniture itself, we have included a chapter on medieval decorating. We hope that this will give our readers a better idea of the settings in which these wonderful objects were meant to be viewed. Only when we can envision the medieval world as a physical whole can we begin to develop a reliable image of the lives of the people who lived in it. Certainly we believe that a more realistic view of the physical world of our medieval ancestors will help us to understand their way of life and the hardships and limitations their world imposed on them.

As in the previous book, we have been forced to make slight standardizations in the dimensions to compensate for irregularities in the original pieces, because of wear this furniture has suffered; well-meant, if historically incorrect, repairs; and the ravages of time. All of the plans are drawn to accurate scale, which in many cases will enable the craftsman to enlarge them to full size, allowing them to be used as templates from which the work can be copied directly.

The chapters on woodworking and metalworking that appear here are revised and updated from our previous book. Please take time to read them. They contain much new information that will help you make more authentic-looking and historically accurate medieval furniture.

In this new volume we have added projects that will challenge the skills of the reproduction craftsperson. For the metalworker, there are plans to build an accurate medieval lockset, and for the woodworker, there are a number of pieces with wonderful period carvings, including the quintessential element of medieval woodworking, the linenfold panel.

At the back of the book is an expanded and revised resource list to help the home craftsperson find hard-to-locate items, like proper medieval-style nails.

As in the previous book, there is information on locating many of the sites where the original furniture shown in this book can be viewed in person. If you have the opportunity, visit the original pieces. No matter how well documented they are here, there is nothing like seeing the original piece in its proper setting.

# MEDIEVAL DECORATING

Furniture of the Middle Ages, particularly pieces made prior to the fifteenth century, are extremely rare for fairly obvious reasons. Objects made from wood and other perishable substances, if constructed from the best material available and carefully wrought, will easily withstand two or three hundred years of normal wear or even neglect. But it is highly unlikely that at the end of four, five, or more centuries they will have survived the agents of slow destruction, fire, war, and simple changes in taste and increasing demands for comfort and convenience. There were far fewer people in the world than today, and a far smaller percent of that limited population could afford any sizable quantity of furnishings.

Above all, the greatest destroyer of furnishings and the spaces that house them is the weather. The cool, moist climate of Britain and northern Europe encourages rot and insect infestation. In the drier climate around the Mediterranean Sea, climactic conditions work to preserve objects. Consequently, it is a curious fact that we know more about the furniture and decorations in Egypt, under Ramses II, and Imperial Rome than we do about domestic appointments in England at the time of King John.

We do know, however, that medieval interiors were never intended to be seen as the rough-hewn, gray spaces that greet the modern tourist. Whether a seat of great power or a prosperous merchant's home, the medieval house had to reflect the social position of its owners in the grandest terms. The master of the house, in consideration of his power and authority, and the lady, in consideration of her family's comfort, demanded that their home contain as many comforts and conveniences as their budget could afford. To set the proper tone for their elevated lifestyle, the greatest care had to be given to the appearance of both public spaces and private living quarters. The walls of every room were finished with a coat of white lime plaster to remove the irregular surface of bare stone walls. After the plaster had dried for a year, the walls were painted and decorated in the latest styles.

Medieval houses of the better class were far brighter and more colorful than is generally recognized. The exterior of Barley Hall, a great half-timbered manor house in York, England, was painted bright red, but most houses, as well as most castles, were simply white-washed till they gleamed. No less surprising, their interiors were painted and decorated to an extent that would, by today's standards, be considered gaudy if not absolutely garish.

The great hall had to be both large and impressive enough to awe the steady stream of visitors, petitioners, and guests who came; walls were lavished with decorative motifs such as bold repeating designs featuring heraldic patterns and family coats of arms. Diamonds, checkerboard patterns, or zigzags reminiscent of flame-stitch fabric were popular; whatever the design of choice, it was almost always picked out in bright, bold colors that made the large, dark rooms look more inviting. Truly grand houses, such as manor halls and castles, were sometimes fitted with wood paneling. The boards, usually pine, were attached vertically to the wall, frequently extending from floor to ceiling or stopping at waist or shoulder height in the manner of modern wainscotting. Whatever its height, the finished wainscot was usually painted as brightly as the walls.

The focal point of every significant medieval room was its fireplace. Providing both heat and light, the fireplace from the twelfth century onward also displayed high-tech innovation. Previously, a central fire pit, which left rooms drafty and smoke blackened, provided heat and light. With the introduction of the chimney, rooms above the ground level could be heated for the first time, bringing bedrooms and private quarters into the mainstream of family life.

If fireplaces created heat, the introduction of window glass ensured that rooms retained their warmth. Exactly when glass became commonplace in private homes is a matter of contentious historical debate. Even the houses of wealthy merchants frequently lacked window glass until well into the Renaissance. In our previous book, *Constructing Medieval Furniture,* there is a fine example of a fifteenth-century window frame from an English merchant's house that clearly never held glass. Installing window glass during the Middle Ages was an obvious display of wealth. In the fourteenth century 1 square foot of glass cost the equivalent of a day's wages for a skilled craftsman; the product's sheer scarcity made its acquisition a near miracle. Were windows in manor houses and merchants' residences no more than holes closed with heavy wooden shutters that plunged the rooms into darkness from November until spring? Or did they contain glass like the windows in fine churches and cathedrals? Were they filled with something other than glass? The answer is probably "all of the above."

By the thirteenth century glass was certainly installed in the private quarters of some manor houses. Rooms of secondary importance and all windows in the homes of the less prosperous probably had windowpanes made from strips of boiled cow horn, oiled linen, or oiled parchment. Although not transparent, all of these materials allowed light to enter a room while keeping out the worst of the elements. What little artificial light there was in the central hall came from hanging chandeliers, several candelabra, or large pricket candlesticks. In other rooms the fireplace and small, hanging oil lamps made of fired clay supplied the only illumination. In castles where the ceilings were high enough to allow smoke to escape, rush torches held in iron rings were sometimes used as sidelights.

The combination of heat and light in the same room throughout the year had been unimaginable in the early twelfth century. But by the end of the century domestic life had changed significantly. As bedrooms and family sitting rooms (known as solars) became more comfortable, there was reason to heighten their visual appeal. The most common form of decoration in these rooms was achieved by marking the surface of a wall with lines to simulate the mortar joints of stone blocks. These strike lines, typically between ¼ and ⅜ inch wide, were usually bright red, although more subtle colors also appeared. The blocks' size varied with the room's size, but 8 inches in height and 14 inches in length were near the average. In the middle of alternating blocks, or sometimes on each block, the painting of stylized flowers or heraldic designs might add a splash of color. Window splays, the areas immediately around window frames, were sometimes decorated with designs entirely different from those on the rest of the wall. If you attempt to re-create a medieval period interior, it is good to remember that medieval paints and color washes would have been flat, lacking any sheen, and that most repeating designs were painted with stencils, which allow a design to easily be repeated indefinitely.

Where more elaborate effects were desired, allegorical paintings depicting scenes from the Bible, fable, and history were favorite subjects. Beasts and birds, both real and fabulous, cavorted and mingled with other subjects. The medieval version of a world map was a popular motif, as were wheels of fortune and scenes of Jesus' miracles. The walls of family chapels also displayed Bible stories, but just as often depicted death, decay, and the perils of Judgment Day—just to reinforce the importance of good behavior. Whatever the subject, the paintings were frequently life-size or larger. In Longthorp Tower in Cambridgeshire, England, there remains a wealth of painted decoration from the early fourteenth century. Here, in a single room 16 feet square, but of extraordinary height, are paintings of St. Anthony, a philosopher and his pupil, a king (possibly Edward III), the seven ages of man, the Nativity, part of the Apostles' Creed, a variety of aquatic birds decorating the dado (the wainscot area of the wall), and the wheel of the five senses, all of which are at least life-size, some larger.

On some occasions it was not profusion of design that attracted a client, but a particular color. It seems that England's Henry III was peculiarly fond of green. Most of the public and the private chambers in the majority of Henry's castles were painted green. In some rooms green walls were decorated with gold and silver stars, other rooms were painted to look as though they were covered with green draperies, and sometimes they were just plain green. Even the queen's rooms were painted green. Henry may have been a weak king, but he had very strong decorative tastes.

In many cases decorations were not painted directly on plastered walls, but on large linen panels.

Lying somewhere between oil paintings and fine tapestries, painted wall hangings were extremely popular among those of middling wealth, who were not rich enough to afford real tapestries but aspired to ape the fashions of the nobility. Painted hangings satisfied a taste for luxury within affordable bounds. To make them as insulative as real tapestries, painted hangings were often backed with woolen cloth. On some occasions the lower portion of a wall was adorned with painted hangings while the upper part had its decorations painted directly on the wall. Instructions for making a painted wall hanging appear in our previous book, *Constructing Medieval Furniture*.

Painted hangings appear in the 1360 inventory of Queen Isabella (mother of England's Edward III), which even includes painted covers for use on the seats and backs of benches. When Eleanor of Castile came to London in 1255 to marry the future Edward I, she covered not only the walls of her apartment with painted hangings and genuine tapestries, but also the floors. Conservative Londoners were scandalized at such decadence. The chronicler Matthew Paris recorded that this excessive pride excited laughter and derision.

Scandalous behavior aside, the desire for a serviceable floor covering is understandable. The heavy tapestries usually found only in the palaces of popes and kings would have been far too precious to walk on. In many medieval houses the ground floor was used as storage and the public rooms were located on the floor above. If this was the case, the floors of the hall and other rooms were no more than wooden planks. In those instances where the hall was located on the ground floor, it is likely that the floor would have been large flagstones. In more elaborate houses decorated tile would have replaced the flags, but in either case the floor would have been laid directly on the damp earth.

In the family quarters animal skins were placed at the bedside and in front of the fire to help keep cold feet warm. Floors in public rooms were left bare or covered with rushes, which during feasts or special occasions were strewn with herbs and sweet-smelling flowers, including basil, chamomile, daisies, sweet fennel, lavender, roses, mint, and violets, to freshen the air.

Theoretically the rushes were swept out and replaced each week, but often as not, they probably remained for weeks on end. Erasmus once observed that "beneath the rushes lay an ancient collection of beer, grease, fragments, bones, spittle, excrement of dogs and cats, and everything that is nasty."

Like their wall-mounted counterparts, bed hangings were made as thick as the householder's purse would allow. On cold winter nights only the weight of the hangings kept the sleeper's body warmth from disappearing through cold stone walls.

Obviously no home was complete without furniture but, curiously, historians have paid scant attention to medieval furniture, some of which exemplified the relatively modern dictum that "form follows function." The shape and size of medieval furniture were dictated solely by its purpose, any ornamentation being applied only to enhance the visual appeal of the piece. Due to technological limitations, medieval furniture often had a tendency to appear overly heavy. The sheer bulk of many of these pieces was relieved by intricate carvings.

Carved details were often picked out in bright colors, and on uncarved pieces, geometric designs and scenes from legend and the Bible were painted in manuscript-style illumination. Like painted wall hangings, furniture was frequently made by monks, who either sold their work to raise money for the monastery or, occasionally, gave it as gifts to noblemen who had provided endowments to their order.

The variety of furniture available to the medieval household was limited enough that most rooms would have appeared bare by modern standards, but it was more than adequate in a time when specialization had not yet become an obsession and in a place where possessions of any kind were few and precious. The most important and often the grandest piece of furniture in a medieval household was the master bed. We know this because it was the item most often bequeathed in wills. Curiously, despite their social importance at the time, there are virtually no surviving medieval beds. For this reason the beds in both this book and our previous one are taken from reproduction pieces.

In addition to bedroom furniture, the house's most impressive furnishings were usually found in the great hall. Here, the primary pieces of furniture were the high table and the armchairs for the lord and lady. Other members of the household important enough to sit at the high table probably had chairs without arms. The staff ate at collapsible tables and benches that could be cleared away between meals. The only other piece of furniture likely to be in the hall would be a dresser for linens or a "cup board," a tiered side table used to display the family's collection of pewter and silver. Even in well-to-do merchant families a half-dozen spoons, a few silver bowls, several ewers (pitchers), and a few silver-rimmed wooden drinking bowls known as mazers were an impressive collection of luxury goods.

Noblemen and merchants, required to travel on business, often had more than one house but seldom more than one set of furnishings. Even the most powerful lords were required by their position and general political instability to travel frequently, but they, too, had only a single set of furniture, which accompanied their every move. One did not leave anything of value behind, not even in a fortress manned by a garrison. Consequently, virtually all medieval furniture had to be portable. Chairs and tables, along with bed hangings, tapestries. and tableware, were packed into chests, coffers, and bourges (leather trunks) and loaded onto wagons, packhorses, and oxcarts that lumbered across the country from house to house. Confirmation of this nomadic lifestyle can be found in accounts such as those of France's Catherine de Médicis. In the inventory of her furniture we read, in reference to the sumptuous town house that Jean Bullant had built for her in the Rue des Deux-Ecus and the Rue du Four, that when she desired to eat there or stay in it, which was very often, she had the necessary furniture brought in, and her officers carried it back after her departure.

With so much moving it hardly comes as a surprise that trunks and chests were the most numerous pieces of furniture in the medieval household. Each different size and style had its own specific purpose and name. There were chests to store fine clothes and fur, ambries

to keep leftover food, and coffers to hold jewels and gold. The more exalted the contents of the chest, the more highly decorated and ornamented its exterior was likely to be. Among the highest levels of society, small coffers intended to hold jewelry were often covered in tooled leather, jewels, carved ivory, and chiseled gold ornaments—the chests were nearly as valuable as their contents. When the larger chests were not used to transport household goods from place to place, they stored clothes and linens in much the way that closets and dressers do today. Much of the remaining furniture in manor houses and castles were built-ins. Storage closets, like the one found here in the chapter on the York Minster Cabon, and window seats, popular because they provided a well-lighted place for ladies to do needlework and other handicrafts, were permanent fixtures built into the stone walls of the building. Even sinks and hand troughs, where they existed, were built directly into the wall.

With its brightly decorated walls and painted hangings around beds, as well as heraldic banners, carved and painted furniture, and massive stone fireplaces, the medieval manor was a place filled with bright color and rich design. Although undoubtedly not up to twentieth-century standards of health and convenience, the homes of the medieval rich were far from the cold, decayed gray spaces that we now associate with castles. All things considered, it is unlikely that in eight or nine centuries our own homes will appear nearly as inviting as surviving castles and manor houses do today.

# WOODWORKING

A few general observations and suggestions about woodworking methods and materials will facilitate the construction of the furniture described in this book.

## MEDIEVAL WOODWORKING

During the Middle Ages most furnishings were fashioned from freshly hewn, or green, wood—the technique of aging and curing wood was unknown. Working with fresh wood simplified the woodworker's tasks. Green wood clogs modern power tools, but it aided the use of primitive hand tools made from a grade of metal far inferior to that used in modern implements. Furniture fabrication in the woodland eliminated the need to move wood from one place to another. It may seem silly today, but in a labor-intensive society the elimination of any needless effort makes labor more efficient.

Working green wood demanded methods of construction different from those that we will use when working with cured wood. The medieval woodworker prepared sections of furniture that were to be joined with dowel pins by drilling holes that were slightly misaligned. The shrinkage of the drying wood lined up the segments. Modern lumber will not contract; holes can therefore be drilled in a straight line.

The medieval forest often sheltered temporary manufacturing communities. Woodsmen felled trees; sawyers shaped them into boards either by cutting them with saws (hence the title sawyer) or by forcing them apart with wedges and sledgehammers; craftsmen then created practical items from the fresh lumber. Coopers formed barrels and buckets, carpenters fashioned furniture, and wrights produced wheels and carts.

## REPRODUCTION TECHNIQUES

Some medieval methods can be used by the modern woodworker. When visible work is executed with hand tools, the authenticity is enhanced. Beveling the edges of a board with drawknives and spokeshaves replicates the original and vicariously transports you to the remote forest shop where it was created.

Using hand tools requires some experimentation. Reserve the custom milled oak you ordered to make that wonderful chest, and practice first on scrap lumber.

## GENERAL CONSTRUCTION

Medieval construction techniques were of the type that architect Frank Lloyd Wright once called "cut and butt." The rudimentary tools and technology of the Middle Ages necessitated that basic assemblage be simple. The only procedure in this book that would not be considered elementary is the excessive use of rabbet joins on the Ambry.

### Doweling

Maple, because of its hardness, makes a superior commercial dowel. Use any species of wood to build your furniture, but hold it together with maple or birch dowels. Whittle your own doweling—if you are a true medievalist—or purchase it at any lumber, hardware, or hobby store.

The first step in fastening a wood joint with a dowel is to align the segments to be joined, clamping them securely. Select a drill bit identical to the size of the specified doweling on the materials list. If the construction plans do not specify locations, consult the drawings to determine where to drill the holes. To

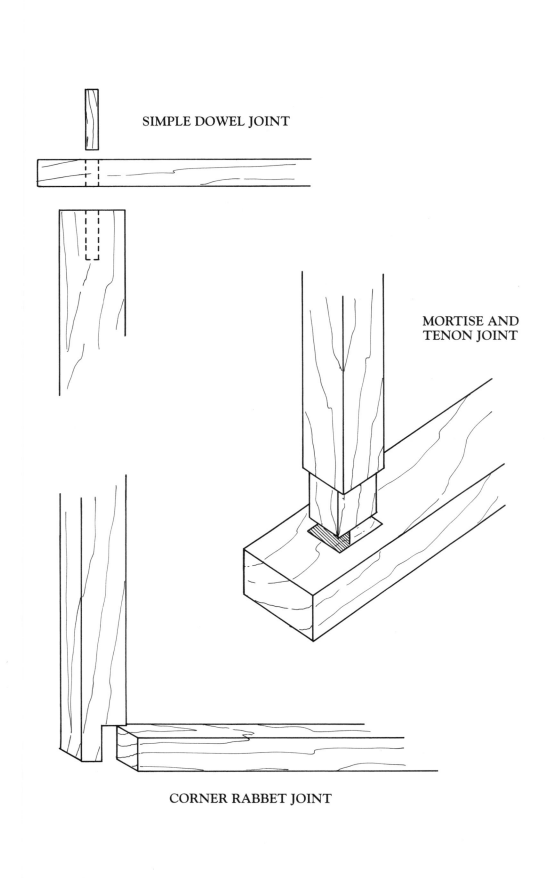

SIMPLE DOWEL JOINT

MORTISE AND
TENON JOINT

CORNER RABBET JOINT

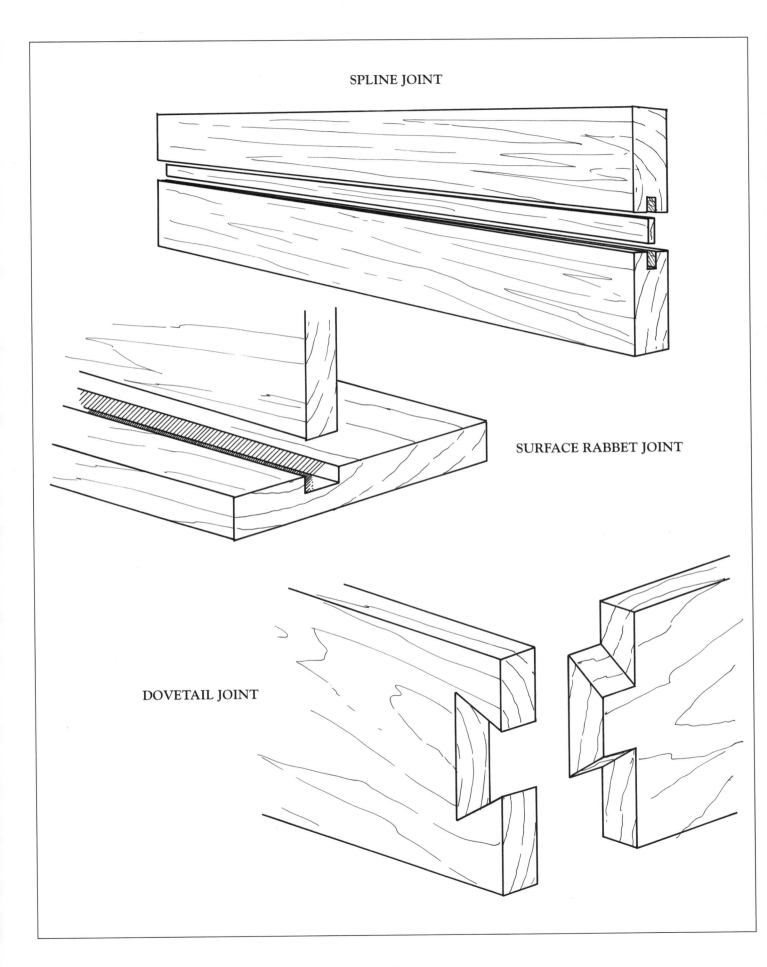

SPLINE JOINT

SURFACE RABBET JOINT

DOVETAIL JOINT

prepare the dowel, cut a length no more than 1 inch longer than the depth of its designated hole. To ease entry, slightly round the end of the dowel. Light sanding or rubbing with a bar of soap will permit it to be tapped smoothly into place. Tap the dowel gently into the drilled hole with a wooden mallet—four or five soft strokes should lodge a 2-inch dowel. Too snug a dowel may break off before it is seated, or it may eventually split the surrounding wood. Too loose a dowel may cause the piece of furniture to wobble and eventually come apart.

### Clamps

The use of clamps is frequently recommended in this book to hold segments of furniture together while a work is being assembled. Best for this purpose are long bar clamps, or cabinet clamps. They generally extend far enough to press together even the largest section of furniture.

The metal jaws of clamps may bite into the wood and leave deep scars that will need to be sanded out later. To prevent such marks, pad the jaws of the clamp with a thin piece of wood slightly larger than the clamp's jaws.

## WOOD

Oak and pine are the staple woods in the furniture industry today, as they were for the construction of furniture during the Middle Ages. If you live in the United States or Canada, use white oak rather than red oak. The uneven grain in red oak complicates carving. The costlier white oak's straighter grain cuts smoother and is a better choice if carving is involved. White oak resembles the English oak used to originally construct many of our choices for this book. Exotic woods, such as walnut and lime, are occasionally suggested for our projects. Finding these woods may be difficult; alternative materials will also be recommended.

Pine boards may warp over time. A pine project requires a straight-grained, knot-free fir. A clear, straight wood looks better and is less likely to warp.

### Timber

Tree species have not changed in the past millennium, but the way in which boards are cut has evolved. In medieval times, trees were plentiful and tools were primitive, so the boards used in the production of furniture were thicker and wider than today's mill-cut lumber. To duplicate medieval dimensions, it will be necessary to have your wood custom milled. The expense of custom-milled wood is justified in the quest for authentic-looking furniture.

Using custom-milled lumber will give your furniture a medieval look. At times the structural integrity of the piece compels the use of bulkier lumber, or chunkier boards may be needed to make it fit together as it is shown in the schematics.

Recycling old lumber can evoke the period look without ordering oversize boards. In the demolition of old barns and houses, planks and beams—often in dimensions larger than can be found in new material at any price—surface. A number of architectural salvage firms across the United States and Great Britain offer old construction materials; a few of these are listed in the resource guide at the back of the book. To locate other firms, look under "salvage" in the telephone directory, check with local historical or preservation groups, or search the Web.

### Joined Lumber

Modern mill-dimension lumber will never approximate ancient timber. A solution is to glue together standard-cut boards to produce thicker or wider stock without the expense of ordering custom millwork. Many lumbermills and most cabinet shops will glue up standard-dimension lumber to provide boards of any width and thickness, executing joints that will be as strong as the wood itself and inconspicuous when they are incorporated into the furniture. The practiced woodworker and the adventurous beginner may find that the most cost-effective solution is to glue their own boards. Spread a thin, even coat of cabinetmaker's glue on the faces that are to be joined, let it set for three or four minutes, and then press the glued surfaces together, clamping them tightly. Take care when you tighten the clamps; excess glue may ooze out around the edges as the boards are being pulled together. An extra pair of hands is a help; keep a damp rag handy to wipe glue off the edges of the boards. The next day, remove the clamps to find a board as strong as if it were a single piece.

Gluing boards together for greater width is more challenging. Of the several ways, the simplest is to glue the edges and clamp them as just described. Care is needed to not only clamp them tightly together but to hold them flat while the glue dries. The resultant seam will never be as strong as its components and may fracture with age or if subjected to undue stress.

Dowels or splines can unite the boards to strengthen this seam. Doweling and splining, though not particularly difficult, do require the proper tools and a few trial runs. You will find instructions for doweling boards together in the chapter on constructing the Merrills Board, because doweling is integral to the construction of that piece.

Determine which edges of the boards are to be joined together by finding the straightest and squarest edges on the boards with which you are working. Stand the boards in a vise, one at a time, and locate and mark the center of the board. Using an adjustable square as a guide (by setting the square just slightly less than half the width of the board), place a pencil on the front edge of the square, and slowly move the square and pencil simultaneously along the length of the board.

When the edges have been marked, place the boards side by side in the vise so that the edges to be joined together are both facing up. Using the adjustable square, mark a line across both boards at intervals of 4 to 6 inches. Allow for the fact that your boards are probably longer than they will be when they are cut to their final length. Do not dowel closer than 2 inches from the final edge of the board. Designate the location of each dowel with an X.

To ensure that the holes for the dowels are drilled exactly in the center, and perfectly straight, it is best to use a doweling jig. Jigs are available from any good hardware store, lumberyard, or tool store and are not terribly expensive. Certainly, if you plan to do much flat doweling, they are a worthwhile investment. Position the doweling jig directly above the center of the X that marks the position of the dowel, and drill the pilot hole to the proper depth. Under normal circumstances a ⅜-inch dowel, sunk 1 inch to 1½ inches into each board, is adequate. If you are doweling a chest lid, or some other structure that will apply a lot of stress on the joint, sink the dowel 2 or 2½ inches into each board. For heavy stress joints use a dowel ½ inch in diameter. If you do not have access to a doweling jig, use a nail or center punch to mark the center of the X. This will guarantee that the drill does not slip off-

center. Holding the drill plumb and level, drill the hole to the proper depth as described above.

Cut the dowels ⅛ to 3⁄16 inch shorter than the combined depth of the holes and slightly round the ends of the dowels.

When all the pilot holes have been drilled, place a few drops of white glue in each hole in one board, and tap the dowels into place. Now place a few more drops of glue into the corresponding holes on the opposite board and a small bead along the edge of the board, and set the point of the dowels into the mouth of the corresponding pilot holes. Gently tap the boards together with a wooden mallet, or pull them together with cabinet clamps. In either case, be certain that the dowels are pulled together evenly along the length of the board; if they are forced out of line, they may crack or break. When the boards touch, pull them snugly together with cabinet clamps, if possible.

## ABOUT THIS BOOK'S DRAWINGS

The original pieces of medieval furniture, with few exceptions, were the models for the drawings in this book. Most of the furniture is not in square or even symmetrical because of the methods used in making medieval furniture and the assault of time. To compensate, we have standardized dimensions and removed many of the slight variations intrinsic in rudimentary building.

The drawings, however, are true to scale. Fragments of carving or other detail can be enlarged on a photocopier to the needed size and transferred as a pattern directly onto the surface of the wood. If such an enlargement would be of specific benefit, such as in reproducing patterns for carved or cutout work, it is noted in the individual chapter.

We have featured the wood grain pattern wherever possible. This makes the drawings prettier and accurately indicates the direction of the wood grain—an important consideration if there is some question as to the direction of the grain in a panel or a particular board's orientation.

# Metalworking

Hinges, banding straps, locks, lock plates, forged nails, and several styles of pulls and handles constitute the hardware used on this book's furniture. Broad metalworking instructions are provided in this chapter; the procedure for fabricating these articles does not vary from project to project. Guidelines for any nonstandard work will be covered in the individual chapters.

## TOOLS

In the Middle Ages cabinet hardware was created by a blacksmith working with forge and anvil. Reproduction of hardware by the original methods is ideal, but most of us lack a forge. We will, therefore, reproduce the same look with tools that can duplicate some of the smith's methods in a modern shop; other items will be made with the use of completely modern equipment.

To construct the metalwork in this book requires only a few simple tools. A band saw with a metal cutting blade is ideal for cutting the metal. In its place a jigsaw or reciprocal (saber) saw, with metal cutting blade, will do.

A heavy vise and two shaping hammers—ball peen rather than claw—will also be needed. One of the shaping hammers should have a 10- to 12-ounce head and the other a 16- to 18-ounce head. Flat, round, and triangular steel files will be required for finishing the metal. Each shape of file should be available in at least two different grades (one for coarse work and one for finishing) and in two sizes (medium and small). At the very least, you will need small fine-grade files to get into tight corners.

You probably don't have access to a real forge; therefore, you will need a welding torch to heat the metal for shaping.

Of the two suitable types of welding torches, the better is a combination oxygen-acetylene torch. It simplifies metalworking, because it quickly provides great amounts of heat. Acceptable but less efficient is a single-tank acetylene gas torch, which will take a much longer time to heat the metal to the point of malleability. The ubiquitous hand-held propane torch simply will not provide the necessary heat to accomplish our projects. A pair of welder's gloves and goggles will shield your hands and eyes from the searing metal.

A mandrel is needed to curve the heated metal into decorative shapes. A mandrel—two round metal pins, each ⅛ inch in diameter and 2 inches in length, inserted into a metal base—is easily made from stainless or cold-rolled steel.

The diagram at the end of this chapter will guide you. Cut a steel base that is 1 inch thick and 4 or 5 inches in length to a width that will conform to the jaws of your vise (at least 1 inch wide). Drill three ½-inch holes in the mounting block. Holes one and two should be spaced ¼ inch apart, and hole three should be ½ inch from hole two. These holes hold metal pins, which should be set firmly but remain free enough that they can be relocated when necessary.

You can always engage a local blacksmith or iron-monger to fashion metal findings for your medieval furniture if you lack the equipment or the skills necessary for these projects. Several reputable blacksmiths and sources for premade period hardware appear in the resource guide at the back of this book.

## MATERIALS

The metal used in these plans is usually of a type called flat stock—sold in straps or sheets that are wider than they are thick. Other kinds of metal are round stock, which is a round bar of steel, and square stock, which is a square steel bar.

The various sizes of the assorted types of metal stock necessary to our projects are commercially available. Metal thickness will usually be provided in standard dimensions of inches. The materials list at the end of each chapter will detail the amount and dimensions necessary to manufacture the hardware for each piece of furniture.

## FORGING METAL

We suggest making several trial pieces before you actually attempt any of the finished hardware, if you are new to forging metal. Start by bending a piece of flat stock 1¼ inches wide and ⅛ inch thick into a 90-degree angle. Many of the hinges and bands on the furniture covered in this book need this stock size piece of metal. Shaping a right angle is both a simple procedure and one that will have to be performed every time a hinge or a band laps around a corner on an article of furniture.

### Bending Right Angles

Insert a segment of flat stock, at least 1 foot in length, vertically into the jaws of the vise, with 2 or 3 inches of stock protruding below the jaws of the vise. To avoid a crooked bend, the stock must be at right angles (90 degrees) to the top of the vise.

Heat the 2 inches of stock immediately above the vise's jaws in preparation for bending. As you move the tip of the flame around on the area being heated, do not hold it on one spot or the stock may melt at the point of contact with the fire. A pink-red glow indicates that the metal is ready to be formed. It is helpful if one person heats the metal while another does the actual forging. Preserving the metal's heat, allows it to be shaped more effectively.

To form the right angle, hammer where the heated stock meets the vise's jaws while gently pulling the stock's free end toward the forging surface (the top of the vise) with a pair of pliers or a set of vise grips. To clarify this, imagine that the metal is as flexible as a long, thin piece of wood. If you clamp one end of a thin piece of wood in a vise, you can easily flex the opposite end. You do essentially the same thing with a piece of metal by heating it in order to make it flexible. Strike the surface of the newly formed angle two or three times directly at the angle of the bend where it lies against the vise. The resultant sharp corner fits snugly against the wood's edge. Practice will yield worthy results.

### Using the Mandrel

The mandrel is used to shape the loops on each half of the hinge where they are joined together with a pin and to forge decorative curls on hinges and straps.

A good practice exercise is to heat 1 or 2 inches at the end of a section of flat stock and to insert the end between two closely set mandrel pins. Gently tug on the tip of the bar and lightly strike the hot metal with a forging hammer—while steadily applying heat. Slowly pull the metal into loops of any size. The hotter the metal, the more malleable. Practice forming loops that fit snugly around the mandrel pin, the exact dimensions for accepting hinge pins.

### Hinges

Strap hinges, some of them essential to the banding that holds the furniture together, anchor many of the chest lids shown in this book; most are made of ⅛-inch-thick flat stock.

The two halves of the hinge are usually joined together with three interlocking loops, one on the hinge's shorter end and two on the long end. Joined together with a pin, this position of the hinge is called the spine. Use a band saw (or other saw) to cut out the metal fingers (tangs) that are used to shape the loops as shown on the drawings on the next page. Mold the loops on the mandrel after removing the burrs from the sawn edges. To ensure that the hinge operates properly, comply with any variations in the directions concerning the length of the tangs and position of the loops.

Both butt hinges and flat hinges are used on the furniture shown in this book; they differ slightly in the shape of the spine, but their basic construction, encompassing the arrangement of the tangs on the hinge stock, is identical. Diagrams on both types of hinges appear at the end of this chapter.

### Hinge Pins

To fashion the hinge pins, use a section of round stock that fits snugly, but not tightly, into the holes in the hinge spine. Cut the pin about 1 inch longer than the hinge's width. Clamp the pin vertically in a vise so that only about ⅛ inch of metal projects above the vise's surface. Heat the pin's tip. Strike the hot end of the pin with the flat end of the forging hammer until it balloons slightly, like a mushroom cap. Round the edges with the ball end of the hammer. After the pin has cooled, insert it into the hinge. Trim the pin, if necessary, so that slightly less than ¼ inch extends

# HINGE CONSTRUCTION

## LAYING OUT THE TANGS

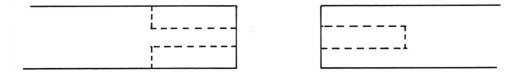

## CUTTING THE TANGS

## FORGING THE BUTT HINGE

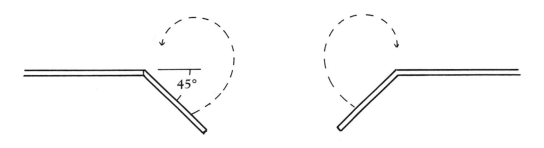

45°

## COMPLETED SECTIONS OF BUTT HINGE (SIDE VIEW)

# HINGE CONSTRUCTION

## FORGING THE FLAT HINGE

## COMPLETED SECTIONS OF FLAT HINGE (SIDE VIEW)

## COMPLETED SECTIONS OF BUTT OR FLAT HINGE (FRONT VIEW)

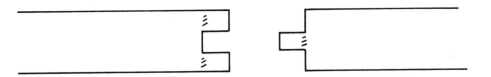

FORMING THE HINGE PIN          THE COMPLETED HINGE

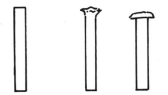
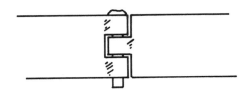

beyond the hinge's end. Invert the assembled hinge on a forging area, so that the unflared end of the pin faces upward. Heat the exposed end of the pin, and carefully flare it with the forging hammer; beating too tightly against the hinge might cause it to bind.

The ends of hinges and their associated straps and bands are occasionally formed into ornamental shapes; the mandrel is an invaluable tool for this job. In this volume we will address this item in the chapter dealing with the construction of the Cathedral Cabon.

## Banding

Allow several extra inches of metal when creating hinges or bands that extend around the sides of a piece of furniture. Some of the length will disappear in the act of bending the metal at the corners.

Be patient when banding a furniture case; bend one corner and fit it into place before marking the position of the next bend. Heating and bending alter the length of the metal stock in unpredictable ways.

## Forging Tip

To distress the smooth exterior of metal bar stock, lay it on the vise or an anvil and heat 3 to 4 inches of its length at a time with the torch, marring the surface and edges with the round end of your forging hammer. Eliminate the regular edges of the metal, but do not distort or misshape the stock.

## Lock Plates

A plate called an escutcheon shields the area around the opening in the wood through which the key is inserted. Escutcheons are usually constructed of flat stock that is $1/16$ inch thick, far thinner than the hinges and bands on a chest. Patterns for lock plates accompany the furniture drawings. The lock plates can usually be cut out of flat stock. The edges of the plate can then be heated, distressed slightly, and filed smooth.

## NAILS

Applying hinges and hardware requires fairly large quantities of hand-forged nails. Simple cut nails lack the large heads necessary to secure the hardware.

Medieval nails were often longer than the thickness of the wood into which they were driven. The expedient solution to this problem was simply to curve over the end of the nail on the interior of the chest, which also added strength. Such nails were called clinch nails. Some modern reproduction forged nails are too brittle to bend without breaking; if you are unsure whether they can be clinched, experiment on a scrap of wood. It is technically possible to make nails by hand; we commend your persistence if you do, but we don't recommend it. Rather, purchase nails of the right size, length, and head style from a supplier of reproduction nails. Several sources of reproduction nails, on both sides of the Atlantic, are listed in the resource section at the back of this book. One of them even supplies clinch nails.

## METAL FINISHES

To give a uniform dark finish to your newly fashioned metalwork and to prevent it from rusting, we suggest a natural oil finish. There are two ways to finish metal objects. The first utilizes olive oil—the same substance that was used as a finish on medieval woodwork. Clean the forged metal thoroughly with a wire brush, and then coat the surface evenly with olive oil. Apply an even heat to the metal for 30 to 45 seconds, either with a torch or a kitchen stove. Heat it just to the point where it cannot be touched. Blacken the oil; do not burn it off the metal. Allow the metal to cool naturally, and wipe it with a clean, dry cloth.

The second method is not dissimilar to the first. Fill a large metal pan to a depth of $1\frac{1}{2}$ to 2 inches with heavyweight oil—used motor oil is perfect for this purpose. Heat the metalwork with a torch until it is hot, but not glowing. Quench the hot metal in the pan of oil. Wipe the excess oil from the metal.

# WOODCARVING

Easily worked and readily available, yet tough and durable, wood has been a basic building material for thousands of years. Wood was once used to make everything from kitchen utensils to church decorations, and the traditional skills of the woodcarver were vital to the community. Much woodcarving was probably done by ordinary people who fashioned everything from bowls and spoons to furniture and plowshares for their own use. There are clear signs, nevertheless, of the artistry of woodcarvers in the beautiful wooden boats of the Norse invaders and in early churches (though the oldest surviving example of church carving in Britain—at South Cerney in Gloucester—dates back only to the twelfth century).

It was in the Middle Ages, however, that ornamental carving really flourished, for the thousands of churches that were built in the fourteenth and fifteenth centuries provided a wealth of opportunities for carvers to show their skill in decoration. Although they continued to fashion all the items demanded for everyday life, the medieval woodcarvers began to create the beautiful rood screens, bench ends, and other ecclesiastic furnishings that made the Middle Ages the golden age of carving.

Like stonemasons, medieval woodcarvers worked in teams or schools under a master carver—many wood carvers were actually stonemasons as well. Some of the carvings that they made are simple scrollwork. Some are religious icons. The medieval church also housed the unconscious fantasies of the age. With chisel and gouge, master carvers created weirdly wonderful creatures—dragons, warriors, severed heads, hermaphrodites, and one-legged sciapods who used their limbs as sunshades—as well as the common scenes of daily life that they saw all around them.

Sadly, church patronage, which had brought the woodcarvers so much work, halted abruptly during the English Reformation in the sixteenth century; with it ended the great age of ornamental carving.

## THE CARVER'S CRAFT

There are three basic styles of woodcarving: incised, relief, and in the round. In incised carving, also known as chip carving, the design, usually a very simple one, is cut into the wood. The first project in this book, the Merrills Board, is carved with simple incised lines. Relief carving is technically the opposite of incised carving; here the area around the design is cut away to leave the design standing in high relief. Seven of the projects in this book involve relief carvings, three of which are linenfold panel carving, which is covered as a separate section below. Carving in the round, the final technique, is actually the sculpting of wood, an advanced form of traditional whittling. One of our projects, the sixteenth-century Spanish Settle, involves fully formed, carved figures.

The carving, as with the general construction, becomes more complex as the book progresses. It is best, therefore, to commence with projects near the book's beginning. As with all of the techniques described in this work, it is wise to experiment on a piece of scrap wood before moving on to the finished piece. Creating a prototype certainly takes time, but carving is about patience and persistence; if you are an inexperienced carver, it will prove to be time well spent.

### Incised Carving

The simplest form of carving occurs in this book only in the construction of the Merrills Board; we deal with incised carving in that chapter.

## RELIEF CARVING

1. Transferring the Design: Enlarge the carving plans in this book on a copying machine to make an accurate template that can be transferred directly to the wooden panel. The exact degree of enlargement varies from piece to piece, but the scale will be listed in the individual chapter.

The hatched part of the drawing, in all cases, is the area to be cut away. After the transfer of the design to the wood, accurately indicate the hatched areas to prevent confusion while carving.

2. Establishing an Outline: Begin by cutting around the edges of the design with a sharp carving knife that is held at a 90-degree angle to the wood. Too deep a cut will cause the knife to slip in the tough oak grain. A first cut of 1/32 inch is sufficient. Penetrate several times; in each instance sink the blade slightly deeper into the wood until after three or four passes you have reached a depth of nearly 1/8 inch.

Introduce the knife into the area to be cut away by placing the blade on a 45-degree angle to the wood, about 1/8 inch from the original cut. With several passes of the knife, remove a V-shaped sliver of wood around the entire design. Be sure that you cut this sliver of wood from the hatched area of the drawing. Enlarge this initial cut to a depth of 3/16 inch. The width of the cut is irrelevant because the entire hatched area will be eliminated.

3. Removing the Waste Wood: Now that the edges of the carving are established, remove the entire hatched area of the design to the depth of 3/16 inch. Two possible approaches for removing the excess wood suggest themselves. Certainly the easier is to use a Dremel tool with a router attachment. The most proper historical approach is to use small chisels or spoon-shaped gouges to remove the superfluous wood. Chisels require care; do not cut too deep or too fast. The chisel's sharp edge can easily pierce the walls of the design, possibly ruining the sharp edges of the design itself.

After removing the excess wood, clean up the edges and corners of the design with a fine chisel or carving knife. A small chisel will also remove marks left by a Dremel tool on the surface of the wood.

4. Background Pattern: In medieval as well as later incised carving, the background area of the design (the area from which wood has been cut away) is often textured with a waffled pattern.

Composed of a series of tiny inverted pyramids, arranged in a 1/8-inch center grid pattern, this overall field simulated depth and prevented loose wood fibers in the carved wood from chipping away. Such designs are encountered on the background of the Writing Slope, behind the small carvings at the top of the Cathedral Cabon, and around the leg designs on the Barrel Chair.

The waffled texture was impressed into the wood by tapping a nail lightly into the surface of the wood at close intervals or impressing several points into the wood at one time with a small, punchlike tool with a textured face. A leatherworker's tool, designed for exactly this purpose, can be adapted for use on soft wood. Working with oak, however, calls for a small nail, a tack hammer, and infinite patience.

After the carving work is finished, the corners and edges cleaned with a sharp knife, and the background textured, the entire carved area is sanded lightly to eliminate splinters, loose wood fibers, and sharp edges.

## WOOD SCULPTURE

Fully rendered carvings, as mentioned above, are used only on the Spanish Settle. We have included this somewhat complex process here rather than in the chapter on the Spanish Settle itself.

1. Transferring the Designs: Cut the blocks of wood to the dimensions shown on the plans.

Transfer the drawings of the sculptures (two dogs and two lions) onto all four faces of the blocks. All four faces of both designs are shown in the plans, so this should be a relatively easy operation. Do note that there are a left and a right facing version of each of the animals, so the drawings will have to be turned over to produce one of each pair.

2. Roughing Out a Figure: Cut away the sharp corners of the block so that it begins to take the shape of the animal. Cut away only enough wood so that the carved area meets the outline of the figure. Next, carve away excess wood around the main elements of the figure, such as between the legs, around the muzzle, and in front of the lion's shield. Now begin to shape the limbs of the animal by rounding the legs and the haunches and defining the recesses between the hips and the body. Begin to form the lion's tail and mane at this point.

3. Finishing the Figures: These figures are not terribly lifelike, nor is the carving fully developed. The lions' haunches remain rather flat where they touch the outside of the blocks. Much of the detail on the dogs' faces has been worn away by the constant wear of

human hands. Decide whether to leave the dogs' faces with a soft, worn look or to give them the detail that they undoubtedly once had.

Execute the finishing details such as the dogs' collars and the lions' shields with either carving knives or a Dremel tool, whichever you are more comfortable with. Cut between the animals' toes, around their eyes, and through the waves in the lions' manes with a small V-gouge. Make the edges around the dogs' collars, as well as the wavy, incised line on the collars themselves, with a V-gouge, but detail the rounded edges on the collars with a fine file or sandpaper.

4. Finish shaping the animals, then sand their entire surface to eliminate any knife marks. Smoothly finished figures will look more like the originals, particularly the worn dogs.

## CARVING LINENFOLD PANELS

Historical Background: No one knows how the tradition of the linenfold began. The voluminous folds of heavy medieval clothing figure prominently in almost all medieval art, from painting and sculpture to stained glass. The first carved linenfold panels seem to have appeared sometime before the mid-fifteenth century and remained popular for another two hundred years. The linenfold design from the front of the Paneled Coffer serves as a working model for this project. It is a relatively simple pattern and not terribly different from the linenfold panels used in the Settle (see the photograph in the color section). The panel is reproduced here at 50 percent actual size; you can enlarge the drawings and transfer them directly to the wood panel. These are not particularly complicated linenfold designs, but if you are a novice woodcarver, make several practice pieces in a soft wood, such as pine or fir, before you test your skills on a finished piece of oak.

1. Transferring the Design: Enlarge both the front and the end views of the design and transfer them to the panel. Transfer these designs to the face and both ends of the board to see through the peaks and valleys of the design as you carve away excess wood. Center the design on the board's face, allowing for the edges and rabbets that project beyond the design itself.

2. Roughing Out the Design: With a table saw or radial arm saw, cut the rabbets around the edges of the panel to firmly establish the area of the board that will be worked into a linenfold pattern. This eliminates the need to rework the edges of the board once the delicate carvings have been executed. Work the undulating

shape of the linenfold to the top and the bottom edges of the design area; cutting out the shaped ends comes later.

If you are lucky enough to have a radial arm saw, remove some of the excess material from the face of the panel itself, as shown in the drawing of the preliminary grooves. Using a table saw necessitates turning the panel on its face; take extra care not to cut too deep or too close to the finished surface. The original implements were chisels and gouges. If you use strictly traditional tools, be very careful not to cut too close to the finished lines, either on the panel's face or in the depth of the folds. Remove a few centimeters of wood with each pass; do not take a large bite.

3. Shaping the Panel: When the bulk of the excess wood has been removed, you can actually begin to give the folds in the panel their final shape. First, be certain that the surface that will form the top of the low-lying ribs (that is, the very center of the three valleys that run through the length of the panel) is smooth and even. Plane this area with a sharp, narrow chisel, a miniature molding plane, or sandpaper. The tops of the four raised ribs should already be flat and level because they are actually the original surface of the board.

Next, redraw the ribs that run down the center of the low-lying areas of the panel. Follow the instructions above on establishing an outline, in the section on relief carving, to delineate the edges of the ribs, both those on the surface of the panel and those in the low-lying areas. The ribs will stand out in clear, sharp relief from the surrounding areas.

With a U-shaped gouge or a large round file, shape the concave hollows in the panel. Use the file if you are unsure of your ability to control a gouge. Be careful not to remove too much wood; you still have to shape the convex curves on either side of the ribs.

Work the convex curves of the design with a carving knife or a shallow U-shaped gouge held upside down. A small triangular file, whose shape allows you to penetrate the tight recesses next to the low-lying ribs, can also be used. When the ribs and the concave and convex shapes of the panel surface have all been worked, lightly sand the panel surface. Be careful not to soften the carving's crisp lines. Some knife marks can show; they still appear on original pieces after centuries of wear.

Carving the Ends: This job is relatively easy, because there are no undercuts or complicated back folds on these panels. Sketch in the shape of the top

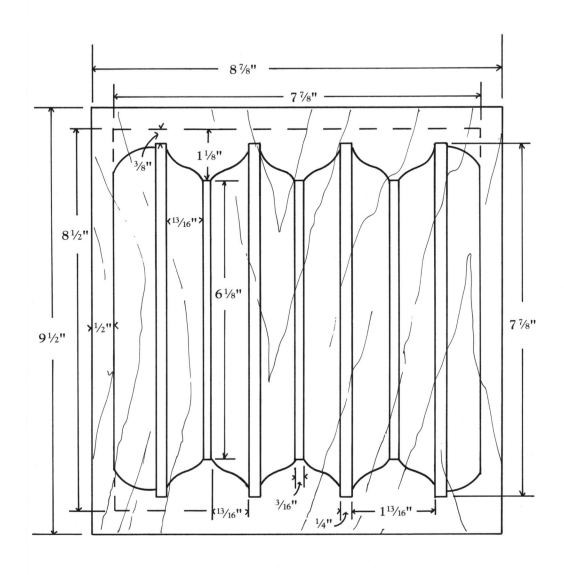

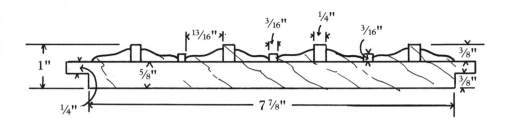

**CARVING THE LINENFOLD PANEL**

18

and the bottom ends of the panels, using the templates as reference. The panel is no longer a flat surface; you will not be able to simply trace the template onto it.

Following the instructions above for establishing an outline, in the section on relief carving, establish the edges of the panel ends. When you have cut the ends free to approximately half the designated depth, begin to remove the waste wood at the ends of the panel with a sharp chisel. Be very careful not to cut into the delicate ends of the ribs. Repeat the procedure until you have revealed the panel's full depth. Use a carving knife to clean up any rough spots around the edges of the panel, then smooth out the background with a sharp chisel and sandpaper.

# LOCKS

The mechanical lock has been used to protect the contents of chests, cabinets, and trunks since the early Middle Ages. Since the tenth century they were common enough that even the Vikings routinely installed them on their sea chests. The design of these early locks was so successful that, except for minor refinements, the standard domestic lockset remained almost unchanged until the end of the nineteenth century. Any lock that can be operated with an old-fashioned skeleton key is based on the same design as the medieval lock.

Sadly, virtually all the locks that originally protected the contents of the chests and the cupboards shown in this book have been removed or replaced. Medieval locks are extremely rare because the delicate mechanism of a lock can easily fall victim to rust and corrosion. In many instances, heavy, surface-mounted hasps or simple wooden turn buttons have obviously been retrofitted to pieces of furniture that still have a lock plate that, quite obviously, once covered a lock.

There are two possible approaches to equipping medieval furniture with working locks. The first, and by far the better, is to reproduce a medieval lock; the second is to adapt a newer lockset to the piece of medieval furniture. If you opt for authenticity after investing so much effort in your chest or cabinet, follow these instructions to re-create a medieval lockset. Remember that although locksets are relatively simple to build, their limited technology leaves their security factor lacking. (Translation: These locks will keep honest people honest, but they won't keep out the bad guys.)

The lockset below has been adapted from a number of surviving period locks. Although the mechanism itself is extremely simple, pay careful attention to both the drawings and text to understand the lockset well enough to build it. This lock can be adapted for use on the Tax Box, the Hewn-Timber Chest, the Paneled Coffer, and the Cathedral Cabon; it is also perfectly suited for installation on the Fourteenth-Century Reading Desk, the Oxford Chest, and the Vestment Chest, found in our previous book, *Constructing Medieval Furniture*.

## CONCEPT OF THE MEDIEVAL LOCK

Medieval locks of the type shown in this chapter were built differently than are their modern counterparts. Today's locks are set on the inside of a piece of furniture (that is, on the inner face of a drawer or a chest), and the exterior keyhole is covered with a decorative plate, known as an escutcheon. The medieval lock was built directly on the back of the escutcheon plate. A small section of wood was chiseled away from the chest's face, forming a hollow into which the locking mechanism could be recessed. The completed lock and escutcheon were mounted to the front of the chest with nails. To prevent the escutcheon and its accompanying lock from simply being pried from the chest's face, locks were often mounted with "clinch" nails, which were longer than the thickness of the board into which they were driven. The excess nail protruding through the chest's inner face could be bent over, or clinched, on the inside, making the lock far more difficult to remove.

## MATERIALS

Most of the lock, except the spring, the lock bar, and the key, can be constructed from steel flat stock that is $1/16$ inch thick. Shape the spring from a piece of $1/32$-inch-thick spring steel. Using an old hacksaw blade to make the spring seems to work adequately in modern reproductions of medieval locks. Cut the lock bar from a ¼-inch-thick piece of steel.

## LOCK PLATE AND HASP

The drawing of the exterior view of the lock shows the location of the keyhole and the opening through which the hasp staple passes. A typical hasp and a hasp staple are shown in the drawings. Specific instructions for constructing hasps and escutcheon plates will appear in those chapters requiring locksets.

There are seven rivets on the escutcheon's face, each bearing a letter or a letter and a number designation. The particular functions of these mounting points for the locking mechanism will become clear as you build the lock.

## MECHANISM OVERVIEW

The interior view drawing shows the lockset as it appears when completed and ready to set in place. The jagged bar, shown here as a hatched area and marked A, is the lock bar, the piece that actually locks the hasp into place. The looped piece marked B, fitted around the bar, is the spring that prevents the lock bar from simply falling open if the chest is tilted or jiggled. The rather fish-shaped plate marked C is no more than the framework that holds two simple gates (known to the medieval locksmith as "wards") around which the key must pass on its way to the jagged bar, and a small tubular collar that holds the key's tip in place. There are no moving parts hidden inside framework C. The small plate marked D is a third ward around which the key passes.

## THE KEY

The key, as shown in the drawing, is designed to fit through the series of three wards. Locks with differently shaped wards would require a key with a different configuration. How the key passes around the wards is shown in the drawings. To personalize a lock, alter the size and shape of the key and the wards through which it must pass on its way to moving the lock bar. Some medieval keys had amazingly complex wards, but the actual locking mechanism was just as simple as the one shown here.

## LOCK OPERATION

Lock drawings 1, 2, 3, and 4 reveal the key as it opens the lock. Refer to these drawings before and during the construction of the lock, to completely understand its operation. In drawing 1 the key is inserted through the keyhole, and the collar steadies it. The removal of both the spring and the staple end of the hasp from drawings 3 and 4 clearly delineates the key in operation. In drawing 3 the key pushes against the lock bar, moving it out of the hasp staple. The key continues its journey past the lock bar in drawing 4; after its 360-degree rotation, it can be removed from the lock. To relock the chest, simply reinsert the key and turn it in the opposite direction.

## LOCK PLATE CONSTRUCTION

The individual chapters provide lock plate dimensions and design. Be sure that the keyhole and hasp staple hole are arranged so that they conform to the dimensions of this particular lockset. Alternatively, adapt the locking mechanism to the configuration of the holes in the particular lock plate of the piece of furniture you are building.

## LOCK BAR CONSTRUCTION

To ensure your chest's security, cut the lock bar from heavy stock. Cut the lock bar from ¼-inch-thick stock to the dimensions indicated in the lock bar drawing. The thickness of the metal requires the use of a band saw with a metal cutting blade. File any burrs from the edges of the lock bar.

Next, cut two lock bar supports from the same ¼-inch metal. Be sure that the lock bar passes easily through the slots in the supports. To shape the rivets on the end of the lock bar supports, use metal files. Begin with a fairly coarse file and work down to a fine-toothed file to smooth your rivet enough to pass easily through a hole in the lock plate. Note that these rivets are square, rather than round. This prevents them from turning once they are riveted to the lock plate. Be sure the shoulder at the rivet's base is square and flat. The rivet must pull tightly against the lock plate so that the lock bar supports will remain firmly in place.

When these three pieces are finished, lay them aside.

## THE SPRING

Using a band saw with a metal cutting blade, cut a 4⅜-inch length of 1/32-inch-thick spring steel to the configuration shown in the drawing of the spring before bending. Be aware that spring steel is very hard; work slowly in order not to break the saw blade or the spring. Note: In drilling the mounting hole shown on this drawing, it is advisable to drill two holes about

## INTERIOR VIEW

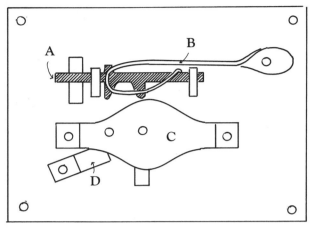

## EXTERIOR VIEW, REDUCED SCALE

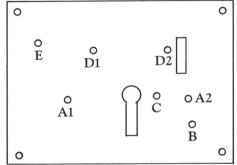

## LOCK IN OPERATION

1

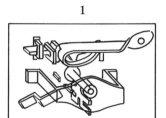

2

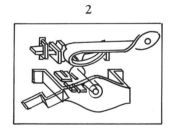

3

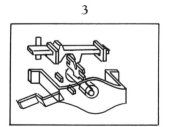

4

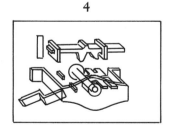

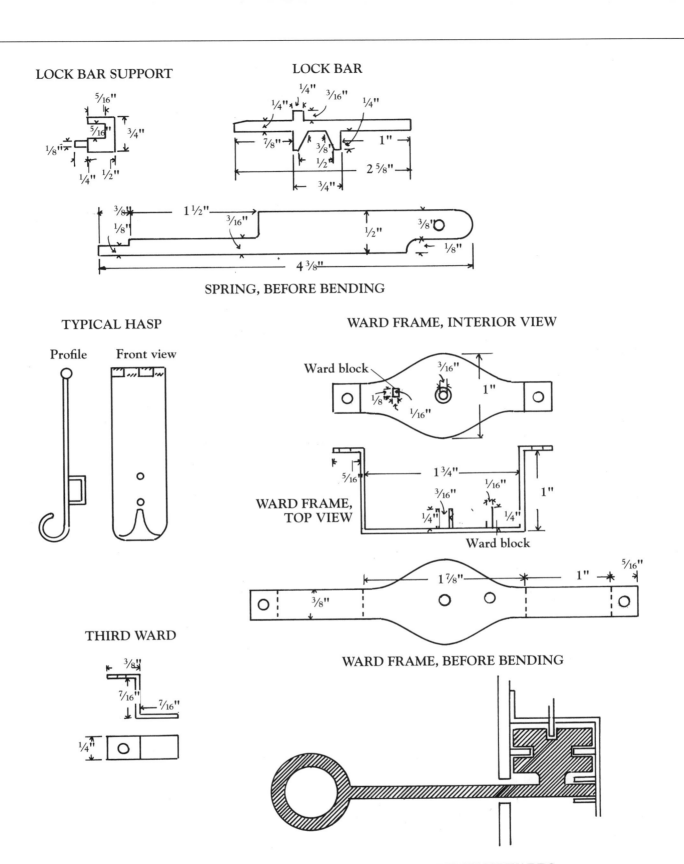

LOCK BAR SUPPORT

LOCK BAR

SPRING, BEFORE BENDING

TYPICAL HASP

Profile     Front view

WARD FRAME, INTERIOR VIEW

Ward block

Ward block

WARD FRAME, TOP VIEW

WARD FRAME, BEFORE BENDING

THIRD WARD

KEY PASSING THROUGH WARDS,
VIEW FROM BENEATH

23

¼ inch apart at this end of the spring. A second rivet will ensure that the spring is not loosened and pushed aside.

Heat 1½ inches at the end of the spring in which you have drilled the mounting hole or holes until the metal glows red. At a point about ¾ inch from the end of the spring, twist the spring a quarter turn with a pair of pliers. This will fashion the "ear," which will attach the spring to the lock plate. Be sure the ear lies as close as possible to the edge of the spring with the notch cut out of it.

Next, heat and bend the small hook near the spring's opposite end, according to the spring drawing. Note that the metal is bent a quarter turn before it is shaped into a hook; this prevents having to curve the metal laterally. When the spring is finished, this hook fits over the lock bar. Finally, heat an area of the spring about 1 inch on either side of the large offset, and bend the large loop as shown in the interior view drawing. A second, very small loop in the narrower end of the spring allows the spring to hook over the lock bar's top and exert a slight downward pressure on it.

At this point all the tensile strength (the springiness) leaves the spring. To replace it, heat the entire spring until it glows and then quench it in a pan of water.

## MAKING THE KEY

To ensure the smooth operation of the lock, make the key before the locking mechanism is attached to the lock plate. The shaft of the key is a 3-inch length of 3/16-inch round stock. Cut the head, or teeth, of the key from a piece of ⅛-inch-thick flat stock. When you have cut the teeth, weld them to the shaft at the location shown on the key drawing. The handle of the key can be as elaborate, or as simple, as you like. Our handle is a simple ring bent from a heated length of 3/16-inch round stock and welded to the shaft.

## WARD FRAME CONSTRUCTION

The ward frame, marked C on the interior view drawing, can now be cut from 1/16-inch-thick flat stock and heated and bent to shape according to the drawings of the ward frame before bending and the top view of the ward frame. For instructions on heating and bending metal, see the metalworking chapter. Drill a ⅛-inch hole in each of the ears to facilitate the attachment of the ward frame to the lock plate.

Next, cut a ¼-inch length of thin-walled steel tubing, and weld it to the center of the interior face of the ward frame. The location of this cylinder can be clearly seen on the interior view and the top view drawings of the ward frame. This cylinder holds the key in its proper position when the lock is being opened or closed; when the ward frame is riveted to the lock plate, the cylinder must be directly behind the circular opening at the top of the keyhole.

Cut two rectangular ward blocks from 1/16-inch flat stock as shown in the interior view and the top view drawings of the ward frames. Be sure that the ward blocks pass easily through the notches in the key. Shaping the rivets on the ends of the blocks resembles working on the lock bar supports, but these rivets must be round rather than square. Begin with a fairly coarse file and work down to a fine-toothed file to give your rivet a smooth surface that will pass easily through a hole in the lock plate. Again, be certain the shoulders at the base of the rivets are square and flat to ensure that the ward blocks do not turn once they are riveted in place. The rivets can be welded to the ward frame once they have been peened in place on the lock plate.

Drill a 1/16-inch mounting hole for the ward block in the ward frame to the left of the key cylinder, as shown on the interior view of the ward frame. To ascertain this hole's exact position, place the end of the key in the cylinder and position the ward block in the proper notch in the key. Place the ward frame in position on the interior surface of the lock plate and replace the key in the cylinder. Position the ward frame so that the key can be removed and reinserted through the keyhole without difficulty. Clamp the ward frame in place on the lock plate, and determine the position of the ward block that mounts on the face of the lock plate. If the key is not in the lock for this phase of the operation, the ward block may not align with the key. Remove the key and the ward frame, and drill and mount the second ward block. This rivet is marked C on the exterior view drawing.

Reposition the ward frame on the lock plate and insert the key. Mark the locations of the ward block's mounting holes on the lock plate. Remove the ward frame and drill the holes in the lock plate. These will hold the rivets shown as A1 and A2 on the Exterior view drawing.

Remount the ward frame and position it with two small rivets. Again, make sure the key fits into the ward frame and passes both of the ward blocks.

The final ward, shown as D on the interior view drawing of the lockset and detailed in the third ward drawing, passes through the small slit in the center of the key. Bend this ward from a heated piece of 1/16-inch-thick flat stock. Be sure that the key can pass around it when it is fitted against the lock plate. Drill a hole in the ward's tail, and a corresponding hole through the lock plate's face, and rivet them together. This appears as rivet B on the exterior view drawing.

## ATTACHING THE LOCK BAR AND SPRING TO THE LOCK PLATE

To guarantee that the lock bar lines up with the key, place the key in the lock before positioning the lock bar on the lock plate's back.

Position the lock bar on the lock plate so that the end falls across the hasp staple hole as shown in the interior view drawing. Set the lock bar supports in place on the lock bar so that the rivets are beneath the lock bar. Be sure there is enough distance between the lock bar supports to allow the spring to set between the small ear on the upper left corner of the lock bar and the lock bar support on the right (see the interior view drawing). The lock bar must also be positioned so that the key will move it from left to right as it is locked and unlocked. The key's only contact on the lock bar should be with the downward pointing teeth; it should not touch the bottom of the bar itself.

Mark the positions of the rivets on the lock bar supports, and drill 1/8-inch holes in the lock plate at the proper position. With a small file, rub the holes square, then insert the rivets and peen them over. Note: If you do not have jewelers' files, file the rivets round, mount them in round holes, and weld them into place to ensure that they do not shift. Place one of the lock bar supports in its proper hole, and peen over the rivet on the lock plate's face. Insert the lock bar and the second lock bar support into place, and peen over the second rivet. These holes will correspond with the rivets marked D1 and D2 on the exterior view drawing. The lock bar should now move freely back and forth in front of the hasp staple hole.

Set the spring in position on top of the lock bar. Clamp the ear on the end of the spring to the lock plate, and open the lock with the key. The key should

lift the spring out of the way so that the lock bar can pass beneath it. If the ear on top of the lock bar is too long to pass under the spring, file it down slightly. Be sure the key does not require too much effort to turn. When the lock operates satisfactorily, mark and drill a hole or holes to accept the rivet or rivets that will hold the spring in place. If you use only one rivet, position the spring so that it exerts a very slight pressure on the lock bar before you place the rivet. If you use two rivets, drill and install the rivet nearer the spring's long end, and then, using the first rivet as a fulcrum, apply a slight pressure on the lock bar and mark and drill a hole for the second rivet.

Now the lock can be locked and unlocked with relative ease. After hollowing out an appropriately wide and deep trough on the face of the chest, permanently mount the lock with clinch nails.

## LOCK SET WITHOUT A HASP

Locks such as those on the Cathedral Cabon (and the Reading Desk in our previous book) do not have a hasp. Instead, the lock bar simply slides behind the stile nearest the lockset, making it impossible to open the door. We recommend attaching a small metal plate to the back of the stile to prevent the lock bar from tearing away the wood on the edge of the stile.

## ALTERNATIVES TO THE MEDIEVAL LOCK

We have a suggestion if constructing a lock scares you. For medieval cupboards with standard doors (such as the Cathedral Cabon), adapt a small surface-mounted lockset known as a rim lock, a type that was common on nineteenth-century interior doors. A rim lock will require only minor modification to serve on these cupboard doors.

Open the lock box and remove the catch normally operated by the doorknob, leaving only the key-operated dead bolt in place. Replace the cover on the lock box, and screw it to the cupboard door's inner surface so that the keyhole in the door aligns with the keyhole in the lock box. A slight repositioning of the keyhole in the door to correspond with the dimensions of the lock box may be in order.

# FINISHES

Much of the furniture produced during the Middle Ages was ornately painted in bright colors with designs and figures; the concept of a clear finish of the type applied to most furniture today was completely unknown. The beauty of natural wood, however, was also appreciated. A natural finish was achieved by smoothing with sharkskin—a natural and very effective form of sandpaper—or scraping with the edge of a flat metal fragment. Even today expert furniture makers use a cabinet scraper to obtain the smoothest possible finish. A smoothed item was immediately utilized. The unintentional mellow tones of the wood were simply a bonus of aging. If you want your re-created furniture to have a truly period look to it, do not finish it with sandpaper. The finish made by a good cabinet scraper looks authentic and adapts much better to a natural oil finish.

To create the wear-and-tear look of the centuries, the furniture can be aged artificially. Wear corners away with a wood rasp and randomly strike the surface with a length of chain or a cloth bag full of nails. Or lightly sandblast the entire work to eliminate some of the soft wood. A final leveling with the cabinet scraper will soften the damage of the aging process so that the surface doesn't look too new. But remember, we are not forging antiques; we are having fun making period furniture.

## CLEAR FINISHES

Centuries of use have softened the surface tones of surviving medieval furniture. To counter the effects of natural oils and dirt transferred to the surface of the wood from human hands, cleaning was occasionally done with a rag soaked in olive oil. Repeated applications of oil invested the wood with natural moisture, prevented it from cracking and splitting, and acted as a natural adhesive for tiny bits of dust. Alternating layers of oil and dust gathered in corners and crevices but were worn off of the main areas. The visual richness of such furniture is difficult to re-create artificially. Oil alone or mixed with a little coloring agent such as wood stain (see below) will give the most authentic-looking finish.

Being true to the original is the best finish, applications of olive oil, tung oil, or boiled linseed oil. Coat the wood lightly until it repels the oil, and then buff to a low luster with a soft cloth.

For a more penetrating oil finish, mix four parts of one of the oils mentioned above to one part spirits of gum turpentine. (Mineral spirits or artificial paint thinner will dry out the wood.) A slightly warmed—not boiled—mixture penetrates best. Prudence dictates the use of an electric stove, not gas. Darkening the natural color of the wood makes it look older. Add a spot of tinting color, of the type used to tint paint, or wood stain to the oil and turpentine mixture. Be careful; only a few drops significantly change the color of a pint of finishing oil. Test tinted oil on a piece of scrap wood before applying it to finished furniture. Apply a second coat of boiled linseed oil to cover the penetrating coat.

To prevent the wood from drying out, periodically apply additional coats of oil. Apply oil every three or four months during the first two years. Once or twice a year thereafter will suffice. Forced-air heating dries out furniture faster than hot water heat.

Occasionally shine your furniture with a furniture polish containing lemon oil, which will help the polish soak into the wood. Avoid a polish listing wax in the label's contents section. To deepen the antique look, use the traditional formula of Genuine Old English polish. The dark brown tint of Old English scratch cover will dramatically darken the wood over successive applications, richening the finish.

To stain newly created medieval furniture, try this fairly authentic period recipe (this is recommended for use on oak only, because the stain reacts with the high concentration of tannic acid present in the wood). Submerge well-rusted iron in equal parts of water and vinegar. Real iron will perform better than modern steel. In one to two months the vinegar and water solution will absorb the pigmentation from the rusted iron. After several months, remove the iron from the solution and filter the liquid through a fine cloth to remove any rust sediment. Staining with the clarified liquid produces a finish that varies from near black to a wonderfully mellow silvery brown. The exact color of the finish depends on the strength of the liquid and the amount of acid in the oak. Test the stain on scrap wood before applying it to finished work, but don't worry about color differences; in furniture that has actually survived for centuries, the surface tones vary from board to board. When the stain has dried, apply a natural oil finish as described above.

## PAINTED FINISHES

The articles of furniture in this book have a natural wood finish, but many medieval pieces were originally painted, the edges and carvings often picked out in colors that contrasted to the body of the piece. If you are considering painting your medieval furniture, paint discarded pieces to see if you like the effect. For those who decide to proceed, we will provide a medieval paint recipe. Prior to the invention of oil-based paint in the late fifteenth century, egg tempera was the medium for painting wood, metal, paper, leather, and cloth. Use it on any project in this book that needs painting.

Artists in the Middle Ages produced specific colors with extremely poisonous ingredients—white lead, copper sulfate, and many other dangerous pigments. Inexpensive powdered pigments of the type used in preschool are safe substitutes. They may not produce a paint with a perfect consistency, but close examination of period paint and manuscript illuminations shows how historically correct a little variation in texture can be.

To prime an area for egg tempera, lay in a ground coat of gesso—a water-based primer sold in art-supply stores. Apply the brush strokes evenly in the same direction, especially if a large area is being gessoed. Fresh eggs, pure ground pigments (available in art-supply stores), and distilled water constitute modern egg tempera. Egg yolk binds the pigment to the gesso ground. To extract pure yolk, separate an egg and ease the yolk into your palm. Gently roll the yolk repeatedly from one hand to the other. As you cup the yolk in one hand, wipe the excess white from the other palm.

The drying yolk will toughen after eight to ten transfers. Gingerly pinch the thickened yolk sac as it rests in one hand, and suspend it over a spotless shallow bowl. Free the yolk to spill into the bowl by piercing the sac with a sharp knife. Discard the yolk sac.

Blend pure ground pigment into the egg yolk mix to create a pleasing color. Pulverize the pigment into the egg with a mortar and pestle, or by grinding the back of a spoon against the side of the mixing bowl. Thin the paint with a few drops of water if it becomes too thick to work easily. Water also clarifies the colors. Using denatured alcohol in place of water hastens the drying and helps preserve the paint. Egg tempera treated with alcohol must be stored in the refrigerator and will still have a shelf life of only five or six days. Dried egg tempera needs no varnish if it is sheltered from the weather. A dried egg yolk glaze is nearly as hard as varnish.

Working with egg tempera takes practice; painting an entire piece of furniture or a wall hanging can be taxing, but it is the correct period approach to the job.

## ALTERNATIVES

Can't get the hang of painting with food? Try artist's oil paint or latex paint to decorate a wall hanging, or substitute regular interior oil or latex paint to embellish furniture. Choose a commercial paint with a flat finish; flatting agents are available to kill the natural sheen of oil paints.

# MERRILLS BOARD

Board games have been popular throughout history; there are records of board games in ancient Egypt, first-century Sri Lanka, and Viking Norway. Our ancestors used board games for both entertainment and gambling, whiling away the idle time that is today largely occupied by television. During the Middle Ages the most popular games were chess (largely played by the nobility), draughts (now called checkers in America), and Merrills (later called nine-men's morris). Merrills, known in Germany, Russia, and even southern Africa, was popular enough to be represented in illuminated manuscripts and in an exquisite tapestry dated about 1510, which is now on display in the Louvre.

Here we see a Merrills board and a board for another game, which no one has been able to identify, carved into the lid of an oak barrel. The straight edges of the barrel lid tell us that it was intended to hold food or other solid objects, rather than ale or wine. This artifact, along with thousands of others, was recovered from the wreck of the *Mary Rose,* flagship of Henry VIII's great fleet of warships. When the *Mary Rose* sank unexpectedly in the mouth of Portsmouth harbor in July 1545, she took the entire crew of 415 and all their possessions to the bottom with her. Since recovery operations began in the 1980s, over thirteen thousand items have been recovered from the wreck, including this Merrills board that some bored sailor undoubtedly carved into a barrelhead to pass the time. The other game board, located lower on the lid, and looking a bit like a miniature shuffleboard court, has yet to be identified. It is, however, the opinion of the authors that it may be a variation of the still popular English pub game known as shove-ha'penny, a game so addictive it was outlawed during the sixteenth century.

Although this project is hardly fine furniture or great art, it is a wonderful example of the type of impromptu work that must have been found everywhere in a world where mass production did not yet exist. An easy project for the beginning woodcarver, it can be made in a day or two but provides endless hours of period entertainment for the entire family.

## CONSTRUCTION NOTES

This barrelhead, as is still true with most casks meant to hold consumable items, is made of oak and held together entirely with wooden pegs. The crossbar, running perpendicularly across the three main boards, was located on the outside of the lid, where it helped to secure the lid to the barrel. The presence of a crossbar, combined with the squared-off edges of the lid itself, tells us that this keg contained solid food, rather than wine or ale (in which case the lid would have been fitted in a slot in the barrel staves to make it watertight).

The game boards are carved on the inside of the lid, indicating that the lid itself had been discarded. Because the three boards in the lid are pegged together, the game board could be made without the use of a crossbar.

### Materials

The three main boards of the lid are all ⅝ inch in thickness, while the crossbar is only ⅜ inch thick. All pegs are ¼ inch in diameter and were probably made of ash.

### Setting Up

Cut the four boards to length, but do not cut the three boards in the lid to shape until they have been joined together with dowels.

# MATERIALS

## WOOD
All wood is oak.

| PART | NUMBER OF PIECES | THICKNESS | | WIDTH | | LENGTH |
|------|------------------|-----------|---|-------|---|--------|
| face boards | 2 | ⅝" | × | 6" | × | 17" |
| face board | 1 | ⅝" | × | 4" | × | 15" |
| cross brace | 1 | ⅜" | × | 4¾" | × | 17¼" |
| dowel | 1 | ¼" diameter | | | × | 36" |

## OPTIONAL MATERIALS

| PART | NUMBER OF PIECES | THICKNESS | WIDTH | | LENGTH |
|------|------------------|-----------|-------|---|--------|
| canvas | 1 | 20 oz. | 24" | × | 24" |
| brewer's pitch | 1 pint | | | | |

## Doweling

Follow the general guidelines for doweling found in chapter 1 to determine the proper fit of the dowel into the hole. The boards in this project are joined flat; this requires a few words of additional explanation.

Decide which sides of the three boards to join together. The center board will be joined on both edges (to each of the boards forming the outside edges of the circle), and the other two boards will be joined to the center board on one edge. Insert the boards in a vise, one at a time, marking their centers. If the boards are accurate to ⅝ inch thickness, the centerline should lie at 5⁄16 inch from either edge. Set an adjustable square slightly less than 5⁄16 inch and slowly drag both the square and a pencil along the length of the board.

After marking the edges of all three boards, align two of the boards side by side in the vise so that the edges to be united are both facing up. Using the adjustable square, strike a line across both boards at the location of the center of the dowels. Consider that your boards are slightly longer than they will be when the final circle is cut. Indicate the location of each dowel with an X.

Use a doweling jig to ensure that the holes for the dowels are drilled perfectly straight into the center. Zero in with the doweling jig above the middle of the X marking the position of the dowel, and bore the pilot hole to the correct depth. Since the exact length of the dowels used in the original barrelhead is unknown, gauge the depth of your holes according to the length of the dowels. If your dowels are being cut from a long piece of doweling, do not dowel farther than ¾ inch into the wood (to allow the use of a dowel 1½ inches in length).

Use a nail or center punch to mark the midpoint of the X if you cannot obtain a doweling jig. Holding the centered drill plumb and level, drill the hole to the aforementioned depth.

After the drilling of the pilot holes, determine if the three boards are going to be pulled tightly together, as they would have been originally, or if small gaps are going to be left between them, as they are in the barrel lid today after having spent four centuries underwater. Our suggestion is to pull them tightly together. This will greatly strengthen the finished game board.

If the pilot holes fit snugly, it may not be necessary to glue the dowels into place. It is unlikely that glue

# PLAYING MERRILLS

Rules of the game according to the Ryedale Folk Museum, North Yorkshire County, England, organizers of the annual World Championship Merrills Tournament

The board has three concentric squares linked through the center point of each side. This provides twenty-four intersection points arranged in sixteen lines of three, on which the pieces are placed. The play is divided into three stages, but the object throughout is to get three pieces in a line; this is called a mill. On forming a mill, one of the opponent's pieces is removed from the board. The game is won by the player who reduces an opponent's pieces to only two or blocks him or her from moving in the middle stage of the game.

The opening stage of the game begins with an empty board. Each player, in turn, places one piece on any vacant point on the board, until both players have played all nine pieces. If either player makes a mill, that player removes any one of the opponent's pieces, providing that piece is not itself part of a mill. Throughout the game, pieces forming a mill are safe from capture. After a piece is removed from the board, it no longer figures in the game. (Note: Moves and lines of three can be made only along the horizontal and vertical lines on the board, never across the diagonals where no lines are marked.)

The middle stage of the game commences when all the pieces are on the board, except those lost in play. Play continues alternately; each player moves one piece to any empty adjacent point, again with the object of forming a mill and removing one of the opponent's pieces. Once a mill has been formed, it can be opened by moving one piece from the line if there is an empty point next to it and closed by returning it in a subsequent move. Each time a mill is closed, another of the opponent's pieces is removed. In a running mill, opening one mill will close another, so that a piece is removed every turn. If a player is unable to move any pieces because there are no empty points next to any pieces, then that player has lost the game. Otherwise, play continues until one player is reduced to three pieces.

The end stage allows the player with only three pieces to move any one piece each turn to any empty point on the board, regardless of its position in relationship to his pieces. The other player must continue to move to adjacent empty points, unless both players are reduced to three pieces. The game ends when one player, down to two pieces, can no longer form a mill.

was used originally. For optimum strength, however, dribble a few drops of white glue in one board's pilot holes. After tapping the dowels into position, sparingly glue the corresponding holes on the opposite board and place a small bead along its edge. Point the dowels into the mouths of the corresponding pilot holes, and gently tap the boards together with a wooden mallet. Pull the dowels together evenly; if they are forced out of line, they may split or snap.

As the boards touch, snug them together with cabinet clamps, if possible. After the glue has set, repeat the process with the final board.

## Cutting the Circle
After allowing the glue to cure overnight, lay out a circle on one face of the board. If you do not have compasses large enough to scribe a 16-inch circle, sim-

ply tie one end of a string around a small nail and the other end around a pencil. Tap the nail into the board at the center point of the circle, and adjust the length of the string so that it is 8 inches between pencil and nail. Now it will scribe a 16-inch circle.

Fortunately this barrelhead has fairly straight edges. Using a coping saw, saber saw, jigsaw, or band saw, cut around the edge of the circle that you have laid out on the board. Rasp out any imperfections in the circular shape and with sandpaper smooth the edges and round over the corners on both sides of the circle.

## Cross Brace
If you are going to use the cross brace as it appears on the original, cut the board to length as shown on the plans and, with a rasp or sandpaper, round off the corners to a smooth quarter-round shape.

Lay the wooden circle on a workbench with the side you plan to use as the game board facedown. Position the cross brace perpendicularly across the three boards, with the ends of the brace extending over the edge of the circle as shown on the plans. Note: Assuming you have actually pulled the boards of the circle tightly together, the cross brace will extend slightly farther beyond the edges of the circle than is shown on the plans.

Weathering has destroyed the original pegs that held this cross brace in place, but it was not nailed to the barrel lid. You may, therefore, position your pegs as you like, but we suggest using two pegs in each board and staggering them so that they are not in a straight line; this will give you the strongest possible structure. Drill the pilot holes (being careful not to drill into the surface of the workbench) and be certain that the dowels are longer than the combined thickness of the barrelhead and the crossbar. To sand the dowels flush on both the face of the barrel and the cross brace, a little extra length is essential. Using a cotton swab, coat the inner surface lightly with glue, and tap the dowels into place, allowing them to extend slightly through the face of the barrel lid. Wipe off excess glue before it dries.

After the glue has cured, sand the dowels smooth with the surface of the barrel lid and the crossbar. Your barrel lid is now complete.

## Carving the Game Boards

The crude nature of the game boards makes it obvious that they were carved into the barrel lid with a small belt knife. Work with a small carving knife or even a utility knife, or use a carving gouge with a V-shaped blade. This will reproduce the V-shaped cut of the original but allow you better control over the work. In either case, if you are not an experienced carver, practice your carving skills on a scrap piece of wood before you begin work on your finished piece, and refer to the chapter on woodcarving at the beginning of this book.

The inconsistencies of shape and line width are the result of the carver's knife blade moving across the heavy grain of the oak; irregularities in your reproduction may differ slightly but will approximate the spirit of the original.

No matter which carving tools you use, begin by laying out the design of one of the game boards on the appropriate board of the lid, in pencil. The plans for the game boards are reproduced here at 50 percent scale; enlarge them on a copying machine to the proper size and simply trace them onto the lid.

After the design is transferred, secure the board to your work surface so it does not slip while you are carving.

If you use an ordinary knife for the carving, start by making two shallow cuts, one on either side of a line, slightly over $1/16$ inch apart. Work in the direction of the grain of the wood wherever possible. Working against the grain can cause the blade to dig deeper than you want and can cause small splinters to appear around the edges of your cut. Don't worry if the width varies a little; it does on the original. Repeat the process several times, each time sinking the blade slightly deeper into the wood. Do not attempt to cut the full depth of the line in a single pass; the pressure involved can cause the blade to slip. Hold the blade on an angle of approximately 45 degrees so that succeeding cuts will form a V-shaped groove in the board about the same depth as its width. The excess wood should simply lift out where the cuts on the alternate sides of the line meet at the bottom of the groove. Repeat the sequence for all successive lines until the design is completed.

If you use a V-shaped carving gouge, place the bottom point of the V-shaped blade on the guideline; the blade will naturally cut a trough slightly to either side of the line as you move it across the surface of the wood. Work the blade carefully into the wood, rocking it slightly back and forth to allow it to forge its way through the wood slowly. Forcing the blade will inevitably cause it to slip off the guideline. Again, unless you are an experienced carver, do not attempt to cut the full depth in a single pass. Several shallow passes will ensure much better control. The finished V-shaped cut should be slightly over $1/16$ inch in both width and depth. When the first design is completed, transfer the second design onto the barrelhead and repeat the process.

## Finish

To prevent salt water from ruining the contents of this keg, the outside of the lid (and likely the entire barrel) was covered with heavy cloth, probably a lightweight canvas, that had been dipped in pitch. Remnants of this material can still be found on the crossbar and surrounding exterior surface of the lid. To re-create this process, use brewer's pitch—ask about it at a good home brewing store. Melt the pitch as directed, spread a thin layer over the exterior surface of the barrel lid with a flat stick or a putty knife, and before it sets, press a layer of lightweight canvas into the surface. A final, thin coat of hot pitch should then be brushed on top of the canvas.

Like the effect but not the mess of melting pitch? Use "tree paint" (a dressing applied to wounds on trees where limbs have been cut off) in place of the pitch. Tree paint dries, whereas some pitch can remain gooey forever. This finish, though not the most aesthetically impressive, is certainly historically accurate, and will spark curiosity. The face of the lid can then be treated with boiled linseed oil.

Alternatively, simply oil the entire lid with boiled linseed oil. To age the piece, add a bit of dark-colored, oil-based wood stain to the linseed oil. Allow the wood to absorb its fill of oil, and wipe off any excess before it dries.

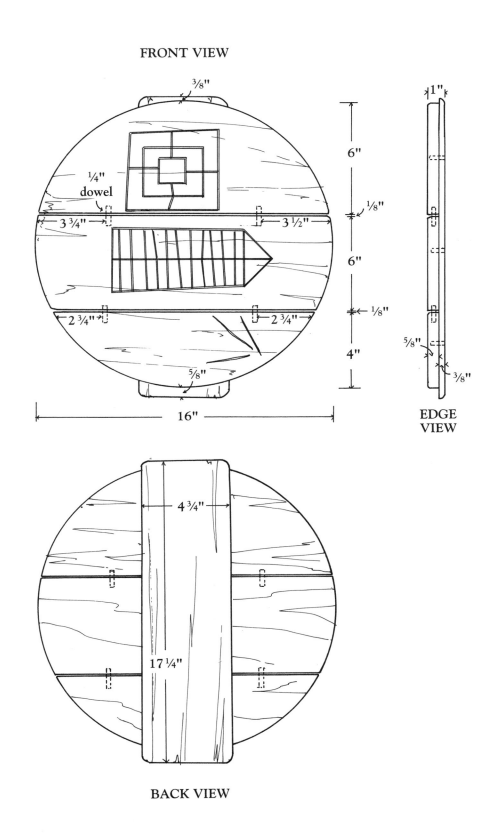

FRONT VIEW

⅜"

6"

¼"
dowel

3¾"     3½"

⅛"

6"

2¾"     2¾"

⅛"

4"

⅝"

16"

1"

EDGE
VIEW

⅝"

⅜"

4¾"

17¼"

BACK VIEW

33

## MERRILLS BOARD DETAIL

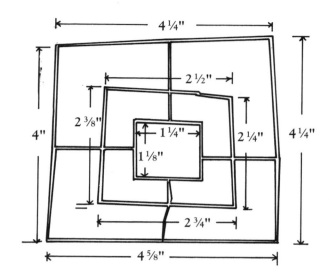

## UNKNOWN GAME BOARD DETAIL

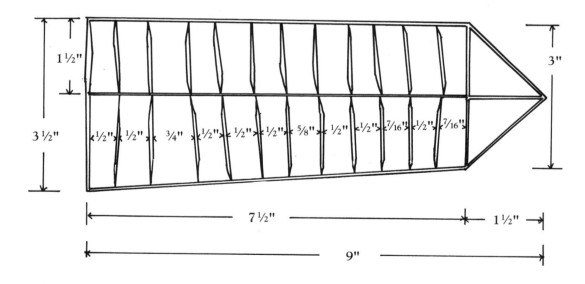

# Project 2

# TAX BOX

Although there is certainly nothing visually striking or structurally complex about this tax box, it is historically an almost unique piece—worthy of a place in this book. The box was hewn from a single block of English oak and fitted with a rudimentary iron lid and hasps. The workmanship is so basic that the piece is nearly impossible to accurately date. A reasonable guess places it between 1300 and 1600.

Looking like primitive safes, lockboxes like this were once hauled from village to village on the estates of great lords, and from town to town by government tax collectors, as they made their rounds to collect tax money from peasants and merchants. When a tax collector, frequently known as a "factor," arrived in a town or village, he set up temporary headquarters at a convenient public meeting place, usually an inn or tavern that also offered him accommodations.

Over the next several days local inhabitants were required to come and pay their taxes. As they paid, the factor checked their names off the tax roll. Anyone who failed to make the required appearance without valid reason found his name on another list, that of the local sheriff. The small capacity of this box reveals the limited scope of the medieval cash economy. Tax collectors did not have keys to open the box, and it is unlikely that a factor had more than one tax box because multiple boxes increased the chances of robbery. This meant that all the coins collected during the days, or weeks, the tax man traveled his circuit had to fit in an area 5¾ inches square and 7¾ inches deep. Neatly filled with modern English pennies, which are slightly smaller than the American penny, the box holds about sixty-one pounds sterling, approximately one hundred dollars at the time of this writing. Certainly it is reasonable to assume that even as late as 1600, a penny was the largest coin a peasant or simple laborer was ever likely to see. They probably would have paid with halfpennies or farthings, which would have made the final tally even less.

## CONSTRUCTION NOTES

The numerous irregularities in this tax box make it fairly obvious that it was cobbled together by the local blacksmith—probably on short notice. Although asymmetrical, the finished product looks strong and imposing.

### Materials

The oak block from which this box was hewn obviously came from a large tree. The grain pattern tells us that this box was cut from no more than a quarter of the area of the trunk, possibly less. Although the box could be replicated from a number of oak planks glued together and worked down, it should really be made from a single block. The best place to find a piece of wood of suitable size is a sawmill or a slab mill; the owner may cut a piece to your specifications.

Alternatively, find someone who is cutting down a large oak tree and buy a section of trunk slightly over 2 feet in diameter. If you are lucky, whoever is cutting down the tree might agree to cut the chunk to 17 inches in length—this will save later work. Try not to get a section too near the root—the grain becomes irregular near the ground, making the wood difficult, if not impossible, to work.

If the tree is dead, the wood may already have begun to dry. If it is completely green, allow it to dry for a few months, or even a year, before splitting it into sections.

To split the trunk into quarter sections, you will

# MATERIALS

## WOOD
All wood is oak.

| PART | NUMBER OF PIECES | THICKNESS | | WIDTH | | LENGTH |
|------|------------------|-----------|---|-------|---|--------|
| body | 1 | 11" | × | 11" | × | 16¾" |

## METAL

| PART | NUMBER OF PIECES | THICKNESS | | WIDTH | | LENGTH |
|------|------------------|-----------|---|-------|---|--------|
| lid | 1 | ⅛" | × | 8" | × | 8⅛" |
| hinge, left side, back section | 1 | ⅛" | × | 1¾" | × | 19" |
| hinge, right side, back section | 1 | ⅛" | × | 1⅞" | × | 19" |
| hinge, left top section | 1 | ⅛" | × | 1⅞" | × | 9½" |
| hinge, right top section | 1 | ⅛" | × | 2¼" | × | 9½" |
| hasp strap | 1 | ⅛" | × | 2" | × | 16" |
| left hasp | 1 | ⅛" | × | 2" | × | 11" |
| right hasp | 1 | ⅛" | × | 1⅞" | × | 9¼" |
| left hasp catch | 1 | 5⁄16" diameter | | | × | 8" |
| right hasp catch | 1 | 5⁄16" | × | 5⁄16" | × | 8" |
| top band | 1 | ⅛" | × | 1⅛" | × | 49" |
| coin slot | 1 | 1⁄16" | × | 1¼" | × | 6" |
| hinge pins | 2 | ¼" diameter | | | × | 2¼" |
| lock plate | 1 | ⅛" | × | 6½" | × | 7¾" |
| forged nails | 19 | | | | | 1½" |

need a sledgehammer and two splitting wedges. Set the section of log on end, with the most even surface facing down. Be sure it is on a solid surface—thick concrete is best. With a marking pen and straightedge, divide the face of the log roughly into quarters. Place one of the splitting wedges on one of the lines, 3 or 4 inches from the outer edge of the log. Tap it into the surface of the log with the sledgehammer. When it is far enough into the surface to stand without being held, drive it into the log with the sledgehammer. After it has sunk to about half its depth, the log should begin to split (with luck, along a nearly straight line). Place the second wedge in the split, slightly nearer the center of the log than the first, tap it into place, and repeat the process. As the crevice in the log opens, the first wedge can be easily removed. When the log is split in half, take one of the halves and split it, too, in half. You should have at least one section of wood of an appropriate size to make your tax box.

If the wood seems fairly dry, begin to make the box immediately; if not, decide whether to prolong the cure for a few more months or attempt to work the wood green. Either can be done, but green wood is harder on modern tools than well-cured wood.

**Shaping the Exterior**
Whichever approach you take, the exterior of the box will need to be shaped with an adze or hatchet; do so immediately. Placing the rough-hewn block on a sturdy work surface, chip away at the exterior to give it a roughly square shape that tapers slightly inward at the bottom, as shown on the plans. Use of a hand planer will cut the time involved in this job by 90 percent; otherwise there are few choices but to do it the traditional way. If you have elected to plane the block, give the finished product an authentic look by putting a few shallow hatchet marks in the surface and eliminating the plane marks with a sharp chisel.

When the basic shape has been reached, the next step is to chamfer the edges, either with a router or a chisel. If you use a chisel, cut the chamfer in the direction of the grain so that the chisel does not bite too far into the wood and cause a large chunk to split off. In this instance the chisel is the better tool for the job; with it you can give the chamfer an irregular wavy quality to make it look like the original.

Note the shallow indentations at the bottom edge of two sides of the box, which serve no apparent function. Possibly the man who made the original intended to put them on all four sides as decoration but gave up

on the idea; we will never know. These can be easily cut into the block with chisels. The inner surfaces of the indentations are not rounded; they are fairly straight—as though a bite had been taken out of the base. We suggest that the hollows be roughed out with a chisel and finished with a rasp and files of decreasing coarseness.

The final step on the exterior is the narrow offset around the top, intended to receive a metal band. In the drawing of the front of the box, this offset is clearly visible because the band has rusted away. On the rear view we can see that the band has survived, giving the top of the box a smooth, clean line.

The simplest way to cut this recess is to mark along the bottom edge with a pencil and a straightedge and, laying the box on its side, to cut the line to the appropriate $3/16$-inch depth with a sharp chisel. Repeat the process on all four sides so that there is a narrow line cut into the surface of the wood all the way around the box, $1\frac{1}{8}$ inches below the top edge. With a pencil, mark the depth of the cut ($3/16$ inch) around the top surface of the box, and gently and carefully chisel away the necessary wood. You are now ready to hollow out the interior of the box.

With a marker and a straightedge, lay out the $5\frac{3}{4}$-inch-square coin receptacle. Most of the wood in this hole can be removed with a drill. A large, commercial drill press will ease the job, but a hand drill or even a brace with a spade bit (closest to the tool used originally) will work well. No matter which type of drill you use, be sure the block is securely braced before you begin drilling. If the drill bit catches in the grain of the oak, the block may begin to spin. If you are using a drill press, the block will have to be clamped; if you are using an electric hand drill or a brace and bit, a good, strong friend should do nicely. Begin with a small bit to get as far into the corners as possible, then move to large spade bits to remove the bulk of the wood. The hole is $7\frac{3}{4}$ inches deep, so do not drill any deeper than $7\frac{1}{2}$ inches, or there will be drill marks on the bottom of the coin box.

When as much of the wood has been drilled away as possible, remove the remaining pieces with a chisel. If your chisel is sharp, the walls and corners of the box should smooth out with relatively little effort. Don't worry about chisel marks on the walls; they appear on the original. Cleaning up the bottom of the box will be a miserable job, but once the drill marks are gone, don't worry about getting the bottom smooth; again, the original is not.

Finally, the top view with the lid removed shows a shallow recessed area around the coin box. This recess is just large enough, and deep enough, to receive the lid so that it lies flush with the surface of the box. If you choose to cut it now, you will have to cut the lid to fit the hole; if you make the lid first, then the recess can be cut to match the lid shape. We feel the latter is the best approach. When the time comes, position the lid, with the hinges and hasps attached, on the box; mark around the outer line of the lid; and remove the hardware. You could use a router or Dremel tool with a router attachment to remove the ¼ inch of excess wood, or you can remove it with a chisel in the same manner as the recess around the outer edge of the top. If you use a chisel, be careful; you are now working into end grain, which is far more likely to split or tear. Without a router, this may prove to be a miserable little job. However you approached it, the woodwork is now finished.

## Ironwork

Most of the ironwork on this piece is ⅛ inch thick. The hinges and hasps can be cut from strap iron, and the lid itself from a piece of flat stock. Those pieces that are made of different stock, such as the coin slot and the hasp catches, are all dealt with individually below.

## Lid

Cut the basic shape of the lid plate from a sheet of ⅛-inch flat stock. Mark the hole for the coin slot, and drill away as much of the excess stock as possible. File away the remaining metal to the shape of the coin slot.

## Hasps and Hinges

Following the instructions in the chapter on metal-working, cut the basic shapes of the hasps and hinges from strap metal or flat stock. The ends of the hinges that lie on top of the box will have to be shaped to fit across the top of the hasp brace; cut them about ½ inch longer than they appear on the diagram.

The ironwork on the original box (seemingly forged by a smith of limited talent) is very irregular in thickness as well as shape. The modern craftsman can file or grind away the edges of the metal pieces and sand them smooth to give them a hand-forged look. Alternatively, heat the metal and hammer the edges slightly round and irregular.

Forge the spines on the hinges and the hasps as instructed in the metalworking chapter, and fit them

together, but do not permanently attach the hinge pins.

Mark and cut the coin slot in the crossbrace that attaches to the hasps so that it is the same size as the coin slot in the lid. Weld the hasp brace to the lid so that the coin slots align. Limit the welds to the area that will be covered by the ends of the hinge straps to prevent their appearance on the finished product.

Position the lid and the hinges on the box so that you can locate the place where the ends of the hinges will have to be bent to fit across the top of the hasp brace. Heat and shape the same as you would any bend. Make the first curve at the lid's rear in the right place for the spines of the hinges to align properly with the box's back. If the front ends of the hinges are slightly longer, or shorter, than they appear on the diagram, it will not matter, but the hinges must align properly on the box. Because the bends that go across the hasp brace are so close together, this will be tricky—it is best to practice on a scrap of metal before working on the actual hinges.

After the hinges have been bent to fit, weld them onto the hasp brace. The least conspicuous place to put the welds is on the inside edges nearest the coin slot.

## Coin Slot

The coin slot is made from metal hardly half the thickness of the rest of the lid. A strip of strap metal 1/16 inch thick and 1¼ inches wide is the best choice. Heat and form the metal into a rectangle that fits snugly through the coin slot hole in the lid. It will be easiest if the ends of the rectangle join at one corner, rather than in the middle of one side of the slot. Weld the ends together and file away the excess weld. If done well, the junction will remain invisible. Place the rectangular coin slot in a vise with an open end facing upward, leaving about ⅛ inch of metal sticking above the vise's surface. Heat the metal and gently hammer it outward and downward against the surface of the vise to form the curled lip around the top of the coin slot.

Insert the coin slot into the hole in the lid and weld it to the underside of the lid. File any rough edges from the weld.

## Box Top Band

Bend a strip of 1⅛-inch-wide strap metal to fit snugly in the recess around the top of the tax box. Position the loose ends so that they come together underneath one of the hinges. Note: On the plans, the top edge of the hinge is held in place with two nails. If the joint in the band falls at the center of the hinge, these nails will hold the entire band in place.

## Lid Attachment

Position the lid on the box, and if you have not already done so, cut the recess in the top of the box to allow the lid to rest flush against the surface.

Drill holes in the long ends of the hinges in the appropriate place, and put the hinge pins in the hinges and hasps so that the entire lid assembly is joined together. Place the assembly into position on the box, and nail the hinges to the box with hand-forged nails.

## Hasp Catches

The hasp catch shown in the diagram is taken from the left side of the box. Although the two catches are the same size, the one on the left side is made from round stock, while the one on the right is made from square stock.

It may be best, especially for the beginner, to fashion the catches into their horseshoe shape before working the ends to a point. Form the catches around a mandrel (as described in the chapter on metalworking) or around a $\frac{7}{8}$-inch iron pipe. Once they are bent, cut them to length and file the ends to dull points with a file or grinding wheel.

To insert them into the box, drill pilot holes, just slightly smaller than the diameter of the hasp catch, through the sides of the box, at the appropriate locations.

Tap the hasp catches to an appropriate depth. The ends of the catches will protrude into the interior of the tax box. To prevent them from pulling out, bend the interior ends to the side with a metal bar and a hammer.

## Finish

It is doubtful if this box ever had a finish, although time has enhanced it with a lovely dark patina. A coat of dark wood stain followed by a coat of boiled linseed oil is all the finish it needs.

## FRONT VIEW

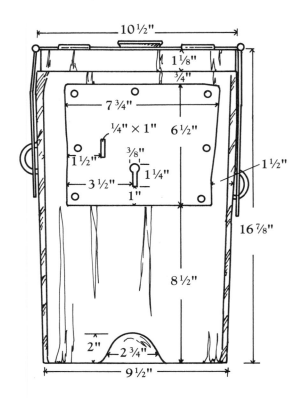

10½"

1⅛"

¾"

7¾"

6½"

¼" × 1"

⅜"

1½"

1¼"

3½"

1"

1½"

16⅞"

8½"

2"

2¾"

9½"

## REAR VIEW

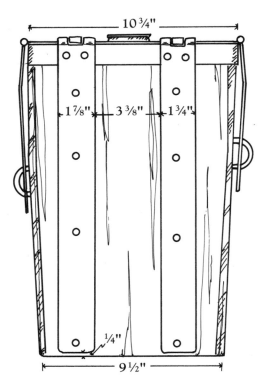

10¾"

1⅞"    3⅜"    1¾"

¼"

9½"

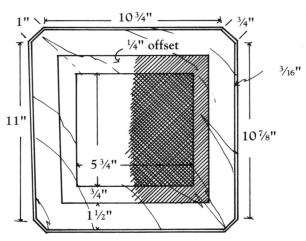

1"    10¾"    ¾"

¼" offset

3/16"

11"

10⅞"

5¾"

¾"

1½"

## TOP VIEW WITH LID REMOVED

## RIGHT SIDE

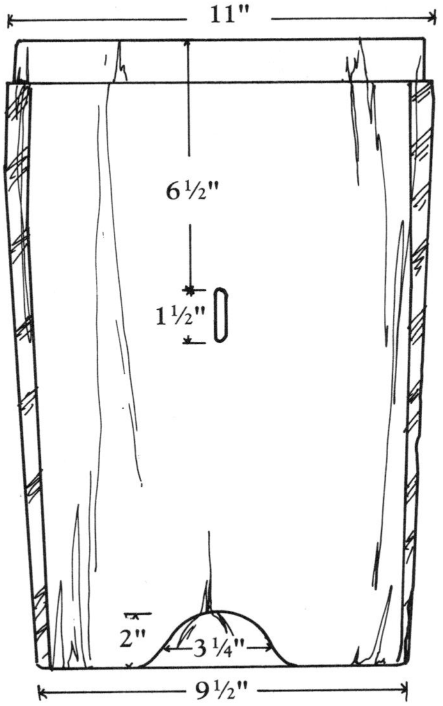

11"
6½"
1½"
2"
3¼"
9½"


## HASP, RIGHT SIDE

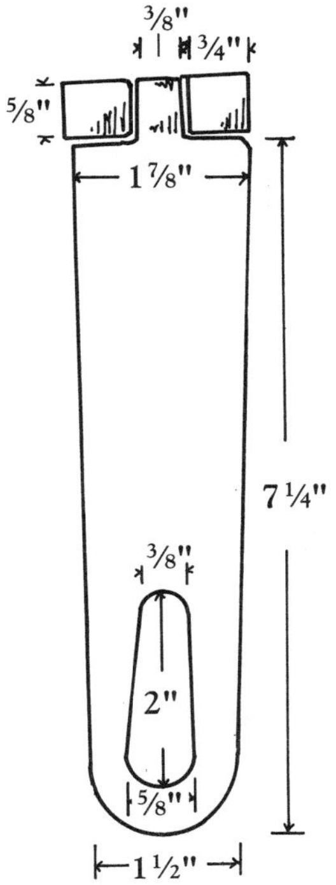

⅜"
¾"
⅝"
1⅞"
7¼"
⅜"
2"
⅝"
1½"


## BOTTOM VIEW

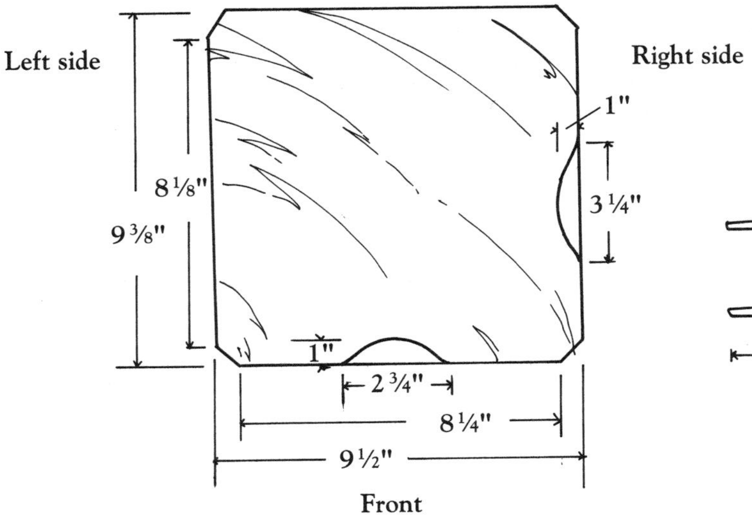

Left side
Right side
1"
3¼"
8⅛"
9⅜"
1"
2¾"
8¼"
9½"
Front


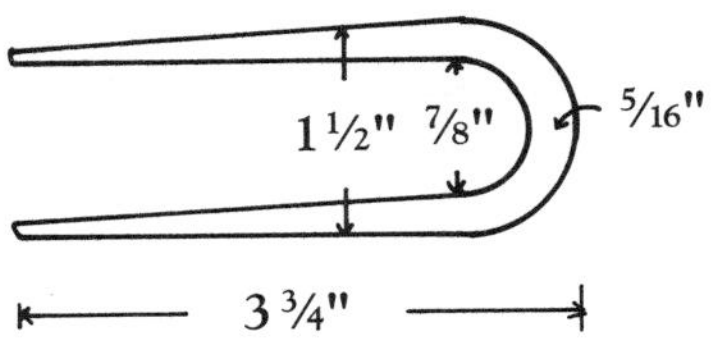

1½"
⅞"
5/16"
3¾"

## LID, LEFT EDGE

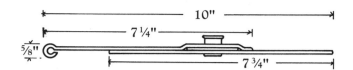

10"

7 ¼"

7 ¾"

⅝"

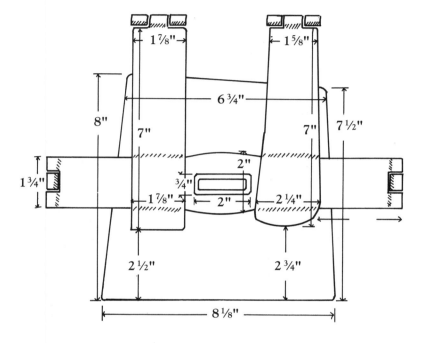

1 ⅞"

1 ⅝"

6 ¾"

8"

7"

7"

7 ½"

1 ¾"

2"

¾"

1 ⅞"

2"

2 ¼"

2 ½"

2 ¾"

8 ⅛"

## LID, TOP VIEW

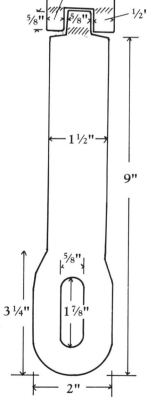

### HASP, LEFT SIDE

7/16"

⅝"

⅝"

½"

1 ½"

9"

⅝"

3 ¼"

1 ⅞"

2"

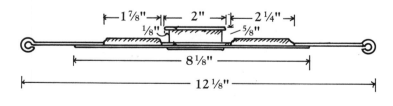

1 ⅞"

2"

2 ¼"

⅛"

⅝"

8 ⅛"

12 ⅛"

## LID, FRONT EDGE

# Project 3

# WRITING SLOPE

From the early Middle Ages onward, writing slopes were common possessions among those fortunate enough to be literate. Not surprisingly, the earliest surviving examples of the writing slope are found in monasteries, where monks copied rare books and works of holy writ and decorated them with the illuminations that are reproduced in many books about the period. By the late sixteenth century the vast majority of the merchant and upper classes had learned to read and write, and the writing slope, which doubled as a traveling office, had become standard equipment for the well educated and well heeled.

The writing slope was far more practical than much of the massive furniture produced during the medieval and Renaissance periods. Lightweight and portable, it could be moved easily as business took its owner on his travels. The flat surface above the lid provided a convenient place to set an inkwell and a sand shaker, which was used like a primitive blotter to dry excess ink from the page. The slope's interior was large enough to hold important papers, ledgers, and personal correspondence as well as quills, a penknife, ink, and a sand shaker.

Although writing slopes date from the earliest years of the mercantile revolution of the thirteenth century, few early examples survive. Fortunately for us, they changed little over the centuries, but it makes exact dating difficult and often impossible. Rarely does a furniture maker date his work for the convenience of future history buffs. In the case of this piece, from the collection of Bolton Castle, however, that is exactly what happened. Directly beneath the lock plate is a carved panel bearing the initials R. S. above the date 1670.

Although part of the S is obscured by the lock plate itself, it is still clearly readable and tantalizes us with clues about the origins and history of this lap desk. The initials probably indicate that it was once the possession of a member of the Scrope family, who held Bolton Castle for many centuries. The date also indicates that the box was not built until twenty-three years after the castle was severely damaged by Cromwell's Roundheads during the English Civil War.

## CONSTRUCTION NOTES

Made entirely of oak, this elegant piece is easy to construct. Its compact size suits even the smallest modern home. Built from only ten boards, it is of amazingly simple construction . Only the carving work adds an element of challenge, but even that is not too difficult .

### Materials

All of the boards from which the case itself is made are $\frac{7}{16}$-inch-thick oak. The 13-inch-wide section used for the writing surface may be difficult to obtain. This can, however, be glued and pegged together from two narrower boards, following the instructions for pegging found in the chapter on the Merrills Board. The two "runners," or feet, on which the chest rests are slightly thinner, at $\frac{3}{8}$ inch thick.

### Setting Up

All of the boards can be cut to size before any assembly begins, because this piece is so simple. Mark each section so it can be easily located when needed; use chalk or light pencil for easy removal from the wood before the application of a finish.

# MATERIALS

## WOOD
All wood is oak.

| PART | NUMBER OF PIECES | THICKNESS | | WIDTH | | LENGTH |
|------|-----------------|-----------|---|-------|---|--------|
| back | 1 | $7/16$" | × | $10\frac{3}{4}$" | × | $26\frac{1}{2}$" |
| front | 1 | $7/16$" | × | $6\frac{3}{4}$" | × | $26\frac{1}{2}$" |
| sides | 2 | $7/16$" | × | $10\frac{3}{4}$" | × | $17\frac{5}{8}$" |
| top | 1 | $7/16$" | × | $7\frac{3}{8}$" | × | $29\frac{1}{4}$" |
| writing surface | 1 | $7/16$" | × | 13" | × | $29\frac{1}{4}$" |
| bottom | 2 | $7/16$" | × | $9\frac{1}{4}$" | × | $29\frac{1}{4}$" |
| runners | 2 | $3/8$" | × | 2" | × | $18\frac{1}{8}$" |

## METAL

| PART | NUMBER OF PIECES | THICKNESS | | WIDTH | | LENGTH |
|------|-----------------|-----------|---|-------|---|--------|
| hinges | 4 | $1/16$" | × | $1\frac{1}{4}$" | × | 3" |
| hasp | 1 | $1/16$" | × | $1\frac{1}{2}$" | × | 6" |
| hasp catch | 1 | $1/16$" | × | $\frac{1}{4}$" | × | $1\frac{1}{4}$" |
| lock plate | 1 | $1/16$" | × | $2\frac{3}{4}$" | × | $3\frac{1}{2}$" |
| forged nails | 69 | | | | | 1" |

**Carving**

Execute the carving before any assembly is begun. Should a carving disaster occur, you can simply replace one board rather than dismantle an entire unit. Begin by carving the decorative edging. Cut a series of incised, scooped-out areas into the lid and the top of the box, as well as along the side edges of the front. Individually, these areas are the size and shape of a quarter section of a pea or a small berry. The carvings vary in size and spacing; if yours are not perfectly symmetrical, don't be concerned—it is the overall effect that counts. The finished carvings resemble a string of beads surrounding the box. The size, shape, and spacing of these beads appear on the front carving detail.

Although these beads can be cut with a round-ended carving gouge, the easiest way to shape them is with a round file, known as a rat-tail file. Simply abrade the edge of the board to the appropriate width and depth, and lightly sand the edges of the beading when finished.

The diagrams of the front carving and monogram plate should be exactly half the actual size of the front panel of the writing slope. Enlarging designs on a copying machine by 200 percent creates an accurate template that can be transferred directly to the wooden panel. These simple, flat carvings are an ideal project for beginning carvers.

Cut away the hatched part of the drawing. To indicate the area to be carved away, follow the instructions for establishing an outline in the chip carving section of the chapter on woodcarving.

After delineating the edges of your carving, remove the entire hatched area of the design to a depth of 3/16 inch. There are several approaches to removing the excess wood. Certainly the easiest is to use a Dremel tool with a router attachment. The proper historical technique is to use small chisels to remove the excess wood. If you use chisels, cut neither too deep nor too fast. The sharp edge of the chisel can easily cut through the fine bands of wood that border the areas you are removing.

Regardless of your approach, clean up the edges and corners of the design with a fine chisel or a carving knife. If you used a Dremel tool, remove any tool marks from the surface of the wood with a small chisel. Lightly sand all the sharp edges of the carvings.

## Case Assembly

With the carving finished, you are ready to assemble the case. Set the sides and front and back panels together on a level surface, with the front and back panels overlapping the ends of the side panels. Square the corners, holding them in position, if possible, with corner clamps.

Fasten the case together with small-headed, forged nails, using four nails along each edge of the front panel and five nails on each edge of the back panel. After drilling pilot holes for each nail, hammer the chest together.

Two random-width boards, running the length of the chest, make the bottom of the case. Nail both these boards and the top board into place. Note that the bottom boards extend 1/2 inch beyond the sides of the case but are flush with the front and rear. The top board extends beyond the sides (1 1/2 inches on one side and 1 1/4 inches on the other) and 1/2 inch beyond the back of the case.

## Runners

Cut the runners that support the writing slope on a slight angle so that the bottoms are slightly narrower than the top. Using a plane or table saw, bevel the edge of the runners to approximately a 30-degree angle, to conform with the dimensions shown in the drawings. Do not bevel the front and back edges of the runners, only the long sides.

After drilling pilot holes, attach the runners to the case with 1-inch-long forged nails. Use six nails to attach each runner to the bottom of the case. Drive the nails through the runners and into the bottom of the case. Countersink the heads of the nails so that they are flush with the bottom of the runners; otherwise they may scratch the table on which the writing slope is set. The ends of the nails will protrude about 1/4 inch into the interior of the case. Bend them over, flush with the surface of the bottom boards.

## Hinges

The brass hinges currently holding the lid in place are clearly replacements, possibly from as late as the nineteenth century. The scars on the lid do not provide outlines of the originals; we recommend using hinges similar to the existing ones. For a more period look, however, opt for hinges of a similar shape made from iron or steel rather than brass.

To fabricate iron hinges, follow the instructions on hinge making in the metalworking chapter. Keep the hinges small and delicate, in accord with the overall look of the writing slope.

## Lock Plate and Hasp

Cut the lock plate from a sheet of 1/16-inch flat stock, and nail it to the chest with four large-headed forged nails. Crimp the nails over on the inside of the case.

Cut and shape the hasp from 1/16-inch sheet metal or flat stock, according to the forging instructions in the metalworking chapter.

The catch on the back of the hasp fits into the rectangular slot in the lock plate. The catch should be formed from a piece of flat stock 1/16 inch thick, 1 1/4 inches long, and 1/4 inch wide. Heat and forge the corners of the catch, and weld the finished catch to the hasp's rear face. File away any excess weld.

As is usually the case with locks of this age, the locking mechanism itself has disappeared.

## Lid Attachment

With the hardware constructed and the lock plate attached to the chest, fasten the lid to the case with your choice of hinges. Locate the position of the hasp so that the catch will align with the catch hole in the lock plate. Cut a small notch in the front edge of the lid at the appropriate location, and attach the hasp with three small forged nails, bending any protruding nail ends flat against the undersurface of the lid.

### Finish

Lightly sand the entire writing slope, and finish it with a dark oak stain and a coat of boiled linseed oil. A smooth writing surface is essential, because this piece is intended to be used as a desk. You may elect to coat the entire piece of furniture with paste wood filler prior to staining and oiling. Paste wood filler evens out the hollows in the oak grain. Read and follow the instructions on the container carefully. If used properly, paste wood filler gives oak a finish as smooth as pine; if used improperly or carelessly, it creates a mess. If you use a paste filler, apply it before you attach any hardware to the chest. Note: Paste wood filler is not as common as it was some years ago; you may have trouble finding it. If your paint dealer is unable to obtain it for you, try a good woodworker's store.

## FRONT VIEW

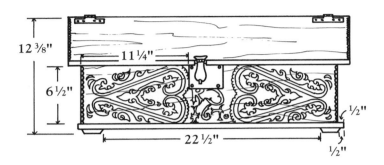

## TOP VIEW

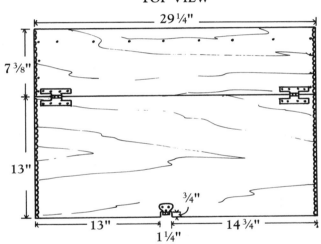

## BACK VIEW

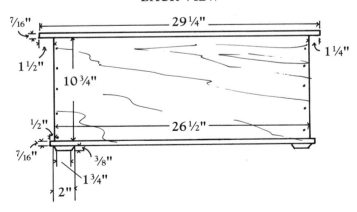

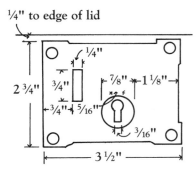

¼" to edge of lid

LOCK PLATE

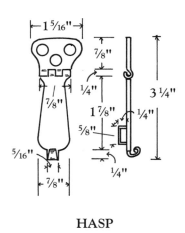

HINGE

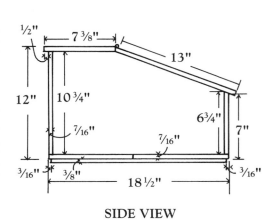

SIDE VIEW

HASP

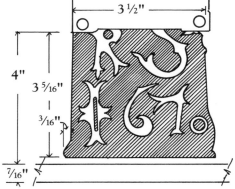

MONOGRAM AND DATE
CARVING

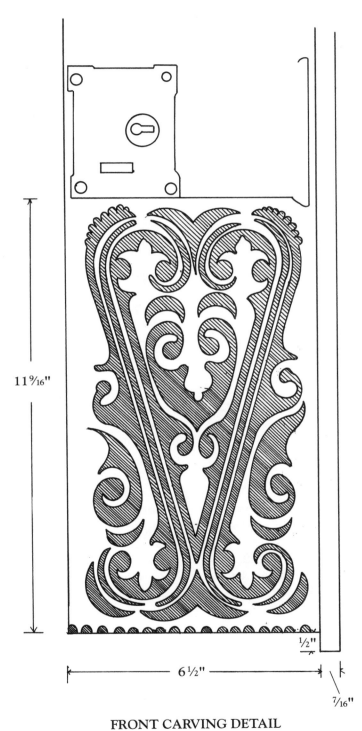

11⁹⁄₁₆"

½"

6½"

⁷⁄₁₆"

**FRONT CARVING DETAIL**

# Project 4

# CHURCH PEW

Kings of direct Norman lineage had ceased to rule England, but the heavy lines and simplistic ornamentation that were hallmarks of the Norman style are clearly evident in the construction of this massive thirteenth-century oak church pew. When last cataloged in the 1920s, it was listed as a bench for invalid monks. The physical evidence suggests a different purpose, however.

During the early centuries of the chivalric nobility, it was not uncommon for great lords to wear their armor to church to show ostensibly that they were ever ready to take up arms in its defense. In reality this power display reminded the church of the kingdom's true rulers. To heighten their grand display, noblemen often brought their falcons into church with them, while lapdogs accompanied their wives.

As the knights shifted uncomfortably, the heavy metal elbow and knee guards of their armor tore at the armrests and seats of their private pews. Such wear is plainly evident on this bench. Although the seat is certainly a later replacement, the tops and inner faces of both arms shows extraordinarily rough wear. Some historians have argued that this occurred when the bench was left outdoors, but there is no such damage on the top rail of the back, nor is there rot on the bottom of the legs, obvious indications of prolonged exposure to the elements. We believe, consequently, that this magnificent bench was once the private pew of a family of warrior nobility who ruled England during the golden years of the age of chivalry.

This bench is one of the many original furnishings still to be found in Winchester Cathedral, Winchester, England.

## CONSTRUCTION NOTES

The construction techniques used in this bench are fairly simple, but exercise care in the order in which it is fitted together. The overlapping back slats and the sheer size of the piece will challenge but need not daunt the competent home craftsman. Although the bench's chunky lines are essential to its imposing appearance, a bench half its length could still produce an impressive piece of furniture—adaptable to a space considerably smaller than Winchester Cathedral.

### Materials

The massive oak framing members of this bench will almost certainly have to be specially milled. It is best to cut all the pieces to length before you begin the relatively simple construction. Allow adequate length for the tenons when you are cutting the horizontal framing members. Mark each piece lightly with a pencil or chalk, and lay them aside for use as necessary. Readying the pieces beforehand cuts down on both confusion and some of the actual construction time.

### Back and Arm Supports: Carvings

Since the back corner posts and the front arm supports involve the most detailed work, make them first. As they are also the only pieces that involve carving, it is better to tackle them before the bench is assembled. If calamity strikes, it will be less frustrating to replace a piece if you do not have to disassemble the entire bench.

Lay out the finial designs on top of the arms and the back supports. The details are reproduced here at 25 percent of their actual size; enlarge them on a copying machine and transfer them directly to the wood. The circular shapes, known as roundels, with the star-

# MATERIALS

## WOOD
All wood is oak.

| PART | NUMBER OF PIECES | THICKNESS | | WIDTH | | LENGTH |
|------|------------------|-----------|---|-------|---|--------|
| arm supports | 2 | 3⅛" | × | 6⅝" | × | 31¼" |
| back supports | 2 | 3⅝" | × | 8½" | × | 52" |
| upper back rail | 1 | 3¼" | × | 7" | × | 11' 1¾" |
| lower back rail | 1 | 3¼" | × | 5" | × | 11' 1¾" |
| back slats | 26 | ½" | × | 6" | × | 16¾" |
| optional center back support rail | 1 | 1¼" | × | 3¼" | × | 10' 7¾" |
| side rails | 2 | 2¾" | × | 5" | × | 14⅝" |
| armrests | 2 | 2¾" | × | 5¼" | × | 14⅝" |
| front seat support rail | 1 | 3¼" | × | 6½" | × | 11' 9½" |
| seat supports | 10 | 3" | × | 3" | × | 16¾" |
| seat | 1 | 1" | × | 19⅝" | × | 12' ¾" |
| dowels | 3 | ⅜" diameter | | | × | 36" |

## METAL

| PART | NUMBER OF PIECES | LENGTH |
|------|------------------|--------|
| forged nails for center of back slats | 26 | 1¼" |
| forged nails for upper back rail | 26 | 2¾" |

shaped designs are the same size on both the back supports and the arms. The stars are easily drawn with compasses. Simply set your compasses to draw a 4-inch circle, move the point of the compasses to the outer edge of the circle, and scribe an arc across the face of the circle. Move the point of the compasses to one end of the arc, and repeat the process. Repeat the process six times to complete the star. Lay out the star before cutting around the roundel to ensure that you have enough wood around the outer circumference to set the point of the compasses. Note: The star design is carved only on the outside face of the roundels on the arms and the front face of the back support posts. When the circles, stars, and vertical post on the back supports have been drawn, cut away excess wood.

In all probability, an ambitious monk originally chiseled the entire design, but there are more efficient approaches to the work. A wide-mouthed, commercial band saw will provide the cleanest possible cut. Otherwise, a jigsaw, saber saw, or even a coping saw will suffice. Cut around the outline of the cross on the back supports and the roundels on the arms, being careful not to pierce the circle.

With sharp chisels, hew away the face of the upright member of the cross on the back support. Note: In the end view drawing the front surface of the vertical post is recessed ⅝ inch behind the rest of the back support. With the point of the chisel or a carving knife, carefully cut around the outer edge of the roundels and across the bottom of the cross, and begin to remove the excess wood. Do not try to remove too much wood at a time. The brittle grain of the oak can easily tear chips out of the roundels. Note that the top of the cross curves outward, almost to the full 3⅝-inch depth of the wood. When you are carving this curve, begin each cut at the top edge of the cross and work downward, toward the roundels.

When the face of the cross has been incised to its proper depth, you are ready to cut the ¾-inch-wide chamfers along the edges. The chamfer tapers to a point at the top of the cross.

Begin each cut of the taper at the topmost point of the cross, and work downward toward the roundel. Work the straight sections of the chamfer between the roundels and the top edge of the back support with a rasp or file, then smooth them with a sharp chisel. Also smooth away the saw marks along the sides of the cross and around the roundels with a chisel or sharp carving knife.

Carve away the hatched area around the stars on the face of the roundels to a depth of ⅛ inch. Cut around the design's edges with a sharp carving knife according to the instructions on establishing an outline in the woodcarving chapter. Here the exact width of the outline cut is irrelevant; the entire hatched area will be removed.

With the edges of your carving established, remove the remaining hatched area to a depth of ⅛ inch. Use small chisels or a carving knife to remove the excess

wood. If you use chisels, cut neither too deep nor too fast. The sharp edge of the chisel can easily chip the star. Clean up the edges and corners of the design with a carving knife, and sand lightly.

The final design element is the ⅛-inch band carved across the top of the back support, just beneath the base of the cross. Lay this out with a ruler, and carve it with a sharp carving knife held at a 45-degree angle. Two cuts ⅛ inch apart should form a V of the proper depth and width. Round the edges of the V slightly with a carving knife, and sand lightly.

**Mortising the Back and Arm Supports**
All of the framing components of the bench are directly connected to the back and arm supports' mortise and tenon joints. The widths of all of the tenons are clearly marked on the drawings, their height being the full height of the timbers from which they are formed, except in the case of the front tenon on the armrest. To prevent this tenon from breaking through the top of the arm, cut it 1 inch lower than the top surface of the armrest. If you doubt your ability to cut a tight, neatly fitting mortise, or want to hide the top of the joint, make the tenons ¼ inch narrower than the height of the timber—but remember that the bench will lack historical accuracy.

Carefully locate the position of all the joints in the back and arm supports. The back supports will each have two mortises on the front face and two more on the inner edge, and the arms will have two on the rear edge and one on the inside face.

Note: Pay special attention to the center back rail, which appears as section B in the drawings. This rail, not original to the bench, was probably added later to provide additional support. Consequently it is only nailed into place, not mortised and tenoned. To eliminate this support would be perfectly accurate. If you include it, add it when the bench is complete.

Cut the mortises after they are drawn in their proper locations. It is easiest to drill away most of the excess wood, not penetrating deeper than the tenon's length. Remove remaining wood with a sharp chisel. Be certain that the walls of the mortise are smooth and flat, and that the corners are square.

**Joining Front, Sides, and Back**
With the top and lower back rails, side rails, and front seat support rail cut to length, mark out the tenon on each end of each rail. Cut the tenons carefully, testing

them frequently for fit. The tenon should sink into its appointed mortise with a few sound taps from a mallet—you should not need a sledgehammer to drive it into place. If a tenon is too tight, it will split the surrounding mortise; if it is too loose, the piece will wobble. When all the mortise and tenon joints fit snugly, it is time to assemble the bench.

## Final Back Assembly
Cut the chamfers on all four edges of the top rail. A cross section of the chamfers can be found in the section B drawing. Note that the chamfers stop $1\frac{1}{2}$ inches short of the back support posts. The chamfers can be most easily cut with a router, but remove the router marks with a sharp chisel.

Both the upper and lower back rails have troughs that are 1 inch wide and $1\frac{1}{2}$ inches deep to receive the back slats. Cut these troughs with the aid of a table saw set to the proper depth. Assemble the rails and the back support posts when the trough has been hollowed in both rails. Now gouge a corresponding trough in the back support posts to receive the slats on the extreme right and left ends of the back. Section C shows that the trough in the back support post is only $\frac{5}{8}$ inch wide, rather than the full 1-inch width of the troughs in the top and bottom rails. The trough in the left back support, shown in section C, is flush with the front edge of the troughs in the top and bottom rails; the trough in the right support should be flush with the rear edge of the troughs in the upper and lower rails. This allows the back slats to be held tightly in position when the entire back is assembled.

Disassemble the back and cut notches in the lower rail to allow insertion of the seat supports. As shown in section C, the seat supports are spaced at approximately 12-inch intervals. The notches should be the width of the seat supports (3 inches) and the same $1\frac{1}{2}$ inches in depth as the trough for the back slats. A side view of the notches is found in section B.

Lay the back on a level surface, being sure that the structure is square. Drill and dowel the rails to one of the back support posts, following the instructions on doweling in the general chapter on woodworking techniques. Remove the opposite back support post. Slide the first back slat into position so that it fits snugly into the trough in the back support. Slide the second slat into position, allowing it to overlap the first slat by approximately 1 inch. You may have to rasp or plane the ends of the slats to get them to overlap properly.

When they overlap by approximately 1 inch, nail the first slat into position by drilling pilot holes into the top and bottom rails and through the slat. Secure the slat in position with large-headed forged nails.

Slide the third slat into position, overlapping the second slat by approximately 1 inch, and nail the second slat into position. Locating this nail, and all subsequent nails, at the point where two slats overlap allows you to secure two slats with each nail. Proceed until all of the slats are in location. If the final slat is slightly too long, simply remove it and trim the excess wood. It is impossible to predict whether the final slat will be a bit too long or too short, because the exact amount the slats overlap varies on the original piece from $\frac{3}{4}$ inch to $1\frac{1}{4}$ inches. Attach the final support post to the back assembly, and dowel it into place.

## Frame Assembly
Temporarily insert the front and side seat support rails into the arms. With a carpenter's square, locate the position where the seat supports will intersect the front seat support rail. Pencil in these locations, and disassemble the front of the bench. Cut the seat support notches in the front rail 1 inch by $1\frac{1}{2}$ inches by 3 inches, as shown in sections B and C.

## Seat and Seat Supports
Again assemble the bench, and cut the seat supports to fit snugly in the notches provided. Note that the seat supports are tapered in the back but notched in the front. With the seat supports in place, cut the seat itself. The current seat, as was undoubtedly true of the original, is made of a single oak board $19\frac{5}{8}$ inches in width. If your search for a similar board is not successful, glue and peg two or three boards together as described in the chapter on the Merrills Board.

After the seat reaches its proper width, make a cardboard template of one end of the bench to fit around the arms and the back supports. The seat rests firmly against the back slats and is flush with the exterior face of the side seat supports. The front edge, however, overhangs the front support rail by $1\frac{1}{8}$ inches. Cut the seat to conform to the lines of the template; it should fit snugly into place inside the arms. The bench must be disassembled to attach the seat. Remove the front of the bench, and reassemble the bench around the seat. Lift the seat to insert the seat supports. When everything fits comfortably, remove the seat and shape the front edge as shown in the end view and section B drawings.

The edge can be formed either with a molding plane or a router fitted with a ¾-inch quarter-round bit. In either case, allow for the ⅛-inch offset at the seat's top edge. Lightly round the seat's bottom edge with sandpaper or a fine rasp.

The seat's span is supported by ten heavy braces spaced at approximately 12-inch intervals. These braces are shown in the section B and section C drawings. They are cut from lengths of 3-inch-square oak to fit into the notches in the front and back rails. Notch the front of each seat support as shown in section B. Next, cut a 1½-by-5-inch arc out of the support's opposite end to lay in the notches in the lower back rail, as shown in section B.

## Final Assembly

Now permanently assemble the bench. Insert the side rails and armrests into the back assembly, and place the seat between them. Laying the arm supports and front rail on a level surface, assemble the arms and the seat support. Making certain that the arms and rail are square, drill and dowel the rail to the arms. Attach the front assembly to the side rails and the armrests, and being certain that the bench is sitting on a level surface and is plumb and square, drill and dowel the remaining joints.

Lift the seat and clamp it to the armrests with cabinet clamps, or raise it as far as possible above the seat support with wooden blocks. Set the seat supports in place, and nail them to the frame with hand-forged nails. Lower the seat into place and nail it to the frame. The original bench has six nails along the front and eight across the rear of the seat, and one nail on each side between the arm and the rear support post.

## Finish

Lightly sand the entire bench. To match the original as closely as possible, coat with an extremely dark stain. Several companies market a stain called Jacobin, which imbues a rich coffee color—the ideal. After the stain has dried, polish the entire bench with boiled linseed oil. If it is still not dark enough, apply several coats of Old English scratch cover polish over several months. This will darken it sufficiently and give it a lovely warm glow.

FRONT VIEW

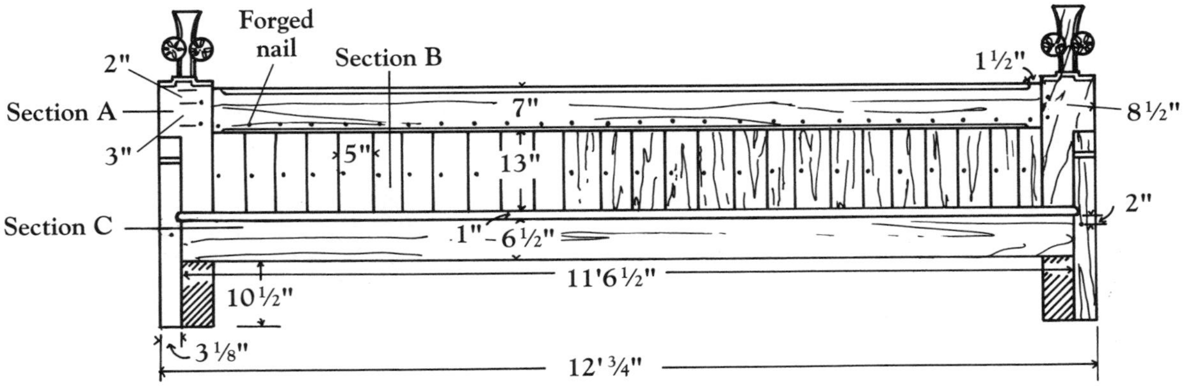

Forged nail
Section B
2"
Section A
3"
Section C
1½"
8½"
7"
5"
13"
2"
1"-6½"
11'6½"
10½"
3⅛"
12'¾"


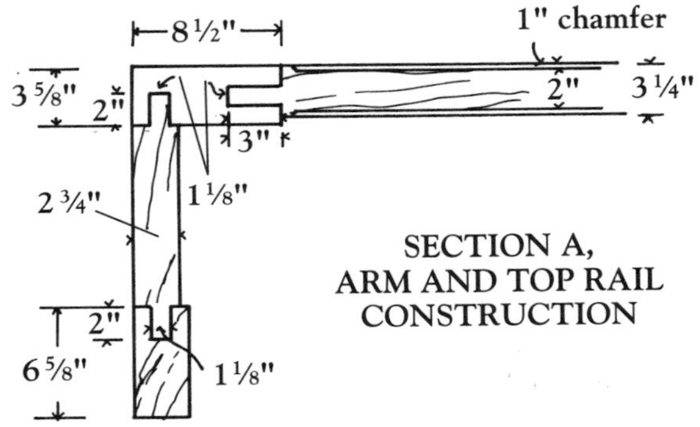

8½"
1" chamfer
3⅝"
2"
2"
3¼"
3"
1⅛"
2¾"
2"
6⅝"
1⅛"


SECTION A,
ARM AND TOP RAIL
CONSTRUCTION

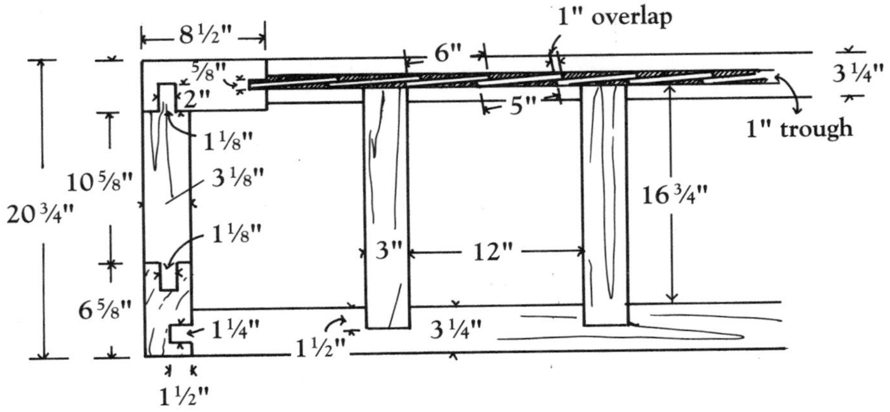

8½"
1" overlap
6"
⅝"
2"
5"
3¼"
1" trough
1⅛"
3⅛"
10⅝"
20¾"
16¾"
1⅛"
3"
12"
6⅝"
1¼"
1½"
3¼"
1½"


SECTION C,
SIDE RAIL, BACK, AND
SEAT CONSTRUCTION

FINIAL DETAIL

PROFILE

END VIEW

SECTION B

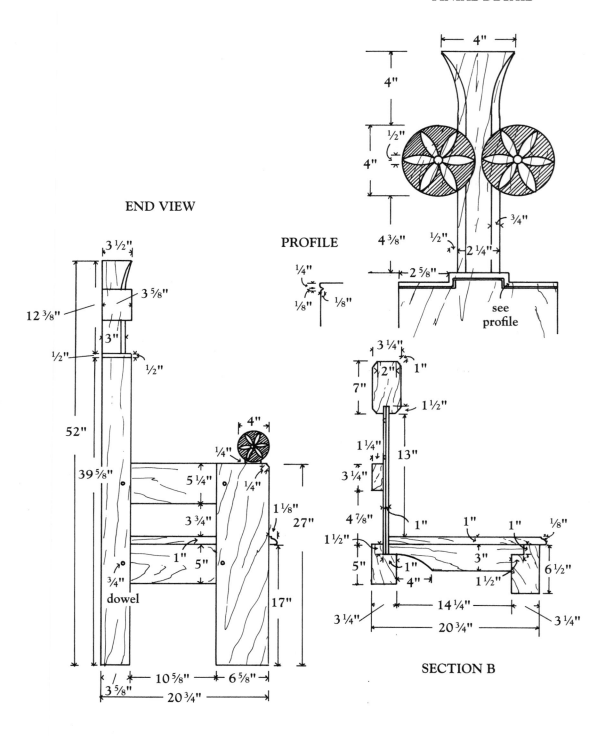

56

# Project 5

# HEWN-TIMBER CHEST

This massive hewn chest is among the most striking pieces in Hereford Cathedral's distinguished collection. The pine planks from which it was constructed appear to have been riven, or split, with wedges, rather than sawn from the tree trunk. The separated slabs of wood were then smoothed and finished into thick planks using only the most rudimentary hand tools. The lid of the chest was hewn from an entire section of tree trunk, the exterior curve of the lid following the natural shape of the tree. The diameter of the tree not only determined the lid's curve, but also the front-to-back depth of the finished chest.

Unlike the simplistic design of the chest's woodwork and strapping, the lock plate is a work of true craft. The elongated square plate is adorned with a lifelike representation of a grape cluster carefully executed with considerable skill.

This chest has been at Hereford Cathedral, Hereford, England, for undetermined centuries, but it may not have originally been designed to be church property. Although the chest has been dated from the mid-fifteenth century, its sheer bulk, unsophisticated design, and lack of ornamentation may indicate that it is actually from one or more centuries earlier. Whatever its age, it was originally almost certainly the property of a minor noble or a member of the rising merchant class, individuals who could not afford the quality of furniture associated with the baronage. If it was the property of a petit nobleman or a merchant, the chest may have come to the cathedral as a part of an endowment or as the property of a novitiate who joined one of the monastic orders associated with the church.

## CONSTRUCTION NOTES

Although the chest is massive, its construction is actually quite simple and straightforward. The only challenges you will face are making the lid and some intricate metal sculpting on the lock plate decorations. Your time and patience will duplicate one of the handsomest chests we have discovered.

## Materials

The heavy pine planks used in the sides, the ends, and the bottom of the chest were, as noted above, split from massive logs. Assuming you do not have access to timbers of the size necessary to split the boards, you will have to have them specially milled to thickness and width. The chest's rather crude look can be best reproduced if you use rough-cut lumber and sand it with a hand sander until it is nearly smooth.

If you choose to use several narrow boards and glue them to the proper width, follow the instructions for joining lumber and doweling, found in the chapters on woodworking and on the Merrills Board. To peg together rough-cut lumber, it will be necessary to plane the edges to ensure a good fit. Although this can be done with a hand plane, planing done on a commercial grade joiner will assure the best fit. Any good lumber-mill will accommodate you.

## Lid

Making the lid offers more limited possibilities. Since it was hewn from a 5-foot-long section of tree trunk that must have been between 28 and 30 inches in diameter, the only practical way to reproduce it is to follow the example of the original. The best way to obtain a log of an appropriate size is to visit a sawmill or a slab mill, where the owner may provide you with a section of tree trunk cut to your needs. He might consent to cut away one side of the log (slightly less than half of its total mass), leaving you with less wood to remove. If you are working with an entire log, you will

# MATERIALS

## WOOD
All wood is pine or fir.

| PART | NUMBER OF PIECES | THICKNESS | | WIDTH | | LENGTH |
|---|---|---|---|---|---|---|
| front and rear | 2 | 1¼" | × | 17½" | × | 50" |
| ends | 2 | 1¼" | × | 20" | × | 21" |
| bottom | 1 | 1¼" | × | 20" | × | 50" |
| lid (tree trunk split in half) | 1 | 28" to 30" diameter | | | × | 52½" |

## METAL

| PART | NUMBER OF PIECES | THICKNESS | | WIDTH | | LENGTH |
|---|---|---|---|---|---|---|
| end lid bands | 2 | ⅛" | × | 2½" | × | 44" |
| hinged lid bands | 3 | ⅛" | × | 2½" | × | 44" |
| hinged vertical case bands | 3 | ⅛" | × | 2½" | × | 60" |

need either a chain saw or a sledgehammer, splitting wedges, and a good deal of patience. Alternatively, you might find a tree that is about to be cut down and offer to purchase a section of the trunk. Fortunately, a large pine tree is easier to find than an oak of similar size.

The first step in shaping the lid is to remove the bark. Starting at one end of the log, use a hatchet to chip away a strip of bark the entire length of the log. Using a chisel or wide putty knife, loosen the bark on both sides of the stripped area. Then peel away the remaining bark.

Once the bark is removed, use a chain saw to cut away one side of the log, leaving a slab slightly over a foot thick. If you are handy with a chain saw, use it to hollow out the lid's interior curve. When most of the excess wood has been removed, begin to smooth and shape the interior of the lid with an adze. With a blade shaped like a garden mattock, but sharp like an ax or hatchet, the adze is the only practical tool for tackling such a project. Mastering this implement takes prac-

tice, but if you start where there is a fair amount of wood to remove, you should be fairly adept by the time you get to the more precise work. The more wood that you can remove at this stage, the quicker the remaining wood will dry, and the easier the final steps will be. You should be able to work the lid to within 90 percent of its finished shape with the adze.

If the log is fairly dry, the remaining work will be easier. If the wood is green, leave it to cure for a minimum of four months (a year is not excessive) before you begin the finishing work on the lid. Trial and error will determine for you when the wood has cured adequately—if your tools drag, or if the wood feels wet, it has not cured enough.

The next step on the lid's exterior requires a drawknife; use it to smooth out any large imperfections or rough spots and to shape the bottom corners. Final finishing work can be done with a carpenter's plane. This will remove any large flaws left by the drawknife. Note that the bottom edges of the lid are rounded.

| PART | NUMBER OF PIECES | THICKNESS | | WIDTH | | LENGTH |
|---|---|---|---|---|---|---|
| horizontal bottom bands | 2 | 1/8" | × | 2½" | × | 66" |
| horizontal end bands | 8 | 1/8" | × | 2½" | × | 19" |
| vertical end and bottom bands | 2 | 1/8" | × | 2½" | × | 97" |
| hasps | 3 | 1/8" | × | 3" | × | 14¾" |
| hasp catch | 2 | 1/8" | × | ½" | × | 8" |
| lock catch | 1 | 1/16" | × | ½" | × | 2¾" |
| lock plate | 1 | 1/8" | × | 11" | × | 12" |
| lock plate ornament | 1 | 1/32" | × | 6" | × | 12" |
| handle rings | 2 | ¼" diameter | | | × | 24" |
| handle staples | 4 | ¼" diameter | | | × | 5" |
| large-headed forged nails | 138 | | | | | 2" |

Finish the lid's interior with a chisel. The concave interior does not need to be as smooth as the exterior. It is infrequently seen, and it is not as smooth on the original chest.

**Alternative Lid**

If you cannot find a log from which to make the lid, have a slab glued up at a lumbermill to the appropriate thickness and width. The lid can then be shaped with the methods described above, a task made even easier with the help of an electric hand plane.

**Setting Up**

Since the construction of the body of this chest is so simple, it is possible to cut all the pieces before beginning the actual construction.

Cut the bottom, the sides, and the ends as shown on the diagrams, but do not cut the angles on the top edges of the front and the back. The actual thickness of the top may vary slightly from one end to the other;

it may be wise to leave the curved edge of the end boards slightly longer than they are shown on the drawings, at least until a final fitting of all the pieces. Note that the grain on the end panels runs vertically, whereas the grain on the sides and the bottom runs horizontally.

**Fitting the Case**

When the side, end, and bottom panels have been cut, set the pieces together as they will appear when the chest is finished. If you have elected to use rough-cut lumber, sand it before the trial fitting. To hold the pieces in their proper position, use cabinet clamps, strap clamps, or even small nails that can later be removed. If you use nails, position them so that the nail holes will eventually be covered by the iron banding.

With the chest temporarily assembled, fit the lid into place. Use a hand plane to begin to cut the angle on the top edges of the front and back panels, slowly allowing the lid to come to rest on the case. Check your fit frequently during this step to see where any adjustments in the thickness of the lid, angle of the top and back, and curve of the ends need to be made. When the lid rests evenly on the case, it is time to assemble the chest.

## Case Assembly

The original chest shows no evidence that anything other than the metal strapping holds the case together. It is likely, however, that some form of attachment was used to assemble the chest before the strapping was applied and that this work is hidden by the strapping itself. We proceed on this assumption.

Mark the centerlines of the straps with a pencil and a straightedge on the sides, bottom, and ends of the chest. These will serve to locate the attachment points.

Use either wooden pegs or nails to join together the pieces of the chest. If you choose nails, we suggest using hand-forged ones in the spirit of medieval construction. Sink the nail heads so that they are flush with the chest's surface and do not interfere with the application of the strapping. There is no need to glue the pieces together; the iron banding will adequately support the chest.

With the pieces held together temporarily with cabinet clamps or strap clamps, be certain that the sides and ends of the chest are square and plumb. Nail or peg (as described in the general chapter on woodworking techniques) the chest together. The end panels and the bottom sit inside the front and the back panels; all the nails or pegs, therefore, will be on the chest's front and back. One nail or peg where each iron band intersects a corner of the chest should be sufficient. This gives a total of nine nails or pegs each in the front and back panels. You are now ready to forge the metal banding.

## Lid Banding

The five bands that run across the top of the trunk are each constructed of a single piece of $1/8$-inch strap metal, the rear ends of three of them forming the top end of the hinge that opens the lid and the front ends forming the hinges, the joint of the hasps, and the lock cover. It will be easiest to begin by forming the two outermost bands, and progressing to the three inner ones.

It is a good idea to cut a wooden template in the shape of the lid's outer surface; use it as a gauge against which to fit the straps as you bend them.

Cut the segments of strap metal to the necessary length, allowing enough to turn 3 inches of the band underneath the bottom edge of the lid. Heat the metal as for any shaping, but heat a slightly longer area than would be necessary to make a bend. By placing one end of the strap metal on an anvil or suitable working surface, and holding the opposite end in one hand, gently hammer the heated area to begin to bend the metal into an arc. Neither shape too tight an arc nor attempt to bend the metal too fast. It is much easier to incline it farther by reheating than to have to remove too tight a curve later. After the band has been shaped into an arc that nicely hugs the template, use a mandrel (as described in the chapter on metalworking) to shape the tight curves around the lid's bottom edges. Repeat the process for the second outer band, and then for the three inner bands, being sure to leave an excess length of unbent metal at the front and rear ends of these inner bands to form the hinge and hasp joints.

## Case Banding

Begin with the short bands that wrap around the corners of the chest. There are eight of these, all identical in size and shape. Cut the stock to length, allowing enough stock to fit beneath the entire width of the vertical bands on the front and the side of the chest. Allowing $1/2$ inch of metal to form the corner bend, cut these straps to $18 1/2$ inches. Bend the straps into an L shape, according to instructions in the metalworking chapter, so that one leg is 11 inches long and the other is 7 inches.

Now form the bands nearest the bottom of the chest, those that run across the entire front and back—but wrap around the sides only as far as the short bands.

With these twelve bands cut and shaped, drill pilot holes through them, position the bands on the trunk, and attach them with large-headed forged nails. Also attach the two outermost bands to the lid.

Next, forge the three bands that run down the chest's front, across the bottom, and up the back. Make the bottom section of these bands $1/4$ inch wider than the actual depth of the trunk to allow them to slip over the horizontal bands on the front and the rear of the chest. Also allow enough extra stock on one end of all three straps to form the lower ends of the hinges. Do not attach these straps to the chest until after the formation of the hinges.

Now make a template for the lock plate. Positioning the band and the lock plate template on the chest, mark the section of the center band that will be covered by the lock plate, and cut it away.

## Hinges

Notice on the side view drawing of the hinge that the spine of the hinge wraps completely around the hinge pin and is buried behind the strap. To accomplish this, notch the flat stock as shown in the drawings.

Place the bands on the chest in their proper location; set the lid, without the bands, on the chest; and mark the level of the lid's bottom on the hinge straps. This line will be the top of the hinge's spine. Lay out the area to be excised from the strap metal according to the hinge detail A drawing, and remove the band from the chest. Lay out the rectangle to be cut from the metal, drill out as much of this area as possible, and file away the remaining excess metal. Following the instructions on hinge making in the metalworking chapter, bend the spine for the hinges and replace the bands on the chest. Note: If the construction of these hinges seems confusing, make paper models of the hinge ends illustrated in the hinge details A and B, and bend them to shape until the concept becomes clear.

Replace the lid and set the bands that form the upper portion of the hinges in place, with the unformed hinge ends falling behind the finished lower half of the hinges. Mark the location of the top line of the lower half of the hinge on the lid straps. Remove the lid straps, and lay out the H-shaped areas to be cut away according to the hinge detail B drawing; be certain that the notches fall below the line of the top of the lower half of the hinge. Bend the spine for this half of the hinge. Repeat the process on the opposite end of the bands to form the top end of the hasp and the lock cover joints according to the hinge detail A drawing. Cut any excess metal on the back end of all the straps to the 2-inch length prescribed in the drawings.

Reposition the straps on the chest's body, and put the lid and the lid straps in place. Check the alignment of the hinges by inserting the hinge pins. Drill and nail the lid straps to the lid, and then drill and nail the straps on the chest itself. When two or three nails have secured each strap in place, remove the hinge pins and take off the lid to allow the body to be turned for insertion of the remaining nails.

## Final Case Bands

Now bend and attach the bands running down the ends and across the bottom of the chest.

When these bands have been nailed in place, set the lid on the chest and permanently install the hinge pins.

## Hasps and Lock Cover

From ⅛-inch strap metal, cut three identical plates to form the hasps and the lock cover. Heat and shape the curled handle and the hinge section of these pieces.

For the two hasps, mark and cut out two rectangular holes, as shown in the drawings, by drilling and filing away excess material. For the lock cover, bend a ½-inch-wide piece of ¹⁄₁₆-inch strap metal to form a three-sided, right-angled figure that is ⅝ inch on the two shallow sides and 1½ inches on the single long side. Weld this piece in place on the reverse side of the lock cover at the same location as the rectangular holes on the hasp covers. Then place these three pieces on the lid with hinge pins, peening over the pins' ends.

## Hasp Catch

From two pieces of ⅛-inch-thick strap metal that is 8 inches in length, form the hasp catches as shown in the drawings. Begin by filing or grinding the ends to points, and then heat and bend the stock to form open-ended rectangles.

Mark the location of the hasp catches through the open holes in the hasps. Drill two holes large enough to allow the hasp catches to be inserted through the metal banding beneath the hasp.

Drill smaller pilot holes through the chest's wooden face. Tap the hasp catches through the chest, and bend the ends to lie flat against the chest's interior.

## Handle Rings

From a 2-foot length of ¼-inch round stock, bend two rings of the size shown in the handle ring drawing. Using a 1¾-inch iron pipe for a forming mandrel will ease this job. Heat the ¼-inch stock, and bend it completely around the pipe twice. Allow the metal to cool, and saw the rings loose. Reheat the rings, and hammer the ends to meet. Then weld the ends of the rings closed.

From additional ¼-inch round stock, form two horseshoe shapes, and cut them to the length shown in the drawing. File or grind the ends to a point. Drill ¼-inch holes through the side bands of the chest at the appropriate location and ⅛-inch holes through the chest's wooden ends.

Placing the staples through the rings, drive the staples through the wood, and bend the ends to lie against the interior of the chest.

## Lock Plate

Cut the lock plate from ⅛-inch flat stock as shown in the drawing. Lay out the key and lock holes on the plate, and drill and file the openings to shape. Also make holes large enough to receive a forged nail in each corner of the lock plate.

The lock plate is decorated with a raised design made from a 1/32-inch-thick sheet of flat stock. Make a forming tool from a ⅝-inch piece of round stock about 4 inches in length. Round one end of the tool into a half sphere. Repeat the process with a ¼-inch length of round stock.

Mark out the lock plate design on the 1/32-inch flat stock. It is easier to make this design in three pieces—the first containing one of the grape clusters and a length of stem, the second with the second cluster and more stem, and the third having only the pod shape where the two stems join.

Lay the flat stock on a flat piece of softwood; pine will work best. Place the large forming tool at the center of one of the grapes, and strike it with a hammer. It should indent the shape of one grape into the metal.

After every one or two grapes are indented, turn over the metal plate to tap out the warps and dents. This is a slow, tedious process.

Form the stems in the same way. A series of taps along the stem line will eventually form the stem. Alternatively, bend a length of ¼-inch stock to the shape of the stem, and lay it along the stem line, slowly tapping it along its length with a hammer.

After the pieces are formed, cut out the shapes and file the edges smooth. Then solder the decorative shapes onto the lock plate.

## Handles

The original handles are gone, but they were undoubtedly formed from either lengths of heavy plaited leather or braided rope.

## Finish

Coat this chest with a dark stain followed by a coat of boiled linseed oil to closely approximate the original finish.

## FRONT VIEW

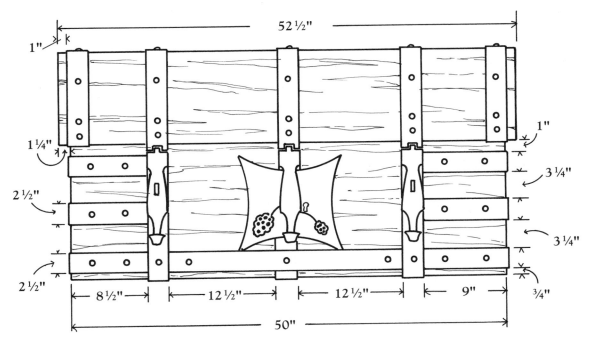

52½"

1"

1"

1¼"

3¼"

2½"

3¼"

2½"

¾"

8½"    12½"    12½"    9"

50"

## END VIEW

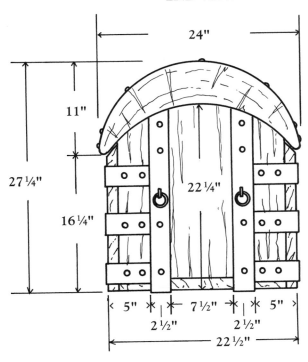

24"

11"

27¼"

22¼"

16¼"

5"    7½"    5"

2½"    2½"

22½"

## CROSS SECTION

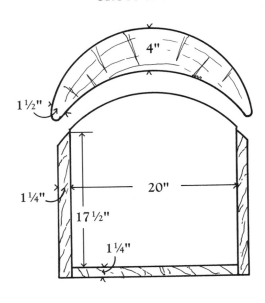

4"

1½"

1¼"

20"

17½"

1¼"

# HINGE

### DETAIL A

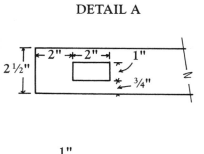

### DETAIL B

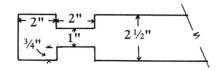

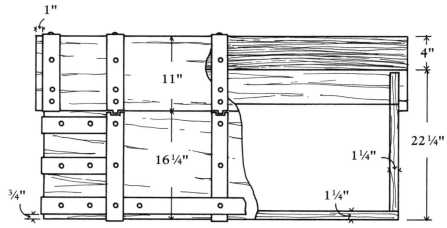

## REAR, CUTAWAY VIEW

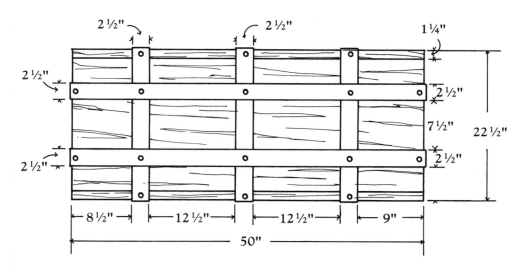

## BOTTOM

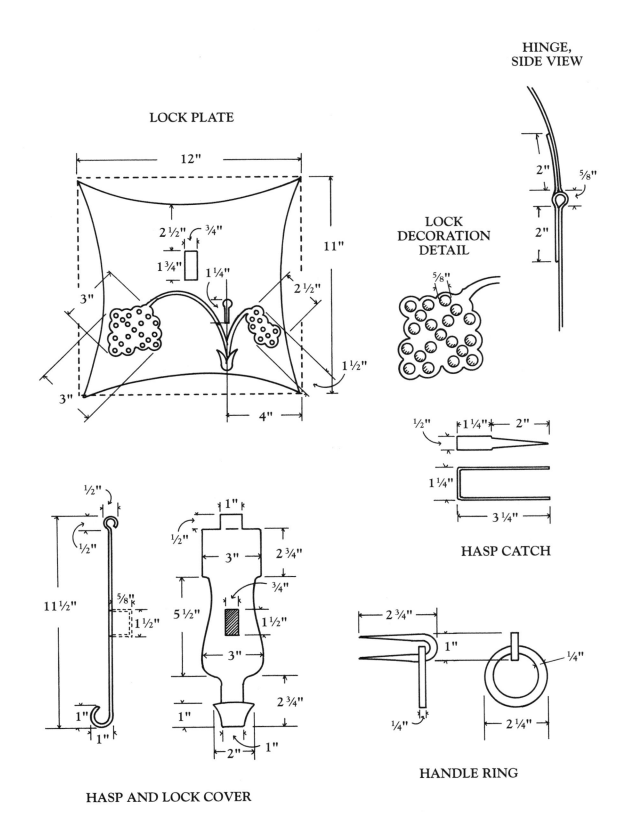

HINGE,
SIDE VIEW

LOCK PLATE

LOCK
DECORATION
DETAIL

HASP CATCH

HASP AND LOCK COVER

HANDLE RING

65

# Project 6

# LIBRARY SHELVES

Throughout much of the Middle Ages, books were so rare that the idea of needing special shelves to house a large collection was inconceivable.

Monasteries, schools (usually run by monasteries), record halls, and even the king's record keepers simply piled their books on tables and in trunks. The invention of the printing press in the late 1440s rapidly changed things, and within a century and a half, even private libraries grew to impressive proportions.

Universities, schools, and churches—eager to organize and display their growing collections of books—built shelves on which to arrange the books by subject, thereby making them easier to access. To protect these valuable books from theft, school governors ordered that books be chained in place. A book could be taken off the shelf and placed on a reading ledge in front of the stack—there and no farther. Chains were attached to each book by means of a small metal plate on the bottom corner of the front cover. When the books were replaced on the shelves, the chain and the attachment plate were left exposed. Since the books were shelved backward, their spines, bearing the title and the author's name, faced the inside of the shelf and were invisible to the reader. Often, in those books still remaining in chained collections, we find shelf numbers, titles, and authors' names written on the edges of the bindings just above the chain plates, allowing researchers to find their books without pulling every volume off the shelf.

These wonderful shelves were built of fine English oak in 1623—too late to be truly medieval, though the appearance and construction of the shelves are identical to the medieval style. The iron chains and rods were in use until 1792, when they were removed. Of the dozens of similar shelves in this library at Oxford University, this shelf unit remains the closest to its original form. The column that can be seen at the left edge of the picture was a late addition and therefore does not appear on our plans.

## CONSTRUCTION NOTES

This piece's basic construction is amazingly simple; only the complexity of the molding patterns and the sheer monumental size of the unit make this project a bit of a challenge. When cutting the shelves and divider panels, allow enough extra length to provide for the rabbet joints where the shelves fit into the end panels and where the divider panels fit into the shelves. The shelves are blind pegged into the end panels; the exact number and locations of the pegs are only guesswork.

Although the original piece has only two shelves, you may want more. Allow for any additional shelves from the beginning of the project by adapting the number of shelves, the rabbet joints, and the length of the divider panels to the desired number of shelves.

Because of this unit's size, be certain you can move it from your workshop to its final location. You may need to construct it in the room where it will be installed.

### Materials

Made entirely of oak, this unit has only one board that is extraordinarily oversized—the end panel on the right of the drawings that anchors the shelves to the wall of the building. It would be unlikely that reducing this panel to the same thickness as the left end panel would compromise the structure of the bookcase, but to do so would require shortening the width of the triangular pediment at the top of the unit by 1¼ inches.

Whatever your decision, buy all the wood for the project in advance. Once you begin construction, you will be amazed at how rapidly the shelf unit takes shape. If you decide that cutting the moldings as shown in the drawings is too complicated to tackle yourself, allow time for your local mill or cabinet shop to make them before you begin construction work.

### Frame Preparation

Trim the end panels to length. Note that the end panels do not mortise into the bottom rails the way the seat does (see the end view drawing).

Cut the top panel, shelves, and divider panels to length, allowing for the rabbet joints where the shelves intersect with the end panels and where the dividers intersect the shelves. Note that the top panel does not fit into the end panels with a rabbet joint; it lies across the top of the end panels, making it the same length as the outside width of the shelf unit (90¼ inches).

Mark the position of the shelves on the inner face of the end panels. The best way to ensure that they are located at the same height is to lay the end panels on a level work surface with their back edges touching, and the inner face of the panels faceup. Be sure that the panels are aligned at the top and bottom. Using a carpenter's square, mark a centerline for each shelf across the face of the two end panels. Move the square ⅜ inch on either side of the centerline to locate the top and bottom lines of the rabbet.

In the same way, lay the two shelves next to each other on your work surface, with the underside of the center shelf, and the top surface of the bottom shelf, facing upward. With the carpenter's square, mark the centerlines of the two divider panels. Move the square ⁵⁄₃₂ inch to either side of the centerline to locate the width of the bottom (the narrowest part) of the rabbet (see the detail D drawing). Repeat this process to locate the position of the divider panels on the top of the center shelf and the underside of the top panel. Ensure that the upper and lower divider panels are in alignment by simply continuing the lines from the underside of the center shelf around the edge and across the top face of the shelf, and then continuing this line onto the underside of the top panel. Note that the top panel is longer than either of the two shelves. To ensure that the divider panels sit vertically when the unit is assembled, be sure that the left end of the top panel extends ¾ inch beyond the left end of

the center shelf before you mark the location of the divider panels.

Using a table saw or a radial arm saw guided by a fence, cut the rabbets in the end panels and shelves to the depth shown in the drawings of details D and E. Flare the rabbets on the shelves to a 45-degree angle (as shown in the detail D drawing) with a chisel, molding plane, or router. Using a table saw, molding plane, or router, chamfer the top and bottom ends of the divider panels to fit in the rabbets in the shelves.

When the rabbets have been cut in the end panels, it is time to cut and install the lower shelf supports. These are identical to the center shelf support shown in the section A drawing, except that they are only 1½ inches thick. Cut two of these supports (don't forget to cut the 1-by-2-inch notch in the top of the support), and drill pilot holes for three dowels (approximately equally spaced) completely through the supports. Clamp them to the end panels directly beneath the rabbet for the lower shelf. To ensure that they are even with the rabbet, it is a good idea to put a board in the rabbet and butt the shelf support gently against the board. When the supports are in place, mark the locations of the pilot holes by inserting the pilot drill through the holes in the shelf supports and drilling just enough to mark their locations on the end panels. Remove the shelf supports and drill ½-inch-deep pilot holes into the end panels. After coating the inside of the pilot holes on the shelf supports with glue, tap dowels through the holes until they extend slightly less than ½ inch through the face that fits against the end panel. Temporarily position the shelf support over the pilot holes to ensure that the dowels line up with the holes in the end panels. Lightly coat the surface of the shelf support and the interior of the pilot holes in the end panel with glue, and tap the shelf support into position. Clamp the support to the end panel until the glue is dry to ensure good adhesion.

### Frame Assembly

The shelves are almost certainly doweled into the end panels. Unfortunately, since the dowels do not come through the outer face of the panels, we know neither where the dowels are located nor how many there are. We suggest that three ⅜-inch dowels be used in each end of a shelf. Aligning the pilot holes will be tricky because you cannot mark directly across the boards you are joining. Instead, we recommend that you use doweling centers. Available from better tool and cabinetmakers' shops, doweling centers allow you to drill

# MATERIALS

## WOOD
All wood is oak.

| PART | NUMBER OF PIECES | THICKNESS | | WIDTH | | LENGTH |
|---|---|---|---|---|---|---|
| left end panel | 1 | 1⅜" | × | 11" | × | 76½" |
| right end panel | 1 | 2⅝" | × | 11" | × | 76½" |
| top panel | 1 | 1⅜" | × | 11" | × | 90¼" |
| shelves | 2 | ⅞" | × | 11" | × | 87" |
| divider panels, top shelf | 2 | ¾" | × | 11" | × | 21" |
| divider panels, bottom shelf | 2 | ¾" | × | 11" | × | 21½" |
| backboards | 12 | 1" | × | 8" | × | 72" |
| baseboard | 1 | 1" | × | 6" | × | 90¼" |
| shelf rail | 1 | 1" | × | 2" | × | 87¼" |
| shelf supports | 2 | 1½" | × | 4" | × | 22¾" |
| shelf support, center | 1 | 2" | × | 4" | × | 22¾" |
| bookrest | 1 | ¾" | × | 11" | × | 88¼" |
| bottom rails | 2 | 2¾" | × | 4½" | × | 42" |
| center support | 1 | 2½" | × | 9½" | × | 30" |
| foot for center support | 1 | 2½" | × | 2" | × | 9¼" |
| seat | 1 | 1¾" | × | 9¼" | × | 89¼" |
| legs | 2 | 1½" | × | 9¼" | × | 21⅛" |
| columns | 2 | 3¼" | × | 3¼" | × | 14" |

| PART | NUMBER OF PIECES | THICKNESS | | WIDTH | | LENGTH |
|---|---|---|---|---|---|---|
| ball finials | 2 | 3¾" | × | 3¾" | × | 4¾" |
| column molding | 1 | ⅝" | × | 1¼" | × | 60" |
| pediment | 1 | 1" | × | 14" | × | 83" |
| crown molding for pediment | 2 | 2" | × | 4¼" | × | 48" |
| top edge molding | 1 | 1" | × | 4" | × | 108" |
| brackets | 2 | 1⅜" | × | 2" | × | 4¼" |
| dowel | 4 | ⅜" diameter | | | × | 36" |

## METAL

| PART | NUMBER OF PIECES | THICKNESS | | WIDTH | | LENGTH |
|---|---|---|---|---|---|---|
| lock plate | 1 | 1/16" | × | 5½" | × | 8" |
| rod | 1 | ½" diameter | | | × | 89" |
| rod brackets | 4 | 1/16" | × | 1" | × | 4 5/16" |
| bracket supports | 2 | 3/32" | × | 6½" | × | 6½" |
| bracket supports | 2 | 3/32" | × | 3¾" | × | 6½" |
| hasp top | 1 | ⅛" | × | 1½" | × | 4" |
| hasp arm | 1 | ⅛" | × | 3⅜" | × | 23" |
| hinge pin | 1 | ⅛" diameter | | | × | 1⅞" |
| knob on hasp | 1 | ⅜" diameter | | | × | 1" |
| hasp latch | 1 | 1/16" | × | 3/16" | × | 1½" |
| optional angle brackets | 6 | 1/16" | × | 1" | × | 1" |
| optional chain | 1 per book | 1/16" diameter | × | ½" × 1½" link | × | 30" long |

pilot holes in one board, insert the dowel centers, position the board in the rabbet, and with the tap of a hammer, punch a small hole in the end panel at the exact center of the dowel.

If you cannot find doweling centers, be careful to locate the dowels at the exact position on the end of the shelf and in the end panel. In either case, the dowels should not be sunk into the end panel more than ½ inch. Check to ensure the depth of the holes. Before you glue the dowels into place, it is a good idea to dry fit the dowels and shelves together to ensure the alignment of the pilot holes. When you are satisfied that everything fits, glue and tap the dowels into the end of the shelf. After the glue has dried, check the length of the exposed dowels; it should be slightly under ½ inch. When the dowels fit securely into the pilot holes, place a little glue in the pilot holes and in the rabbet in the end panel, and tap the shelf into place. Install the 1-by-2-inch rail that supports the front edge of the bottom shelf into the shelf supports before you attach the shelf itself. Repeat the process with the other shelf and the opposite end panel. Be sure that the assembled unit is square and plumb while the glue is drying.

For extra stability, run two dowels down through each end of the lower shelves into the shelf supports. The original piece seems to have small dents along the lower shelf's front edge indicating points where small nails were driven through the shelf and into the support rail.

When the glue is dry, gently move the unit to a location where the bottom of the end panels can be placed against a wall. You will need this extra bit of support to nail the top onto the end panels without the danger of breaking the fragile joints that hold the shelves in place. With the bottom of the end panels firmly against a support, stand the top in position against the end panels, drill pilot holes for five nails on each end, and nail the top into position. Be aware that the top panel is 2¼ inches wider than the end panels. This extra width extends beyond the front face of the unit.

## Back Assembly

While the frame is drying, cut the back panels and the baseboard, which runs along the bottom of the back, to length. Be sure to allow 1½ inches for the lap joint that connects the back panels into the baseboard. Cut the lap joints on one end of the back panels and along one edge of the baseboard. Although the boards shown in the drawing are all 8 and 9 inches in width, it is certain that at least one board will be a slightly odd

width to match the exact width of the case. This board should be placed at the end of the unit nearest the wall (in the drawing of the back view, this would be on the left side of the case). If anything, allow this odd-width board to be slightly wider than needed. You can plane it to the exact width when the back has been attached to the case.

Lay the back panels and the baseboard on a work surface as they will appear when attached to the back of the bookcase. Drill and dowel the back panels to the baseboard, being sure that the boards are tightly butted against each other before they are pegged into place. Do not worry about trimming the ends of the dowels flush with the surface of the baseboard. The back is joined together only at the bottom; the tops are loose, making it very fragile at this stage. Any rough movement can cause the dowels to break. If you must move the back, slide a board under the loose end of the panels so they can be lifted together. It will require three people to move the back—one on the baseboard and one on each end of the board supporting the loose ends of the back panels.

When the glue on the shelf unit is completely dry, turn the unit over so it is lying facedown. Raise the end panels off the floor with 2½-inch-thick blocks so that the weight is not resting on the top panel's front edge. Gently lift the back unit into place on the frame, and arrange it so that it is aligned squarely on the bookcase. Clamp the back panels to the end panels, and drill pilot holes for dowels along the top and the sides of the unit as shown in the back view. The dowels should run into the end panels to a depth of about 1 inch. You may want to lift the back off the case and apply a line of glue around the edge of the case before inserting the dowels. Gently realign the back on the case, being careful not to smear the glue onto the back panels. Tap the dowels into the holes, and saw them off about ¼ inch above the back's surface. When the glue has dried, you may cut (or sand) the dowels flush with the back's surface and plane off any extra width on the back panel.

Now stand the case upright and insert the divider panels between the shelves.

## Bottom Rails

On the original shelves, the bottom rails, which support the bench seat and attach it to the shelf unit, connect a row of eight shelf units along a wall of the library building. Assuming you are putting up only a single bookcase, you will probably want to end the rail

4 or 5 inches beyond the seat support's rear edge. This is the length of the rail shown on the materials list. For decorative purposes, we suggest ornamenting the rail's end either with a simple chamfer to match the chamfer on the rail's side or with a decorative cut to match the shelf support's end.

When you have determined the length of the bottom rails, cut them to the size and shape shown in the front and end views on the plans. Next, notch the ends of the rails that connect with the shelf unit so that the end panels fall in line with the center of the rail. When in place, the rails should touch the shelf unit's rear wall. Locate the position of the mortise hole that will receive the seat support. With a chisel, cut a 1-inch-wide mortise to the length shown in the end view plan. The mortise should be located in the center of each rail. Note that the mortise goes completely through the rail. When the mortises have been cut, clamp the rails to the end panels, and drill pilot holes through the side panels and the rails. Remove the rails, coat the inner surfaces lightly with glue, reclamp them to the end panels, and tap dowels through both pieces.

When the glue is dry, trim the ends of the dowels flush with the surrounding wood. The shelves should now be relatively stable and freestanding.

**Center Support and Bookrest Installation**
Cut the center leg as shown in the section A drawing. Note that the foot is the same 2½-inch width as the support but is made from a separate piece of wood. Since there are no visible dowels, we assume that the dowels run through the foot and into the leg. Cut the tenon on top of the leg. We do not know the exact width of the tenon, but logic dictates that it is no less than ¾ inch and no more than 1 inch.

The center shelf support is the same as the two supports at the outer edges of the shelf, except that it is 2 inches in width rather than 1½ inches. Cut this support and chisel out the tenon to fit snugly over the mortise on the leg's end. Clamp the shelf support in place on the leg, and drill pilot holes as shown in the section A drawing. Remove the shelf support and set it aside until later. There is no apparent point of attachment to connect the center leg to the shelf unit's back, but we must assume that they are connected in some way. Our suggestion is to simply dowel through the back panel and into the center leg. To do this, locate the leg beneath the lower shelf at its proper position, as shown in the front view drawing. Lightly mark the position of the leg on the back panel, remove the leg, and drill pilot holes for three dowels through the back panel along the length of the leg. Replace the leg. While an assistant holds the leg in place, replace the drill through the holes in the back panel and mark the dowel locations on the back of the leg. Remove the leg and sink the pilot holes to a depth of 1½ inches.

Now it is time to replace the shelf support on top of the leg. Lightly glue the inside of the mortise and the top of the leg. Replace the shelf support, clamp it in position, and tap in the dowels. When the glue has dried, cut the dowels flush with the shelf support. You are now ready to attach the center leg to the cabinet.

Lightly coat with glue the inside of the pilot holes and the entire rear of the leg as well as the top of the shelf support. Tilt the shelf unit backward and set the leg unit in place, then return the shelf unit to the upright position. It will be a bit tricky to keep the leg from shifting while you are doing this, so we suggest realigning the dowel holes with a small screwdriver. While an assistant braces the leg, tap three dowels into place through the back panel and into the leg. You may also want to put one or two dowels through the shelf into the top of the shelf support to ensure that it remains square.

The slanted bookrest in front of the bottom shelf is nailed to the shelf support with small hand-forged nails, the heads being sunk flush with the top of the bookrest so that they will not snag the delicate leather book covers. Note that the front corners of the shelf are rounded with a 1-inch-radius curve.

**Seat Construction**
Cut the two legs for the seat from the 1½-inch stock. On the bottom of each leg, cut the tenon to the size shown on the end view and section B drawings. Again, we are not sure of the thickness of this tenon, but it is reasonable to assume it is about 1 inch thick, meaning you will need to remove ¼ inch of wood from either side of the tenon. Insert the legs in the mortises in the rail, and drill and dowel them into place.

Cut the board for the seat 1 inch shorter than the width of the bookcase. The decorative molding, detailed in the section B plan, encircles all four sides of the seat. The easiest approach to cutting these moldings is with the aid of a molding cutter, but you can use molding planes or a router to achieve the same effect. If the molding is simply too complex for your tools, employ the services of your local cabinet shop or mill works.

The seat overhangs the legs too far for the top to have been fitted into place with doweled mortise and tenon joints; the seat was simply nailed in place with two large-headed nails in each end. For stability, cut a shallow mortise and tenon joint and then nail through the seat and into the top of the tenon. There is enough extra wood in the stock to allow for this. Situate the seat so that it rests ½ inch inside the outermost dimensions of the shelf unit's sides, and nail it to the legs. Here, as with the bookrest, the nails were sunk flush with the seat's surface so that they would not snag the clothes of the library's users.

## Pediment and Crown Molding

Cut the two 3¾-inch-square columns to 14-inch lengths as shown on the plans, and set them in place 3½ inches from the back wall of the bookcase in line with the end panels' outermost edges. Mark their locations on the top of the bookcase and remove them.

The footed balls that sit on top of the columns were turned on a foot-powered lathe, probably a pole lathe. The marks left by a lathe that turned at a very low speed are still plainly evident on the turnings. In the photograph it is obvious that the balls only vaguely approach a circular shape. The small foot on which the balls rest is also turned roughly circular. The two bands that encircle the balls are slightly under ¼ inch wide and of a similar depth; the bottom of the groove indicates that they were made with a round-ended lathe tool. Reproducing these balls must be done on a lathe. Again, if you do not have one, visit a cabinet shop. If you go to a commercial woodshop, ask that the balls not be perfectly round; a little irregularity in shape helps retain the period look of the piece.

The molding around the top of the columns is shown in the molding detail C drawing. As with the molding around the edge of the seat and the balls, if you cannot execute this yourself, visit a cabinet shop or mill works. This is, however, this project's simplest molding, and cutting it with a table saw and router should not be too difficult.

When the columns, balls, and molding are prepared, assemble the columns. The corners of the molding are mitered at 45 degrees to fit neatly around the column and secured in place with small nails. The balls are simply tacked on top of the columns with four nails set near the edge of each ball's foot. It is advisable to drill pilot holes in the foot before nailing it to the column top to avoid splitting the turning.

Next, cut the triangular pediment that sits between the columns. The exact length of the pediment is the distance between the two columns, whose locations you previously marked on the bookcase's top. The backboard for the pediment is made from a single oak plank, 1 inch thick and 14 inches wide. If you do not have access to a board of these dimensions, dowel two boards together following the instructions for doweling in the chapter on general woodworking. When you have a board of the necessary dimensions, cut it to a triangular shape 14 inches in height and the distance between the columns in length.

The moldings that go around the pediment's two upper edges are shown in the molding detail B drawing. Approach this molding with the same method you used for the previous moldings. Apply the finished molding to the pediment. You are now ready to put the pediment and columns in place.

Simply toenail the columns into place on the top and end panels of the bookcase. This may not be the most stable method of attachment, but it is the one that the original craftsmen used. You may elect to provide additional support by using small metal angle brackets or by placing several screws into the column through the underside of the top. When the columns are in place, fit the pediment between them to ensure that it does not need to be trimmed down.

Run a line of six dowels along the center of the bottom edge of the pediment; two dowels should fall between each section of shelving. The dowels should be spaced roughly 1 foot apart and be allowed to stick out of the bottom of the pediment by 1½ inches. Stand the pediment between the columns so that its back is in line with the back of the columns. Mark the location of each dowel. Remove the pediment and drill pilot holes to receive the dowels in the top of the bookcase. Set the pediment back in place to ensure proper alignment of dowels and pilot holes. Lightly coat the bottom of the pediment and the dowels with glue, and tap the pediment into place against the top of the bookcase.

The molding around the bookcase's top edge is detailed in the molding detail A drawing. Approach this molding's manufacture as you have the others. Producing molding with chamfered rear edges is a little tricky and is best handled by those set up for the job. When the molding has been completed, apply it to only the front and the exposed side (the left side in the drawings) of the bookcase. Cutting chamfered edge molding to a perfect 90-degree angle takes a little practice, but once you have the knack, it can be done on a simple miter box.

Experiment on a scrap before cutting into the best piece of molding. Nail the molding to the bookcase so that the bottom edge of the molding is flush with the bottom edge of the top panel.

Cut the two small brackets shown in the detail G drawing from 1⅜-inch-thick oak, and nail them to the face of the end panels as shown in the end view drawing. These brackets should be the same thickness as the left end panel. If the right end panel is the full thickness shown in the diagram, align the bracket with the outside edge of the end panel so that it rests against the wall of the room. The original bracket from this end is missing, but the scar remains on the end panel.

## Finish

A rich, dark oil finish will make this bookcase positively glow. Add a little wood stain to the first coat; a touch of red added to the brown will bring the reproduction close to the color of the original.

## Metalwork

*Rod and Rod Support Brackets.* The bookcase has only one rod running along the center shelf's front edge. The chains from both the upper and lower shelves attached to this one rod. The single remaining chain is clearly visible in the photograph. The rod itself is an 89-inch-long piece of brass round stock that is ½ inch in diameter. This is supported by four brackets of the type shown in the drawings of the bracket support and the top and side views of the rod bracket. The bracket supports are cut from 3/32-inch-thick stock. The two center brackets, which will be located at the junctures of the center shelf and the shelf dividers, have four arms of equal length. The other two brackets, which will be located on the end panels, have only three arms, the horizontal arm nearest the end panel having been eliminated.

When the rough shape of the bracket supports has been cut, drill a ¼-inch hole in the center of the support through which the tangs, or ears on the end of the bracket can pass. Drill holes to accept nails near each arm's end as shown in the bracket support drawing. Slightly round all the edges of the bracket support.

The rod brackets are shaped from a piece of flat stock that is 1/16 inch thick. Begin with a piece of flat stock 1 inch wide and 4 5/16 inches long. Allow 1 inch on either end of this for the small tangs that attach the bracket to the bracket support. Lay out the tangs so that they are centered on the bracket. Measuring ¼ inch wide at the base, the tangs nearly taper to a point. Remove the excess metal from around the tangs.

The two ribs that appear on each end of the rod bracket in the top view of the rod bracket are cut into the surface of the metal with an engraver's tool or a round-ended metal gouge. If you do not have an engraver's tool, the easiest way to reproduce these is probably with a Dremel. When the engraving has been completed, bend the tangs 90 degrees toward the face of the bracket (the side with the engraved lines on it). Next, heat the metal and shape it around a 5/8-inch steel bar. Since the bracket is made from 1/16-inch stock, it should not take much heat to make it malleable, and it should work with relative ease. When the bracket is shaped, the tangs should lie back-to-back. File away any sharp edges. When you have the four brackets cut and shaped, insert the tangs through the hole in the bracket support's center, and bend them outward as shown in the side view of the rod bracket.

Plug the bracket located nearest the wall (that is, the bookcase's right end) to prevent the rod from passing completely through it. A small disk of metal seems to have been soldered across the outside end of the bracket on the original unit.

The brackets can now be nailed into place with small round-headed nails. Be sure the brackets are in alignment so that the rod will pass through them.

*Hasp and Lock Plate.* The 24-inch-long hasp is situated on the bookcase so that the 1⅛-inch ear (appearing on the right side of the drawing of the hasp arm) covers the rod's end, ensuring that none of the books are stolen.

The hasp itself is cut from a piece of ⅛-inch-thick stock. Simply enlarge the diagram to get a pattern for the decorative shapes. Allow enough extra stock on top of the hasp to form the hinge's spine. Cut the top end of the hinge from a piece of similar stock. Following the instructions for making a hinge in the chapter on general metalworking, shape and assemble the spine of the hinge.

Shape the hatched areas along the hasp's edge with a file. Hold the file at a 45-degree angle to the surface of the metal, and work the designs as shown. The alternating half-round portions of the design can be made with a large, round rat-tail file. The alternate designs will require a combination of a small rat-tail file and a triangular file. Some of these design elements will be a challenge; practice on a discarded piece of metal before working on the actual hasp.

The small knob on the bottom of the hasp was originally cast. Turning it on a metal lathe will probably be easier. Leave a $1/8$-inch-diameter pin on the knob's bottom to attach it to the hasp. This pin should be about $1/4$ inch long. Drill a $1/8$-inch hole through the hasp as shown in the drawings. Insert the pin through the hole, and peen over the pin's end on the hinge's back.

The latch on the back of the hasp is made from a piece of $1/16$-inch-thick flat stock that is $3/16$ inch wide. Cut and bend it to the shape shown in the drawing, and weld it to the back of the hasp. Nail the hasp to the end panel of the case with five round-headed forged nails as shown in the hasp drawing. Be sure to locate the large ear on the hasp so it covers the rod bracket.

Cut the lock plate to the shape shown in the drawing from $1/16$-inch-thick flat stock. The latch hole must be large enough to receive the latch on the hasp's back. If you are building a lock, refer to the chapter on medieval locks. Otherwise, rout or chisel away enough wood from the end panel so that the latch fits through and lies flush with the lock plate. Nail the lock plate into position with six small round-headed nails.

Should you decide to chain your books to the case, the chain currently used to hold the one book in place has rectangular links that are $1\frac{1}{2}$ inches long and $1/2$ inch wide. We do not know if this chain is original or a replacement, but it is certainly old. The chain is attached to the book by a small metal tab, fitted with a ring, that holds the last link of chain. This tab wraps around both sides of one cover of the book and is held in place with two small rivets. Because of the location of the tab, chained books have to be set on the shelves spine first, causing the titles and authors to be hidden from the browser.

# FRONT VIEW

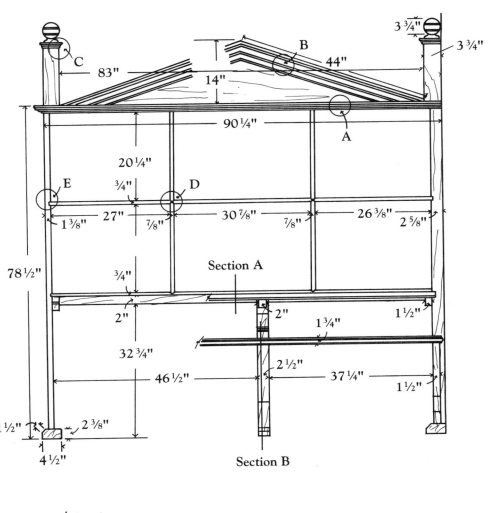

3 ¾"

3 ¾"

C

83"

B

44"

14"

A

90¼"

20¼"

¾"

E          D

1 ³⁄₈"     27"     ⁷⁄₈"          30 ⁷⁄₈"          ⁷⁄₈"          26 ³⁄₈"          2 ⁵⁄₈"

78½"

¾"

Section A

2"          2"          1 ¾"          1½"

32¾"

46½"          2½"          37¼"          1½"

1½"          2 ³⁄₈"

4½"

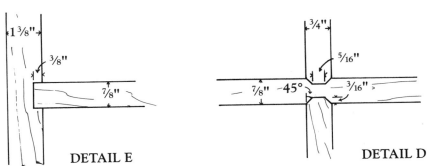

Section B

1 ³⁄₈"

³⁄₈"

⁷⁄₈"

**DETAIL E**

¾"

⁵⁄₁₆"

⁷⁄₈"    −45°    ³⁄₁₆"

**DETAIL D**

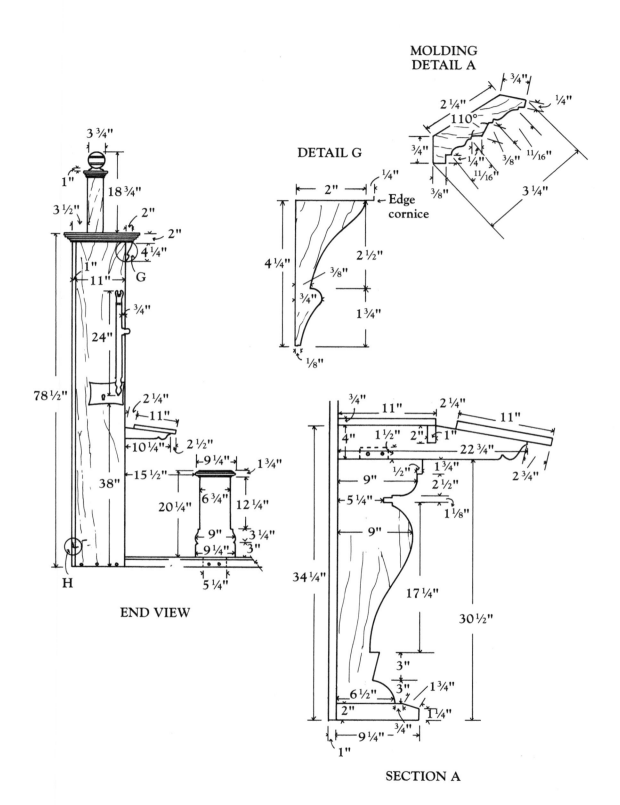

MOLDING
DETAIL A

DETAIL G

Edge
cornice

END VIEW

SECTION A

76

## SECTION B

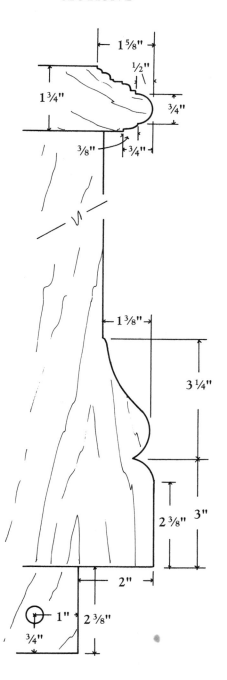

1 5/8"
1/2"
1 3/4"
3/4"
3/8"
3/4"

1 3/8"

3 1/4"

2 3/8"    3"

2"

1"
2 3/8"
3/4"

## MOLDING DETAIL B

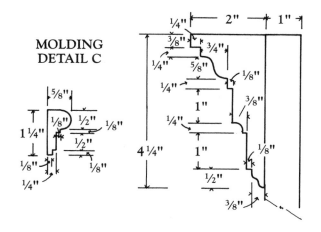

1/4"    2"    1"
3/8"
3/4"
1/4"    5/8"
1/8"
1/4"
1"
1/4"
4 1/4"
1"
3/8"
1/8"
1/2"
3/8"

## MOLDING DETAIL C

5/8"
1/8"    1/2"    1/8"
1 1/4"
1/2"
1/8"    1/8"
1/4"    1/8"

## DETAIL H

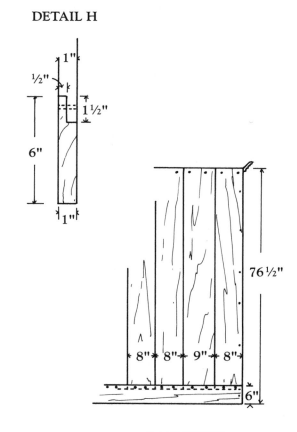

1"
1/2"
1 1/2"
6"
1"

76 1/2"

8"  8"  9"  8"

6"

## BACK VIEW

**BRACKET SUPPORT**

**HASP ARM**

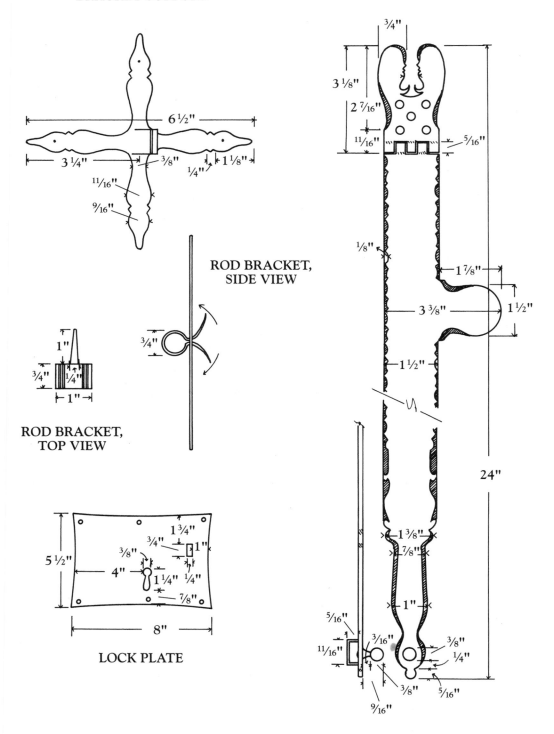

**ROD BRACKET, SIDE VIEW**

**ROD BRACKET, TOP VIEW**

**LOCK PLATE**

# Project 7

# HALF-TESTER BED

As we noted in the opening chapter on medieval decorating, the master bed was often the most elaborate piece of furniture in the medieval household. Not only did it provide a place to sleep, but the size and quality of the bed were prime indicators of the owner's social status. The larger and more elaborate the bed, the more important its owner. The sleeping platform of this bed seems unusually high by today's standards, but until well into the nineteenth century it was not unusual for the high beds of the upper classes to require steps to get into them. The extra height not only kept the sleepers safe from the cold drafts that were ever present in poorly heated homes, but they prevented rats, searching for a warm place to sleep, from jumping into bed with the human occupants.

The presence of a tester, or canopy, indicated that a bed's occupant was of high enough rank to be worthy of privacy and also that he or she had enough money to afford the expensive fabric required to make bed-curtains. The term half-tester indicates that the canopy does not run the full length of the bed as it would in a four-poster.

This reproduction of a fourteenth-century bed is located in the marshal's room at Carlisle Castle on the border between England and Scotland. Because of Carlisle's importance in keeping Scottish raiding parties from crossing into England, its marshal (head of the castle garrison) would have been a man of great importance. This fine bed reflected the grandeur of his position.

## CONSTRUCTION NOTES
Most of the construction of this piece is fairly straightforward. The assembling of the tester canopy and the bed's large size will present a challenge, and the multi-plicity of mortise and tenon joints will require strict attention to the instructions and the plans.

Because of the bed's size, it will be nearly impossible to move even the assembled headboard from workshop to bedroom, and the fact that it does not disassemble makes it almost impossible to move it from one place to another. It may be necessary to build the headboard unit and assemble the bed in the room where it is going to be located.

Anyone contemplating building this bed for use at home may want to consider adapting bed hangers to the side rails so that it can be disassembled. It may also be necessary to attach the canopy with screws so that the headboard can be broken down to be moved through doorways.

To ease into this dauntingly massive project, we will begin by building the footboard. After this and the side rails have been built, you will find the courage to tackle the headboard.

## Materials
This reproduction bed is made of pine, although an original bed of this size and quality would more likely have been built of oak. In either case, all the material necessary to construct this bed should be available without too much special milling.

## Footboard
Cut to length the five boards that form the main panels of the footboard as shown in the footboard drawing. Note that the two wider boards are used at the top and the bottom of the panel. Allow 2 extra inches in length on each board for the tenons. When the boards have been cut to length, mark and cut the tenons on either end. The tenons are to be 1 inch in length and ½ inch in thickness. So that the tenons fit properly

# MATERIALS

## WOOD
All wood is pine or oak.

| PART | NUMBER OF PIECES | THICKNESS | | WIDTH | | LENGTH |
|------|------------------|-----------|---|-------|---|--------|
| footboard, corner posts | 2 | 2¾" | × | 2¾" | × | 44" |
| footboard, wide-panel boards | 2 | 1" | × | 8" | × | 47½" |
| footboard, narrow-panel boards | 3 | 1" | × | 7" | × | 47½" |
| side rail, top rail | 2 | 1¾" | × | 1¾" | × | 75" |
| side rail, center panel | 2 | 1" | × | 8½" | × | 73½" |
| side rail, bottom rail | 2 | 2¾" | × | 2¾" | × | 75" |
| headboard, corner posts | 2 | 2¾" | × | 2¾" | × | 85" |
| headboard, top board | 1 | 2¼" | × | 9" | × | 48½" |
| headboard, bottom board | 1 | 2¼" | × | 11½" | × | 48½" |
| panel divider, stiles | 2 | 2⅛" | × | 3" | × | 46½" |
| headboard, panel boards | 10 | ¾" | × | 9" | × | 14¼" |

into the corner posts, be sure that the tenons are in the centers of the panels; that is to say, form the ½-inch-thick tenon by removing ¼ inch of wood from each side of the board. Note that the top edge of the tenon on the top board and the bottom edge of the tenon on the bottom board are stepped back 1 inch from the board's edge.

Following the patterns given in the footboard and the footboard decoration detail drawings, lay out and cut the patterns on the top and bottom boards. These are simple, flat cuts that can be carried out with a band saw or jigsaw.

After these boards have been cut, begin shaping the corner posts. Lay out the design, shown in the bedpost detail drawing, on all four sides of both posts. Begin forming the onion dome–shaped finials by cutting a 1¼-inch-wide chamfer along the uppermost 5¼ inches of each post, using either a router or a drawknife. Then cut the onion-shaped finials on a band saw or jigsaw. Getting all eight sides symmetrical is a bit tricky; practice on an expendable wood scrap before cutting into the bedpost.

Next, cut a mortise along the inside face of the posts to accept the five boards of the end panel. Note

| PART | NUMBER OF PIECES | THICKNESS | | WIDTH | | LENGTH |
|---|---|---|---|---|---|---|
| headboard, panel boards | 5 | ¾" | × | 9" | × | 16" |
| wing panels | 2 | 1" | × | 7½" | × | 48" |
| tester, side rails | 2 | 1" | × | 4¾" | × | 50¼" |
| spacer board | 1 | 2½" | × | 2¾" | × | 49" |
| cornice molding | 4 | 1½" | × | 2¾" | × | 60" |
| fleur-de-lis ornaments | 2 | 1" | × | 5½" | × | 6½" |
| tester ceiling panels | 9 | ½" | × | 6" | × | 51" |
| bed slats | 12 | ¾" | × | 6" | × | 47½" |
| dowels | 4 | ⅜" diameter | | | × | 36" |

## METAL
Wrought iron or cold-rolled steel.

| PART | NUMBER OF PIECES | THICKNESS | | LENGTH |
|---|---|---|---|---|
| curtain rods | 2 | 5/16" diameter | × | 49" |

## FABRIC
Cotton duck or heavy worsted wool.

| PART | NUMBER OF PIECES | WIDTH | | LENGTH |
|---|---|---|---|---|
| bed hangings | 2 | 54" | × | 90" |

on the footboard and side rail section drawing that the mortise is slightly off-center, so that the panels are closer to the outside of the bed frame. To ensure an accurate fit of the joint, lay the end panel boards on a flat work surface exactly as they will be when they are fitted into the footboard. Measure the combined length of the tenons, and cut the mortise in the corner post to this length. Repeat the process for the other corner post. The combined tenon length may vary slightly from one side of the bed to the other. After the tenons have been cut, assemble the end panels and the corner posts to ensure that they are a snug fit for years of sturdy use.

Disassemble the footboard, and lay the corner posts on your workbench so that the mortises face each other and the sides of the corner posts that will be on the outside of the footboard face down on the workbench.

On the surface that is now the top face of the corner posts, mark the position of the mortises for the side rails as shown in the side view, the side rail, the cross section of the side rail, and the footboard and side rail section drawings. The first of these drawings indicates the height from the floor that the side rails will be, the next establishes the length of the tenons, the third locates the side rail on the corner post, and the last gives the width of the tenons. It is difficult to see on the drawings, but the mortise and tenon on the bottom board of the side rail are 1¾ inches in both width and height, while those for the top board are 1¼ inches in both width and height. The mortise for the center panel is the full 1-inch width of the panel. When the positions of the mortises have been marked on the corner posts, cut them to the depth shown on the side rail drawing. Note that the shallow mortise for the center panel abuts the mortises for the top and bottom rails. The finished mortise should have the shape of two squares connected by a narrow channel.

When the mortises have been cut into the corner posts, assemble the footboard. Insert the five panels into the mortises in the corner posts, making certain that the entire structure is square. Drill 2-inch-deep pilot holes that are ⅜ inch in diameter for two dowels in each end of the top and bottom boards of the end panels. Tap ⅜-inch dowels into the holes, and cut them off just above the surface of the post. No dowels are necessary in the three center panels; the dowels in the top and bottom panels should be strong enough to securely hold the footboard. If you wish, coat the inside of the mortise lightly with glue before inserting the panels.

### Side Rails

Cut the component parts of the two side rails to length following the side view drawing. Allow enough extra length on the pieces to accommodate the tenons as shown in the side rail drawing. The center panel will require an extra ½ inch on each end, and the top and bottom rails will need an extra 1¼ inches on each end. When the pieces have been cut to length, cut a rabbet that is ½ inch wide and ½ inch deep in both the top and bottom rails to receive the side panels. The positioning of these rabbets is shown in the side rail cross section.

Next, cut the corresponding tenons along the top and bottom edges of the center panels. Fit the center panel into the top and bottom rails to ensure a snug fit, and then disassemble them, laying the center panels aside.

Cut tenons on both ends of the top and bottom rails. The mortises on the headboard end of the side rails are identical to those required to fit into the mortises on the footboard, shown in the side rail drawing and described above. Test fit the tenons into the mortises on the footboard to ensure that they fit snugly

with just a few taps of a mallet. On the end of the upper rails that will attach to the headboard, cut a mortise 1 inch wide and 1 inch deep. This mortise will be on the top face of the rail and should begin 1 inch from the tenon end of the rail and extend along the rail for 5 inches. Running the mortise through the tenon will weaken its holding power. When this mortise has been cut, lay the footboard and the side rails aside.

### Headboard Construction

Cut the headboard's corner posts to the length given in the materials list. Note that these posts run to the top of the molding surrounding the tester. Next, lay out and cut the mortises into which the side rails will fit. These mortises will mirror the ones on the footboard. Now, cut a shallow mortise for the wing panels that support the tester frame's sides. These wings, and the mortise into which they fit, are shown in the tester and wing details drawing. Note that the mortise is only ½ inch deep and ⅝ inch wide, but it must be positioned to allow the 1-inch-thick wing to lie on the same plane as the side rail's center panel. In effect, the mortise for the wings will continue the line of the mortise for the side rail panels along the entire length of the corner post; it will just be a little narrower. Cutting this mortise should give you a continuous mortise in the front face of the corner posts, beginning 18½ inches from the post's bottom end and extending through its top end.

This mortise's topmost 5¾ inches must now be deepened to 1¼ inches and also widened to 1 inch in width to receive the tester frame's rear end. Note that it must be widened ³⁄₁₆ inch on each side of the existing mortise so that the wing and the tester frame fit flush.

Now lay out and cut to length the top and bottom boards of the headboard. Be sure to allow 1½ inches on each end (3 inches in the overall length) for the tenons. Cut the tenons to the width and length shown in the headboard detail, front and side views. Now cut the mortises in the corner posts into which they fit. Note that the bottom edge of the bottom board is level with the bottom edge of the side rail and that the top edge of the top board is held 1 inch below the upper end of the corner post, as shown in the cutaway view of the headboard rear edge. Final assembly of the headboard will be easier if the mortise into which the top board fits runs through the top end of the corner posts, as shown in this drawing. In the cross section C drawing, the bottom board (as well as the top board, which is not shown) sits flush with the back of the corner post, placing both of them ½ inch behind the front face of the posts.

Between these two mortises, cut a connecting mortise that is ¾ inch wide and ½ inch deep to accept the flat panels that fill in the headboard. Details of these mortises can be found in the cross section C drawing.

Cut the two divider stiles to length, allowing an extra 1¼ inches on each end for the tenons. Cut the tenons to the dimensions shown in the front view of the headboard detail and the front and side views of the headboard stile. Note that the tenons are 2 inches wide and ¾ inch thick. On both sides of the divider stiles, cut a channel into which the panels will slide. These channels run the entire length of the stiles and are ¾ inch wide and ½ inch deep, as shown in cross section C and the side view of the headboard stile. Note that the channels are set ¾ inch forward of the stile's rear edge. Finally, with a router, cut ½-by-½-inch quarter-round chamfers along the full length of the stile's front edges, as shown in cross section C.

Into the top and bottom boards of the headboard, cut running channels to accept the panels. These channels, like those in the stiles, are ¾ inch wide, ½ inch deep, and ¾ inch from the board's back edge. When the channels have been cut, mark the locations of the stiles on the top and bottom boards. The front view of the headboard shows that the stiles are 13¼ inches from the corner posts and 15 inches from each other. Cut the mortises to accept the stiles in both the top and bottom boards. The stiles should sit flush with the back edge of the bottom and top boards (see cross section C). When these mortises have been cut, assemble the headboard frame. All the mortises should fit together gently with one or two taps of a mallet. If the mortises and tenons have been properly cut, the corner posts, the top and bottom boards, and the stiles should all be flush on the back surface of the headboard. There should also be a continuous ¾-inch-wide channel running around each of the panel spaces.

There are five boards in each of the three panels in the headboard. The widths of the boards vary greatly, but the widths listed in the materials list will add up to the proper height to fill the space. You may use boards of different widths, because it is only the end results that matter. Cut the boards in the two outer panels to 14¼ inches in length and those in the center panel to 16 inches.

## Final Headboard Assembly

When the panel boards have been cut to length, lay the headboard assembly on a level surface, and remove the top board from the frame. Slide the panels into place in the panel frames. Replace the top board, and ensure that the entire structure fits snugly and squarely into place. If you want to glue the mortise and tenon joints, disassemble the entire headboard, glue the joints, and reassemble the frame. There is no need to glue the panels into the panel frame. Replace the top board, and clamp the headboard together left to right and top to bottom, making sure it is square.

Drill two ⅜-inch pilot holes through the tenons on each end of the top and bottom boards, and tap the dowels into place. Cut the dowels slightly above the surface of the surrounding wood. Next, drill one pilot hole through the tenons at each end of each of the divider stiles, and peg them in place.

## Bed Frame Assembly

Before building the tester, it is advisable to assemble the body of the bed; otherwise, it will be nearly impossible to hold the headboard upright while the side rails are being attached.

Lay the headboard on its back on a level surface. Fit the center panel of the side rail into the rabbeted channels on the top and bottom rails. Stand the unit on end, and fit it into the mortises on the face of the headboard. When you are satisfied that the joints on both side rails fit snugly, drill and dowel them to the headboard. Your biggest problem will be holding them square while they are being drilled and doweled. You can overcome this by building a temporary frame in the shape of a right triangle, that can be clamped to the side rails and the headboard while they are drilled and pegged. Leave the frame in place while the glue dries. When the glue is dry, stand the headboard upright, with the triangular brace still in place. Gently allow the headboard to lean forward, resting its weight on the side rails. With the aid of two helpers, carefully lift the side rails so that the footboard can be slid into place. After making sure that the entire bed frame is square, drill and dowel the footboard to the side rails.

## Wings

Following the side view and the tester and wing detail drawings, cut out the two wings that support the tester. Allow extra length for the tenon on the bottom of the wings and the angled tenon on top. Note that the tenon on the bottom, although the full 1-inch width of the board, has a 1-inch notch on the front edge and a 1½-inch notch on the edge that fits into the corner post of the headboard. The tenon on the top is also notched (see the tester and wing details drawing). The long mortise on the corner post into which the wing fits is only ⅝ inch wide, so cut ³⁄₁₆ inch off each side of the ½-inch-deep tenon. When the wings fit snugly into the mortises in the side rail and the corner post, glue them into place, and dowel them through the side rail with ⅜-inch dowels.

## Tester Construction

Cut the tester's two long side rails as shown in the side view, the tester and wing details, and the cutaway view of the tester front edge. Allow enough extra length to cut the tenon on the rear end of these rails.

Since the existing mortise at the top of the corner post is 1 inch wide, the end of the rail should fit easily into place. Only the bottom corner of the tenon should have to be removed to allow it to fit into place. Before it falls into place, however, cut a mortise to fit over the tenon on the top of the wing. When the side rails have been fitted so that their surface lies flush with the wings, glue and dowel them into place, being sure they rest tightly against both the wing and the corner post.

To build the tester's front, cut an L-shaped spacer board as shown in cross section in the cutaway view of the tester front edge. Cut this board to length so that it rests between the ends of the side rails. To establish this length exactly, measure the distance between the side rails at the point where they join the headboard. Do not yet attach this board. On the bottom rear lip of the spacer board, drill two ⅜-inch holes that are 1 inch deep. Locate these holes, which will receive the rod that supports the bed hangings, in the center of the rear lip, ½ inch from the point where the spacer meets the side rail. Drill corresponding holes that are ½ inch deep in the top corner of the headboard's top board. Be sure that these last holes are only ½ inch deep. When these holes have been drilled, attach the spacer board to the side rails with glue and two small nails.

After the tester frame has been constructed, cut and fit the small fleur-de-lis that ornaments the corner where the tester frame joins the wing panels. This decorative element is shown in the tester and wing details drawing. Note that it is made from the same thickness of wood as the wings and the tester side rails. Simply tack it into place with two small nails.

## Cornice Molding

From a length of 1½-by-2¾-inch stock, cut the simple cornice molding that surrounds the tester. This molding is shown in the tester and wing details, the cutaway view of the tester front edge, and the tester front edge drawings.

The molding can be shaped with either a molding cutter or a molding plane. It will be difficult to cut with a router, because it is 1¾ inches deep.

When the molding has been cut, attach it to the front, sides, and rear of the tester frame. Its position in relation to the top edge of the tester will be determined by aligning it with the spacer board on the front of the tester.

## Ceiling Panels

The ½-inch-thick ceiling panels that cover the top of the tester, like the boards in the headboard panels, are of random widths. We have suggested—and this is only a guideline—a standard width in the materials list. Note that these boards are supported by the top of the tester's side rails. It will be easiest to place these boards if the board nearest the headboard is installed first. Plane the bottom rear edge of this board so that it lies flat against the top of the headboard; then tack it in place with four small nails.

Additional boards can simply be laid one after another into place. The final board at the tester's front edge, which rests on the inner edge of the spacer board, will have to be trimmed to width. If cut so they fit snugly in place, the ceiling panels will help to stabilize the tester. There is no reason to nail them into place.

## Bed Slats

Since there is no accommodation for springs in this bed, the bed slats must form a nearly solid platform on which to lay the mattress. These slats can be cut from any width of ¾-inch board, but we suggest a standard width of 6 inches in the materials list. The boards should be cut so that they lie securely across the wide bottom rail of the side rails. Space them so that there are no gaps larger than 1 inch between the slats.

## Finish

The reproduction bed in the photograph is finished with a clear oil finish. If you wish to add a bit of color and richness to your bed, simply add a little wood stain to the oil, as explained in the chapter on finishes.

## Curtain Rod

A length of 5/16-inch iron rod, cut to the length noted in the materials list, will support the bed hangings. Insert one end of the rod into the 3/8-inch hole on the rear edge of the spacer bar and slide it into the 1-inch-deep hole. The other end should easily slide into the hole in the headboard. By simply moving the rod to the back of the hole in the headboard, gravity should hold it firmly in place.

## Bed Hangings

The hangings shown on the bed in the photograph are painted on heavy canvas in the same manner as painted wall hangings. You can find instructions for making painted wall hangings in *Constructing Medieval Furniture*. The stiffness of painted hangings, however, prevents them from being of any real use as bed-curtains. A more practical, and properly medieval, solution would be to use a good wool fabric embellished with an embroidered decorative band around the edges.

The length of material given in the materials list will make a drapery that hangs from the high end of the tester frame to the floor. Cut the fabric to conform to the angle of the tester. Hem the top and bottom edges of the panel only, leaving the unfinished edges of the fabric exposed along the drapery's vertical edges. This is a perfectly medieval approach to the use of cloth. Along the top and bottom edges, sew a 1-inch-wide double-turned hem. Attach a pair of 2-inch-long ties along the top edge of the curtains at 3-inch intervals; tie them around the curtain rod to attach the hangings in place. These ties can be made from hemmed strips of the drapery fabric that are 1/4 to 1/2 inch wide or from lengths of leather thong. Tie them loosely around the rod so that the curtain can easily be moved forward and backward.

If you want the hangings to be heavier than a single weight of fabric, place two identical panels back-to-back. The concept of an inner lining was unknown during the Middle Ages.

## Mattress

The mattress on a medieval bed was no more than a straw-filled bag, which could be refilled as the straw broke down and became hard and uncomfortable. With a little effort, you can fit a modern mattress to this bed's dimensions, or modify the size of the bed to accommodate one.

SIDE VIEW

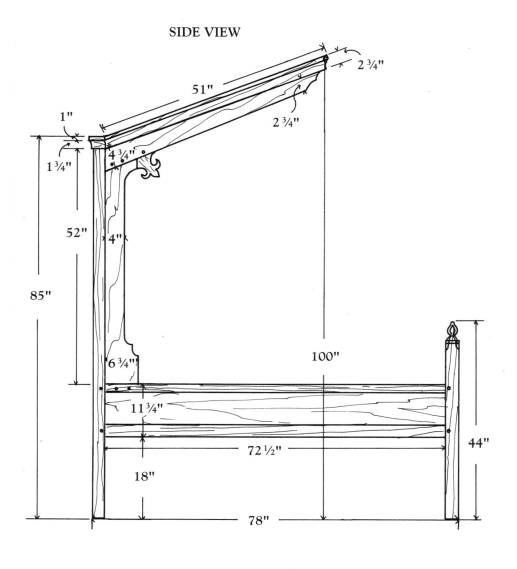

51"

2 ¾"

2 ¾"

1"

1 ¾"

4 ¾"

52"

4"

85"

6 ¾"

100"

11 ¾"

44"

72 ½"

18"

78"

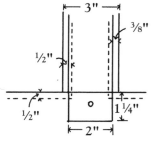

3"

⅜"

½"

½"

1 ¼"

2"

HEADBOARD STILE,
FRONT VIEW

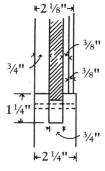

2 ⅛"

⅜"

¾"

⅜"

1 ¼"

¾"

2 ¼"

HEADBOARD STILE,
SIDE VIEW

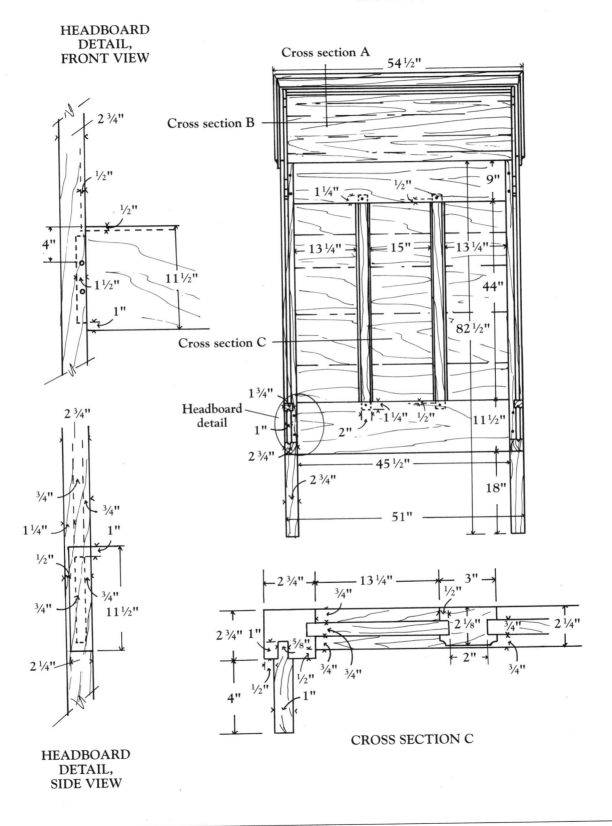

HEADBOARD DETAIL, FRONT VIEW

2 3/4"
1/2"
1/2"
4"
11 1/2"
1 1/2"
1"

HEADBOARD, FRONT VIEW

Cross section A
54 1/2"
Cross section B
9"
1 1/4"
1/2"
13 1/4"
15"
13 1/4"
44"
82 1/2"
Cross section C
1 3/4"
Headboard detail
1 1/4"
1/2"
11 1/2"
1"
2"
2 3/4"
45 1/2"
2 3/4"
18"
51"

HEADBOARD DETAIL, SIDE VIEW

2 3/4"
3/4"
3/4"
1 1/4"
1"
1/2"
3/4"
3/4"
11 1/2"
2 1/4"

CROSS SECTION C

2 3/4"
13 1/4"
3"
3/4"
1/2"
2 1/8"
3/4"
2 1/4"
2 3/4"
1"
5/8"
2"
3/4"
3/4"
1/2"
1/2"
3/4"
4"
1"

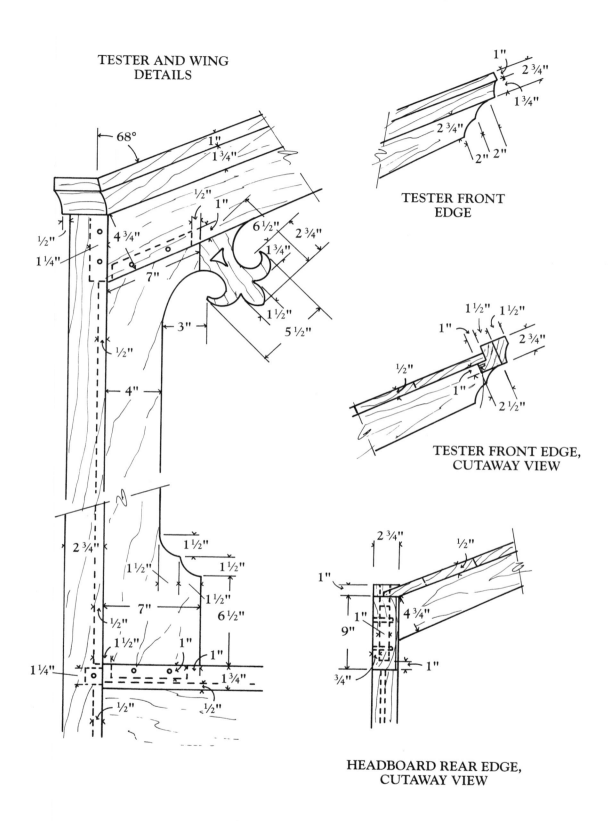

TESTER AND WING
DETAILS

TESTER FRONT
EDGE

TESTER FRONT EDGE,
CUTAWAY VIEW

HEADBOARD REAR EDGE,
CUTAWAY VIEW

## BEDPOST DETAIL

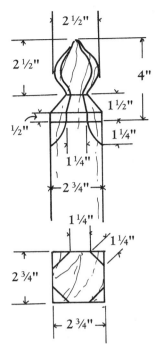

BEDPOST,
TOP VIEW

## FOOTBOARD

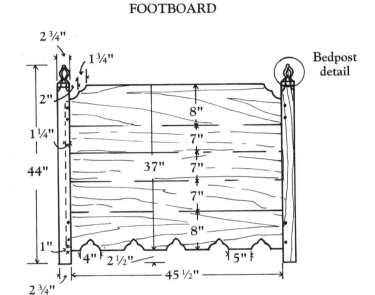

Bedpost
detail

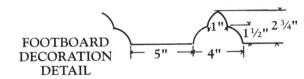

FOOTBOARD
DECORATION
DETAIL

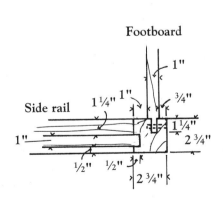

FOOTBOARD
AND SIDE RAIL
SECTION

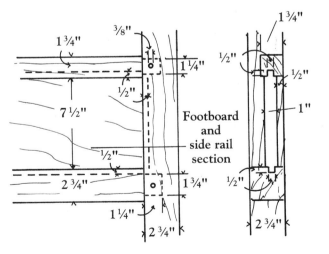

SIDE RAIL

SIDE RAIL,
CROSS SECTION

# Project 8

# AMBRY CUPBOARD

The original purpose of this oak cabinet, which probably dates from the 1500s, is unknown; its design offers few clues as to its use. The delicate design and fine craftsmanship shows that it was a quality piece of furniture, and its small size probably indicates that it was intended for the use of one person rather than an entire household.

The beautiful openwork carving in the door panels was probably once backed with fabric to make the carvings stand out as well as to conceal the contents of the cabinet. Much of the space that this piece of furniture occupies is put to no discernible use; thus the original owner was probably rich enough to invest in an article of furniture that was more decorative than functional.

Although the piece resembles a small bookcase, this was probably not its intended use. The top is too high to use as a reading shelf, a common feature in the period, and a sixteenth-century book owner would probably not have kept them in a cabinet that could be moved so easily—books were simply too valuable to put at risk.

One of the most interesting features of the cabinet is how strikingly modern it looks. Both the construction and the carved designs are startling precursors of the craftsman-style furniture that became popular during the first two decades of the twentieth century.

Although it has long been in Bolton Castle's collection, no one has been able to determine how long it has been there, its place of origin, or its original purpose. This charming piece of furniture remains a mystery.

## CONSTRUCTION NOTES
A cautionary note to the builder: Even without its carved decoration, this cabinet's apparently simple construction is deceptive. Although its square-cut lines and edges seem to be visible, it contains a bewildering array of rabbet joints and lap joints. The use of excessive rabbeting was undoubtedly an attempt to transform fairly heavy timbers into a light and delicate piece of furniture. The photograph reveals that there are no hinges on the doors; the doors pivot on dowel pins. The lines of the cabinet are clean, but building it is not easy. The basic construction techniques are simple, but be prepared to study the plans more than once before beginning work. To simplify the project, we will build the ambry from the ground up.

The ambry's current back panel is clearly a replacement from the nineteenth or even early twentieth century, with no attempt to emulate period methods or design. We have taken an educated guess about the appearance of the original back panel based on the construction of the rest of the ambry.

### Materials
This ambry is constructed entirely of oak. Surprisingly, the boards are the closest to modern mill dimensions of those used in any piece in this book; they should not present physical or economical challenges to the builder.

### Feet
Following the front view and end view drawings and the materials list, measure and cut out the ambry's feet. The foot detail drawing reproduces the sculpted foot at half life-size; it can be enlarged on a photocopier and transferred directly to the wood. When the foot has been cut to shape, lay out the mortise that receives the end panel. As shown on the end view drawing, the mortise is 9½ inches long and begins 1 inch from the back end of the foot. The mortise is ⅝ inch wide

and is located in the center of the foot; this leaves $^{13}/_{16}$ inch of wood on either side of the mortise.

## Side Panels

Cut the side panels to the dimensions shown in the materials list. Lay out and cut a tenon on the bottom of each side panel. The tenon should fit snugly into the mortise in the foot and should be the full 2¼-inch depth of the mortise and ⅝ inch in width. To ensure that the side panels sit in the center of the feet, remove ⅛ inch from either face of the side panel when you cut the tenon to width. Temporarily fit the foot into place to ensure a snug fit.

Moving up the side panel, lay out and cut the mortise that will hold the stretcher, which separates the feet. This 1¼-by-2¾-inch mortise should be located 9⅜ inches above the bottom of the foot.

Now you will cut the first of the rabbeted lap joints that make this project so challenging. Across the top inside corner of the side panel, cut a rabbet ½ inch in height and ¼ inch in depth. A top view of this rabbet is found in the detail B, top corner drawing, which clearly shows that the ¼-inch dimension of this rabbet (the hatched area in the drawing) runs across the ⅞-inch thickness of the board. The ½-inch dimension (the rabbet's height) is on the inside face of the panel and can be seen as the hatched area of the end view with panel removed drawing. After you locate and cut this rabbet, notice the similar rabbets that run down the front and back of the panel. The corner and hinge, section 3 drawing shows the layout of these rabbets, which are ⅝ inch square and 16⅝ inches long. When they have been cut, the bottom corners should be trimmed out square with the edge of a sharp chisel.

A fourth rabbet runs across the panel, from front to back, 13¾ inches from the top edge of the panel (13¼ inches beneath the top rabbet). See the end view with panel removed drawing. This rabbet is ½ inch wide and ½ inch deep.

When all four rabbets have been cut on the inside faces of both panels, the feet should be placed on the tenons, checked for squareness, and doweled into place with two ¼-inch dowels as shown in the end view drawing. Note: The dowels go completely through the width of the feet.

## Stretcher

When the feet have been attached to the side panels, lay them aside and cut a stretcher according to the one shown in the front view drawing. The tenons, which are the full 1¼-inch thickness of the stretcher, are 2⅛

inches in length, allowing them to pass through the ⅞-inch-thick side panel and still have 1¼ inches exposed on the outside of the case, as shown in the drawing. Be sure to squarely cut the shoulders, where the tenon joins the stretcher's body, so that they rest evenly against the inside faces of the side panels when the stretcher pins are inserted. The stretcher should fit snugly, but easily, through the mortises in the side panels.

Copying the stretcher pin drawing, lay out and cut two pins from ⅞-inch-thick wood. Then lay out and cut corresponding mortises (½ by ⅞ inch) in the exposed ends of the stretcher. Situate the mortises very close to the outside face of the side panels, or recess them slightly, so that when the pins are inserted, they pull the stretcher and the end panel firmly together. You should not, however, have to hammer the pins into place.

## Cabinet Floor

Cut the cabinet floor to size as detailed in the materials list. On the front and back of the cabinet, cut rabbets that are ⅜ by ¼ inch. The ⅜-inch dimension, which is visible when you look at the board's edge, is clearly shown in the end view with panel removed drawing. On the ends of the floorboard, the rabbets should be ⅜ by ⅜ inch. The ½-inch-wide tenons on the ends of the board should slide gently into the ½-by-⅜-inch rabbets in the side panels. When you attach the back panel, the floor should position itself.

## Back Panel

The back panel, as we have re-created it, is made from two boards running horizontally across the cabinet's back. The two boards specified in the materials list provide the proper height and length to make up the back of the cabinet. You may, if you wish, peg the boards together to form a single panel. Instructions for joining boards are found in the chapters on general woodworking and constructing the Merrills Board.

The left and right edges of the back panel are rabbeted ⅝ by ¼ inch. The ⅝-inch dimension is visible when you look at the board's edge, as shown in the end view with panel removed drawing. The ¼-inch dimension of the rabbet is visible on the back panel's interior surface.

The rabbet across the top of the panel is ½ by ¼ inch, the ¼-inch dimension running across the board's top edge. The rabbet across the bottom of the panel is ¼ inch deep and ½ inch wide. It is located 1½ inches above the panel's bottom edge, as shown in the end view with panel removed drawing.

# MATERIALS

## WOOD
All wood is oak.

| PART | NUMBER OF PIECES | THICKNESS | | WIDTH | | LENGTH |
|---|---|---|---|---|---|---|
| feet | 2 | 2¼" | × | 2¼" | × | 17⅝" |
| side panels | 2 | ⅞" | × | 11½" | × | 44" |
| stretcher | 1 | 1¼" | × | 4" | × | 44½" |
| stretcher pins | 2 | ⅞" | × | 1" | × | 4¼" |
| cabinet floorboard | 1 | ⅞" | × | 10⅝" | × | 41" |
| backboard | 1 | ⅞" | × | 8" | × | 42" |
| backboard | 1 | ⅞" | × | 8⅝" | × | 42" |
| top and bottom door rails | 4 | ⅝" | × | 1¾" | × | 14" |
| hinge end door stiles | 2 | ⅞" | × | 3" | × | 12½" |
| free end door stiles | 2 | ⅞" | × | 2¼" | × | 12½" |

When the back panel has been rabbeted, it should fit easily between the cabinet's side panels. The left and right edges of the back panel should be flush with the outside face of the end panels. The floor panel should slide into the rabbet near the bottom of the panel and automatically position the top edge of the back flush with the top edge of the side panels. The snug fit of the floor panel into the back panel should hold both in place.

## Frame Assembly
Clamp the cabinet together so that it is square and plumb. Drill and dowel three ¼-inch pilot holes through each side panel and into the end grain of the floorboard. Tap the dowels into place and cut them off, leaving ¼ inch exposed. Sand this down later.

Repeat the process on the back panel, inserting four dowels along the left and right sides of the panel, and five dowels across the back edge of the floorboard.

Locate two of the floor dowels approximately 3 inches from the outside corners of the floor, situate one in the center, and equally space the other two between the first three.

It might be wise to glue the floor and back in place before doweling, because they do not actually interlock with the side panels. When the glue is dry, remove the clamps and set aside the ambry's frame.

## Doorframe
Because the doors swing on dowel pins, rather than hinges, they must be constructed as part of the front assembly, which is then set in place. It will be easiest to build the doors next, and construct the frame around them. We have only detailed the ambry's left door in the drawings, but the doors mirror each other.

Note: The frame of the doors is made from three different widths and two different thicknesses of wood. Cut the top and bottom rails to length, and cut the

| PART | NUMBER OF PIECES | THICKNESS | | WIDTH | | LENGTH |
|---|---|---|---|---|---|---|
| door panels | 2 | ⅜" | × | 10¼" | × | 12¼" |
| top molding | 1 | ⅝" | × | 2½" | × | 42" |
| bottom molding | 1 | ½" | × | 2" | × | 42" |
| front end panels | 2 | ⅞" | × | 3½" | × | 16⅝" |
| front center panel | 1 | ⅞" | × | 3" | × | 16⅝" |
| top filler strips | 2 | ⅝" | × | 2⅛" | × | 17½" |
| bottom filler strips | 2 | ⅝" | × | 2" | × | 17½" |
| top boards | 3 | ⅞" | × | 9½" | × | 12⅜" |
| top board | 1 | ⅞" | × | 8¾" | × | 12⅜" |
| top board | 1 | ⅞" | × | 4¾" | × | 12⅜" |
| top board | 1 | ⅞" | × | 1½" | × | 12⅜" |
| hinge pin dowel | 1 | ⅜" diameter | | | × | 12" |
| dowels | 4 | ¼" diameter | | | × | 36" |

tenons on each end as shown in the left door top view drawing. Trim the excess wood from the face of the board, leaving the tenon flush with the back of the rail. When the tenon has been cut, rabbet a ⅝-by-⅜-inch groove on the back of the rail to receive the door panel. The door panel, sections 1 and 2 drawing shows that the top and bottom rails fit onto the edge of the carved panel without actually holding it in place.

Next, cut the left and right stiles for the doors. Although both doors are cut from ⅞-inch-thick stock, and both are 12½ inches in length, the stile that carries the hinge pin is 3 inches wide and the stile on the door's free end is only 2¼ inches wide. Along the interior edge of both the left and right stiles, plow a ¼-by-1⅜-inch rabbet. This groove will receive both the carved panel and the top and bottom rails. This rabbet is illustrated in both the left door top view and the left door section B drawings.

On the outer face of the stile that carries the hinge

pin, cut a ¼-by-½-inch rabbet, as shown in the left door top view; left door section B; and left door detail.

**Door Panels**

Cut the door panels to the size shown in the materials list, noting that the grain runs horizontally on the panel once it is installed in the door. When the panels have been cut to size, cut a ½-by-⅛-inch rabbet along the left and right edges of the panels. These rabbets are detailed in the left door section B drawing.

Enlarge the outline of the carvings from the left door detail drawing, and transfer it to the fronts of the panels. The panel's front is the side on which you cannot see the rabbets. Carefully black out those areas of the design that will be removed from the panel. These areas are crosshatched on the drawing. A jigsaw will easily remove these areas, but a scroll saw (coping saw) is the most historically authentic tool for the job. Several fairly abstract birds and flowers form the design, but they will appear properly only when the panel has been fully carved. The design is relatively clear on the photograph.

When the piercings are complete, black out the areas to be carved, and then gouge the carvings. The chapter on woodcarving gives good background information on relief carving and chip carving, but here all of the designs are simple crescent shapes (half-moons) cut from the panel's surface with gouges. The carving on the doors can be executed with two gouges, one small and one medium. Executing gouge work in oak requires a steady hand, but the carving offers no complex shapes or angles to contend with. Practice on a scrap of wood before you begin work on the panel itself. Because the panel is only ⅜ inch thick, anchor it firmly to the workbench to prevent the wood from splitting when you work across the grain in delicate areas.

## Assembling the Doors

When the rails, stiles, and panels have been completed, they should fit together easily. Clamp the door together to ensure that it is square, and drill and dowel the stiles in place on the rails as shown in drawing of the door panel, sections 1 and 2. Do not be alarmed when you realize that the panels are thicker than the top and bottom rails; that is the way the original was made.

Note on the left door, top view and left door section B drawings that the stile on the free-swinging end of the door (in this case, the right-hand stile) has been planed to a 5-degree angle. This angle allows the door to open and close without binding against the central panel.

Next, locate the position of the dowels that serve as hinge pins. There is a dowel on the top and bottom of each of the 3-inch-wide stiles. Position the pin at the exact center of the board's thickness, ⁷⁄₁₆ inch from either side and 1⅛ inches from the outermost edge of the stile. The hinge pin can be seen on both the left door, top view and the corner and hinge, section 3 drawings. The pins on the top and the bottom of the door must be in precisely the same location if the door is to swing properly. When you have located the center of the hinge pin, drill a ⅜-inch-diameter pilot hole that is ¾ inch deep. Tap a length of ⅜-inch dowel into the hole, and carefully trim it ½ inch above the surface of the door, as shown in the left door detail drawing. Sand any burrs from the dowels' ends.

## Molding

There are two strips of decorative molding on the cabinet's face, one across the top and the other across the bottom. These are shown in details A and C; molding detail, sections 1 and 2; and section 4. Detail A provides the actual dimensions of the various decorative elements of the molding. All the molding can be cut from ⅝-by-2½-inch stock; the bottom section can then be trimmed to its finished dimensions of ½ by 2 inches as shown in section 4.

## Front Panels

There are three vertical panels on the ambry's front, one on each end and one in the center between the doors. All three panels are the same thickness and length, but the end panels are 3⅓ inches wide while the center panel is only 3 inches wide (see the front view drawing). Cut the panels to length and width as shown on the materials list.

Rabbeting the center panel to accept the top and bottom moldings is relatively easy. Cut simple 2⅛-by-¼-inch rabbets across the top and 2-by-¼-inch rabbets across the bottom of the panel as shown in the section 4 drawing. Trim the width of the rabbeted ends as shown in the center panel drawing. The panel now appears to have a ⅝-by-2-inch tenon on each end. Mark this panel and lay it aside for the moment.

The left edge of the left panel and the right edge of the right panel must be rabbeted to fit into the rabbets on the front edges of the ambry's side panels. The corner and hinge, section 3 drawing illustrates these rabbets, which are ⅝ inch across the face and ¼ inch deep. The opposite edges of these two front panels (that is, the edges nearest the doors) must also be rabbeted to mesh with the rabbets on the stile's edge. As shown in the corner and hinge, section 3 drawing, cut a rabbet ⅝ inch across the face and ½ inch in depth.

There is also a rabbet across the back of all three panels that allows them to lock into position on the floorboard. This rabbet is ½ inch wide and ¼ inch deep and is located 1⅛ inches above the panel's bottom edge. When these rabbets have been cut into the boards, temporarily fit them to the ambry's face. If properly cut, the top of the front panels will be level with the top of the side panels.

The rabbeting of the left and right panels to accept the decorative molding is similar to the center panel. In this case, however, the panels are rabbeted at two different heights. Study details A and C carefully;

the ⅞-inch-wide vertical board that runs the height of the drawing represents the edge of the left front panel. Beginning 2 inches above the bottom of the panel, there is a ⅛-by-⅞-inch rabbet that is cut to fit into the end of the bottom molding like a tenon. Beneath this an additional ⅛ inch is cut away. To ease the confusion, remember that both the ⅝-inch-wide hatched area and the ¼-inch-wide white area, the surfaces from which you have just cut the rabbets, are both part of this same end panel.

When the bottom of the panels have been rabbeted, repeat the process on the top. Begin the rabbeting 2⅛ inches from the panel's top edge. The first channel is ⅛ inch deep and ⅞ inch wide. The rabbet is then deepened another ⅛ inch and run out to the end of the panel. Lay these panels on the worktable so that the left and right panels are in their respective positions. Referencing the center panel, note how the top and bottom of the panel were turned into tenons by removing ½ inch from either side of the rabbeted area. Similarly, cut away ½ inch from the rabbeted area of the end panels, but only on the inside edge of the panel—that is, on the edge that will be nearest the door. Do not cut back the outside edge of the panels.

## Carving the Center Panel

The drawing of the center panel is reproduced here at 50 percent of its actual size. Enlarge it on a photocopier and transfer it directly to the center panel. The crescent-shaped carvings at the top and bottom of the design can be cut with a gouge, in the same way that similar designs were made on the door panels. The remainder of the carvings can be cut with a combination of gouges and carving knives. Refer to the chapter on woodcarving for additional information. The vertically shaded lines of the design are cut a little deeper than the rest of the pattern. Most of the carving is slightly less than ⅛ inch deep, but this 3/16-inch-deep area makes a distinct visual difference. The hatched area sprinkled with tiny triangles is actually textured with tiny pyramid-shaped gouges. A small V-gouge was probably used to make this pattern. Be careful not to make the gouges too large; the size shown on the enlarged drawing is very close to the original size.

## Framing in the Front

Cut the top and bottom moldings to the exact 42-inch length, and notch out rabbets on the outer ends of the moldings to fit accurately over the rabbets shown in

details A and C. Carefully chisel out these notches to avoid splitting the thin oak molding.

Next, cut two lengths of filler strip to bridge the gap between the front edge of the floor and the back of the molding. Initially rip the filler strip to a ⅝-inch thickness and a 2⅛-inch width. Shape the filler strip along the top of the cabinet to the same dimension. Cut the filler strip on the bottom to a width of 2 inches, and then form a ¼-by-½-inch rabbet as shown in the molding detail, section 2 drawing.

Glue the left and right front panels to the ambry's face, clamping them in position while they dry. When the glue is dry, remove the clamps. Clamp the center panel temporarily in position on the front edge of the cabinet floor. Be sure to position the panel in the exact center of the cabinet so that the openings for the doors are identical. Trim the bottom filler strips to fit between the panels, making certain that they fit neatly around any rabbets on the backs of the panels. Remove the center panel and the filler strips.

Lightly glue the front and back of the rabbet on the back of the center panel, the filler strips where they lap over the floorboard, and the entire back face of the bottom molding. Clamp these pieces in place, making certain that the center panel is square and plumb. Position the clamps so that you can dowel the three front panels to the floor of the cabinet as shown in the front view drawing. Adding one or two more dowels to hold the filler strips firmly in place between the cabinet floor and the molding would not be amiss. When the glue is dry, remove the clamps and stand the ambry upright, being careful not to jar the center panel, which is only partly supported.

Set the doors in position, surrounding them with thin cardboard shims to ensure that they are centered between the front panels. Placing a drop of paint on the bottom of the lower hinge pin before lowering the door carefully into place helps to establish the point at which a hole needs to be drilled to receive the pin. Remove the door and drill the hole ½ inch deep. Be sure the hole is large enough that the dowel can swing freely, without being loose. (Hint: Prevent wear to the bottom of the door and the hinge pin alike by placing a thin plastic disk in the bottom of the lower hinge pin hole—cut one from a dishwashing-liquid bottle with a large paper punch. Alternatively, insert a small thumbtack into the end of the hinge pin, but take care not to split your dowel in the process.) Lay the doors aside for the moment.

Clamp the top length of molding in place, and cut the top filler strips to fit neatly between the front panels. Glue the filler strips to the molding, clamp them together, and allow the glue to dry. Do not glue the molding to the front panels.

When the glue has dried, remove the molding and filler strips and set the doors in place, wedging them so that they will remain in position without being held. Place a drop of paint on top of the upper hinge pins, and lower the molding and filler strips into place until they touch the hinge pins. Remove the strip and drill the holes as you did for the bottom of the doors. Now place the doors in position and set the strip on top of them. Temporarily clamp the molding strip in place to make sure the doors swing open and shut without binding. When everything fits, glue the molding in place. The doors are now permanently attached; the front of the cabinet is complete.

## Top

Not only are the boards that make up the ambry's top of random width, but many of them are not square—the top view drawing gives precise detail. Although this may not be the most convenient way to build the top, it adds to the cupboard's quirky charm. The boards listed in the materials list will reproduce the existing top.

Since, like all the ambry's other components, the top boards are rabbeted to fit into the cabinet frame, it will be easiest to cut the rabbets while the boards are still square. As shown in the detail A drawing, the front edge of the top boards must be cut with a ½-by-½-inch rabbet. Likewise, the end boards require similar rabbets where they fit into the side panels. The rear edge, however, should be cut with a ½-by-¼-inch rabbet, the ½-inch dimension being visible on the board's edge. Cut all the rabbets and begin to fit the top boards in place. It will probably be easiest if you place the end boards, both of which are square, on the cabinet and fit the boards between them one at a time. Make any necessary adjustments to the final board before it is set in place.

The front of the ambry is not the most stable structure; it is advisable to peg the top boards together before fitting them permanently. Peg the boards according to the instructions in the chapters on general woodworking and on constructing the Merrills Board. When the top has been pegged together, make minor adjustments if necessary to fit it in place on the ambry. Glue the rabbeted area around the edges of the top, set it in place, and clamp it to the frame. Drill and dowel through the top molding as shown in the front view drawing.

## Finish

The rather mottled look to the cabinet in the photograph probably indicates that at sometime in its life the cabinet was painted. Though much medieval furniture was painted, this cabinet appears to have been painted white, an unlikely medieval color. A natural finish will best complement the ambry. Addition of a stain to darken the piece is entirely up to you.

It is probable that the carved door panels were originally backed with cloth to prevent anyone from seeing directly into the cabinet. Choose a color that will contrast well with the finished wood, and tack the fabric into place around the inside face of the doorframe. Be careful not to nail directly into the delicate carved panel. The frames of the doors are also delicate; have someone apply back pressure with a wooden block before you tack the material onto the doorframe.

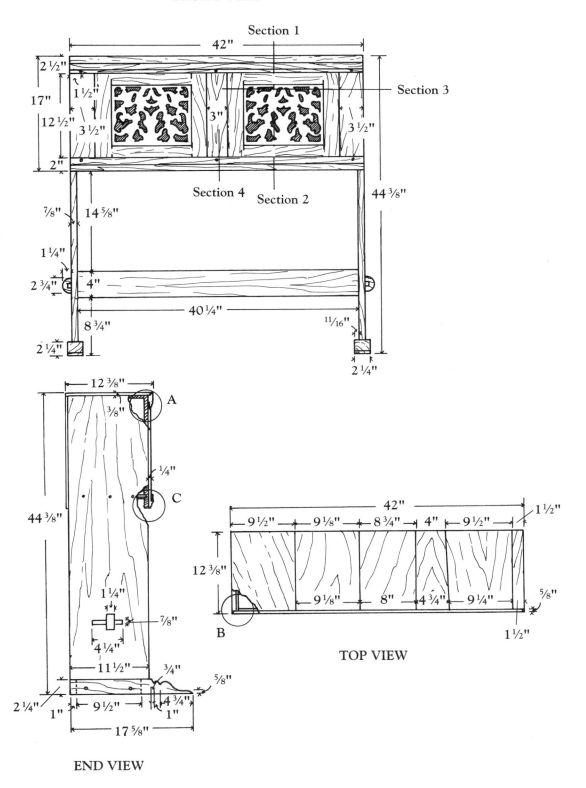

**FRONT VIEW**

Section 1

42"

2 1/2"

17"

1 1/2"

12 1/2"

3"

3 1/2"

Section 3

3 1/2"

2"

Section 4  Section 2

44 3/8"

7/8"  14 5/8"

1 1/4"

2 3/4"  4"

40 1/4"

8 3/4"

11/16"

2 1/4"

2 1/4"

12 3/8"

3/8"

A

1/4"

C

44 3/8"

1 1/4"

7/8"

4 1/4"

11 1/2"

3/4"

5/8"

2 1/4"  1"

9 1/2"  4 3/4"  1"

17 5/8"

**END VIEW**

42"

9 1/2"  9 1/8"  8 3/4"  4"  9 1/2"  1 1/2"

12 3/8"

9 1/8"  8"  4 3/4"  9 1/4"

5/8"

B

1 1/2"

**TOP VIEW**

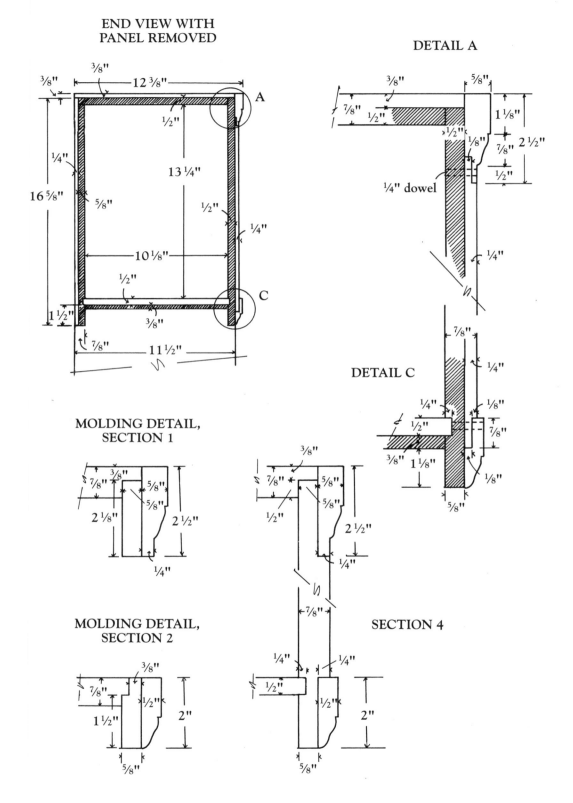

END VIEW WITH
PANEL REMOVED

DETAIL A

¹/₄" dowel

MOLDING DETAIL,
SECTION 1

DETAIL C

MOLDING DETAIL,
SECTION 2

SECTION 4

LEFT DOOR, TOP VIEW

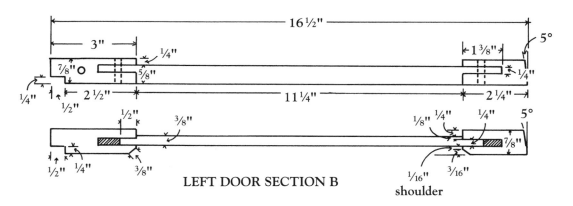

LEFT DOOR SECTION B

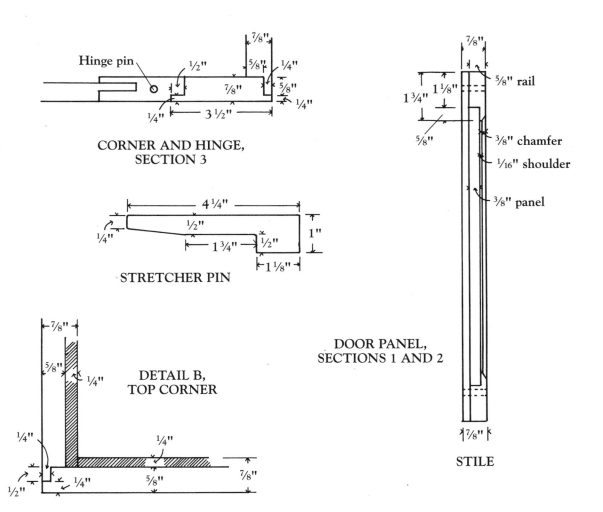

Hinge pin

CORNER AND HINGE,
SECTION 3

STRETCHER PIN

DETAIL B,
TOP CORNER

DOOR PANEL,
SECTIONS 1 AND 2

5/8" rail

3/8" chamfer

1/16" shoulder

3/8" panel

STILE

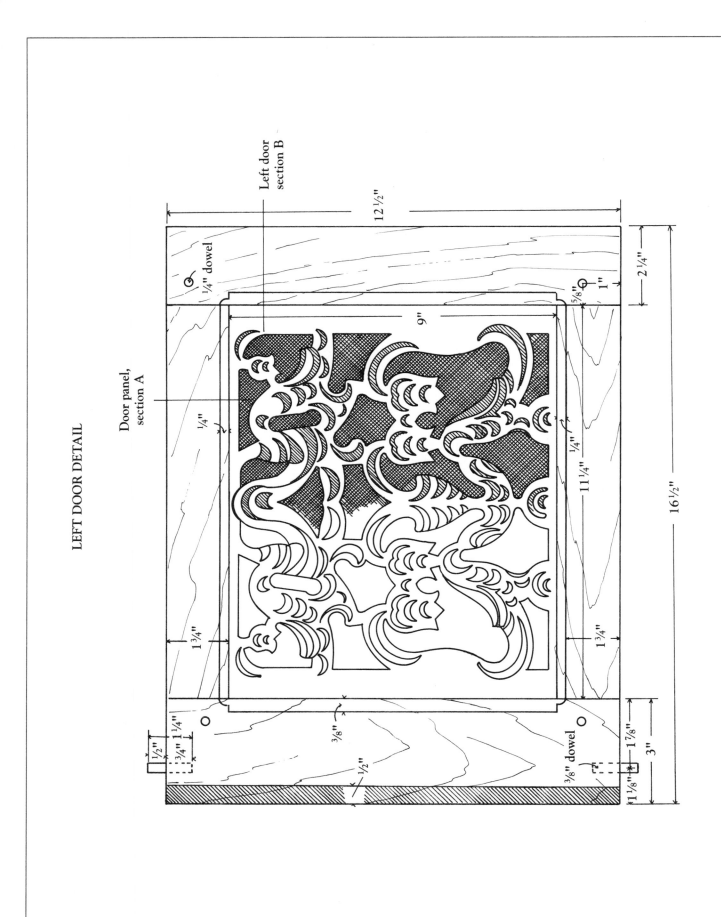

LEFT DOOR DETAIL

Left door section B

Door panel, section A

¼" dowel

12 ½"

2 ¼"

9"

¼"

¼"

11 ¼"

1 ¾"

1 ¾"

16 ½"

5/8"

1"

3/8"

½"

3/8" dowel

½"

¾" 1 ¼"

1 1/8"

3"

1 7/8"

1 1/8"

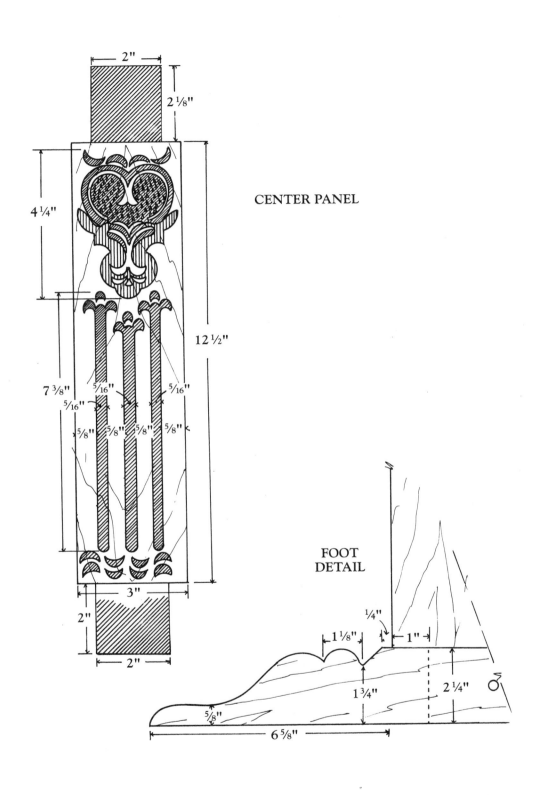

CENTER PANEL

FOOT
DETAIL

# Project 9

# WHEELBARROW

So humble that it hardly merits notice today, the wheelbarrow represented one of the major technological breakthroughs of the early Middle Ages. Before its invention small loads were moved from place to place on sledges, or hurdles—small pallets mounted on skids that could be dragged from one place to another. Hardly designed to prevent back strain, wheelbarrows such as the one shown here did, however, tremendously increase laborers' efficiency. The barrow in the photograph carries a heavy chest, which would otherwise have required the efforts of two men to move.

The origins of the wheelbarrow are obscure, but it certainly did not exist in the classical world, and just as certainly was a common tool by the thirteenth century. It is sad, but hardly surprising, that no actual medieval wheelbarrows have survived. What information we have on the appearance of the medieval wheelbarrow comes almost exclusively from illuminated manuscripts. It is on a number of these manuscript illuminations that this wonderfully re-created fifteenth century barrow, currently on display at Warwick Castle, has been modeled.

## CONSTRUCTION NOTES

Purely utilitarian, most wheelbarrows were crudely built of whatever wood was at hand. Much of this example has obviously been cobbled together from the trunks of saplings or small branches that would otherwise have been used for firewood. Although it looks deceptively simple, the construction of this wheelbarrow, particularly building the wheel, will require patience and attention to detail. As this is a strictly utilitarian piece of equipment, a certain rough-hewn look is not only acceptable, but desirable, in the finished piece.

## Materials

Although this wheelbarrow, like actual historic pieces, is made from a variety of woods, be careful to choose material with good tensile strength that will hold up to the weight and stress of heavy use. Ash and birch are both strong, tough woods that have been traditionally used for tools. The wheel, the hub, the axle, and the sides of the body could be made from either of these. Maple could be used for the cross members of the frame and for the dashboard.

The thickness of the side frames is such that they will almost surely have to be specially milled or glued up from two narrower boards.

## Body

Enlarge the side frame template, either on a blueprint copier or by hand, so that the grid pattern is $1\frac{1}{2}$ inches square. This will provide a full-scale pattern from which to copy the side frames. Lay out the design for the side frames, and use a band saw or a jigsaw to cut the frame to shape. The thickness of these boards will slow the cutting process. Allow the saw to work at its own speed; if you try to push the wood too fast, it will break the blade.

When the rough shape of the sides has been cut, lay out the locations of the two main cross braces and the four small slats that form the barrow's bed. The positions and sizes of these pieces are shown in the side view and the cutaway view of the side drawings. Mark the positions of these framing members on the inner faces of the side frames. Mortise these areas to receive the cross braces and the slats. Note: In the drawing of the top view with dashboard removed, the two main cross braces pass entirely through, and extend $\frac{5}{8}$ inch beyond, the side frames, while the bed slats are only mortised into the frame to the depth of 1 inch. On the cutaway view of the side, the slats are slightly staggered along the frame's side curve. This was probably an attempt to follow the line of the side frame. Likewise, the rear cross brace has been slightly shaped to conform with the angle of the side frame, but you should wait to do this until after the body has been assembled. When the mortises have been roughed out, smooth the sides and corners with a sharp chisel.

Also at this time, drill a $^{13}/_{16}$-inch-diameter hole to accommodate the axle. The location of the axle is shown in the side view of the axle and dashboard. Note that the distance from the front edge of the frame to the axle's center is $1\frac{3}{4}$ inches.

Turn the side frames upside down and mark the position of the legs on the underside of the frame. After cutting out two legs according to the leg drawing, mortise them into the frame in the appropriate locations.

Now shape the rear portion of the side frames into handles. Using the drawings of the side view and the top view with dashboard removed as references, use a drawknife to gently taper the ends of the frame from their full 3-inch width to a finished diameter of $1\frac{1}{2}$ inches. The frames begin to assume their round shape immediately behind the rear cross brace. This is visible in both the top view with dashboard removed and the photograph. The taper begins with no more than a rounding of the corners of the side frame. As you work down the shaft toward the handgrips, the shape becomes more and more circular.

When the side frames have been fully shaped, cut the cross braces and slats. Allow enough extra length on the slats to allow them to fit into the 1-inch-deep mortises in either side frame. Work tenons on the ends of the cross braces to fit them into the side frame. Note that these tenons are the full 3-inch width of the cross braces. The tenons should fit into the mortises with a few light taps from a mallet or with the palm of the hand. Assemble the body of the wheelbarrow to ensure that it fits snugly and is in square. Lay the body aside; do not permanently fasten it together.

**Wheel and Axle**
Begin constructing the wheel assembly by turning the hub from the 3-inch-square stock noted in the materials list. Note on the cutaway view of the wheel front the point at which the hub begins to taper as it nears its outer ends. Allow a $\frac{7}{8}$-inch-wide shoulder at the outermost end of the hub to accept a metal band. As indicated in the side view of the wheel drawing, this shoulder should be 2 inches in diameter. The hub

could be shaped by an expert with a drawknife, but you will probably find a lathe much more practical for the purpose.

When the hub has been turned, mark the center point on each end of the hub. Using a hand drill or drill press, bore a $\frac{3}{4}$-inch hole that is 4 inches deep into both ends of the hub. Be careful that this hole runs absolutely straight into the hub; if it veers even slightly off-center, the wheel will not turn properly. It is expedient, if not historically accurate, to use a lathe with a boring chuck to ensure that the hole runs straight and true.

Mark the center of the hub around its entire circumference. Along this line, indicate the positions of the six spokes. On a 3-inch-diameter hub, the spokes will be located on $1\frac{9}{16}$-inch centers. The mortises to receive the spokes should be 1 inch long, $\frac{5}{8}$ inch wide, and $\frac{1}{2}$ inch deep. Carefully cut the mortises straight into the hub. If the spoke mortises deviate to the left or right, the spokes will not stand straight, and the wheel will lack strength. Use a drill press, if possible, to remove most of the excess wood from the mortises while the hub is clamped in a drill press vise. This will help ensure that the holes are straight. Clean up the sides and corners of the mortise with a chisel.

Cut the six spokes to the dimensions given in the cutaway view of the wheel front. Note that the tenons are the full $\frac{5}{8}$-inch thickness of the spoke, but the tenon's width is less than the width of the spoke itself. Fit the spokes into the wheel one at a time. It will probably require some individual fitting; be sure to mark each spoke and the mortise into which it fits. Since these parts are not interchangeable, trying to find which spoke goes into which mortise can be extremely frustrating.

Now you are ready to make the wheel's outer rim. Scribe a 12-inch circle on a piece of cardboard, and lay out the six sections of the wheel as shown in the side view of the wheel. Sequentially mark the pieces one through six, and cut the template apart. Use the parts as patterns for the six segments of the wheel, allowing $\frac{1}{8}$ inch of extra wood on each end of each segment. This extra wood will allow you to sand or rasp away the wood, a little at a time, until the segments of the wheel align perfectly to form a 12-inch circle.

Form a circle out of the segments of the wheel; then position the hub, with the spokes attached, on top of it. Note: To do this, you may have to make a temporary table with a hole in the center through which the end of the hub can pass. This will allow the spokes to rest on the edge of the rim. If the spokes are

# MATERIALS

## WOOD
The woods are ash, birch, and maple.

| PART | NUMBER OF PIECES | THICKNESS | | WIDTH | | LENGTH |
|---|---|---|---|---|---|---|
| side frames | 2 | 3" | × | 12" | × | 52" |
| cross braces | 2 | 3" | × | 3" | × | 20¾" |
| slats | 4 | 1½" | × | 1½" | × | 16" |
| legs | 2 | 2" | × | 4" | × | 5¼" |
| wheel hub | 1 | 3" diameter | | | × | 14" |
| spokes | 6 | ⅝" | × | 2¼" | × | 4" |
| wheel rims | 6 | 2¼" | × | 1¾" | × | 6" |
| dashboard top rail | 1 | 3" diameter | | | × | 22½" |
| dashboard supports | 2 | 2" diameter | | | × | 15½" |
| dashboard support posts | 2 | 2" diameter | | | × | 15" |
| dashboard support posts | 3 | 2" diameter | | | × | 14¾" |
| dowel | 1 | ¼" diameter | | | × | 36" |

all the same length and are set straight in the hub, and if the six sections of the wheel fit properly, the spokes should nest perfectly into the wheel. Trim spokes that are a bit long; replace any that are too short. When the fit is as good as possible, mark the locations of the spoke tenons on each section of the wheel—again marking which section of the wheel will be attached to which spoke. Remember that they are not going to be interchangeable.

Cut the mortises in the wheel's rim. With the location of the spokes well marked, remove them to ensure their proper fit into the rim mortises. When all the parts fit, you are ready for the final assembly of the wheel. Many small wheels such as this were held together only by the pressure of the iron tire against the wheel's rim. If gluing the pieces together reassures you, do so. You may also want to join together the segments of the outer rim with small nails or screws. On a wheel for a large vehicle, these rims would have been pegged together, but on a wheelbarrow, such effort would have been unlikely.

If you glue the wheel together, hold the pieces in place with the aid of a strap clamp, wrapped around the wheel's outer circumference, to be sure that the segments are clamped tightly while the glue dries. You should be able to nail or screw together the wheel segments on either side of the strap clamp without any difficulty. When the glue is dry, remove the clamp.

## METAL

| PART | NUMBER OF PIECES | THICKNESS | | WIDTH | | LENGTH |
|---|---|---|---|---|---|---|
| axles | 2 | ¾" diameter | | × | | 7½" |
| iron tire | 1 | ⅛" | × | 2¼" | × | 38" |
| hub bands | 2 | ⅛" | × | ⅞" | × | 6½" |
| forged nails for axles | 2 | | | | | 3" |
| forged nails for dashboard | 14 | | | | | 2¼" |
| forged nails for legs, optional | 4 | | | | | 3" |

### Tire and Hub Bandings

Application of the metal tire, and the bands around the ends of the hubs, is a job for a professional blacksmith. To ensure that the wheel is held tightly together, the tire and bands must be forged slightly smaller than the diameter of the wheel and hub. These rings are then heated until they expand, dropped into place, and quenched with cold water so that they shrink tightly around the wood. A good smith knows how to do this. Ask horse owners or a local riding stable for the name of a smith or farrier.

### Axle

After the tire and the hub bands are in place, install the axles. Slightly round one end of the ¾-inch dowel, and lightly sand the portion of the shaft to be driven into the hub. This will allow it to tap into the hub more easily. If the axle and the hole in the hub are exactly the same size, the axle will not fit into the hole; if the axle fits too easily, it will be loose and will break under the pressure of a heavy load. A proper fit will need to be slightly tighter than a good mortise and tenon joint, but if it is too tight, the pressure of driving the axle into place could cause the hub to split. A light coating of soap or oil will help to ease the axle's path into the hub. When the axle is in place, drive a nail through the hub into the axle to keep it from turning inside the hub under the weight of heavy loads. Drill a pilot hole through the hub and the axle, about 2

inches from the end of the hub. Drive a nail into the hole. If you can find or make a forged nail long enough to protrude through the opposite side of the hub, use this, and crimp over the nail's exposed end.

### Alternative Axle

We do not normally suggest alternative (that is, more modern) methods of constructing medieval objects, but here we make an exception. If you plan to use your wheelbarrow, replace the wooden axle with a metal one, which has a tensile strength greater than even the best wood can offer. Many medieval barrows used metal axles, a more durable alternative.

Replace the wooden axle with a ¾-inch piece of steel round stock, or even a ¾-inch segment of heavy-walled, welded steel tubing. It should fit snugly into the hub but turn freely in the frame. It is permissible to pin it to the hub in the same manner as we suggested for the wooden axle. To disguise the fact that you are using a steel axle, simply cut each axle ¾ inch shorter than the body's outside width, and plug the ends of the axle hole with a short length of ¾-inch wooden dowel.

A radically modern approach to installing the axle is to sleeve the hole in the frame through which the axle passes with a metal tube. This prevents the axle from wearing away at the surrounding wood. But although a metal axle is viable medieval technology, sleeving the socket is not.

## Body Assembly

Remove one of the side rails from the body of the wheelbarrow. Place the axle into the socket in the rail still holding the cross braces and slats. Set the remaining side rail back in position and tap it into place. The ends of the hub should just touch the inside of the frame without binding. Lay the bed of the wheelbarrow across your workbench so that the wheel hangs over one side of the bench and the handles over the other. This should allow the body of the barrow to rest firmly on the workbench. Now that the body is square, drill two pilot holes, large enough to accept a ¼-inch dowel, through the side rails and tenons of each of the main cross braces, and dowel the body together.

Turn the wheelbarrow upside down and insert the legs into their mortises. On the wheelbarrow in the photograph, the legs are held in place only by the tightness of the mortise and tenon joint. The legs are also loose. We suggest using two forged nails to anchor the legs. Drill pilot holes through the side rails and tenons on the legs, and nail the pieces together. The wheelbarrow now lacks only the dashboard to complete it.

## Dashboard

Gather together the component parts of the dash, including the top rail and seven support posts. With a drawknife, slightly chamfer the ends of the top rail as shown in the drawing labeled dashboard top rail, bottom view. When that is finished, taper the ends of the support posts as shown in the drawing of the dashboard support post. Note that these posts come in three slightly different lengths. The length is measured at the narrowest end of the taper, just above the 1¼-inch-diameter peg. The points where these measurements have been taken are clearly shown on the side view drawing of the axle and dashboard. There are two 12½-inch-long posts, two 12-inch-long posts, and three 11¾-inch-long posts. Do not be too concerned if the exact lengths vary a little; assembling the dash requires a little play in the posts. If you are taking a medieval approach, and plan to hew the parts for the dashboard from saplings, use a spokeshave to make the support posts roughly square before you cut the tapers on the end. Although the posts themselves are square, the pins on the end are round.

The next step is to drill the holes in the barrow's frame into which the support posts will fit. The locations of the posts are clearly noted in the dashboard top view drawing. Mark the center of each post. Setting the correct angles on the posts so that they

all meet at the top rail and at the correct height is difficult. The four corner posts (those that attach to the side rails of the wheelbarrow frame) are set at a 65-degree angle. The three posts in the center are set at a 75-degree angle. To help you hold the drill at the proper angle, cut a triangular template from a 1-inch-thick board, which is then set in position on the wheelbarrow frame and used as a drill rest. Begin with a small hole to ensure that the pilot runs at the correct angle. When you have the pilot hole in position, graduate to a 1¼-inch-diameter hole saw. All the holes should be 1½ inches deep. After drilling the holes, position the support posts. If necessary, adjust the lengths.

Now comes the hard part. Locate the holes on the underside of the top rail as shown in the bottom view of the dashboard top rail. If you compare this drawing with the top view of the dashboard, as well as the actual standing support posts, this should be manageable. Getting the precise angle on the holes in the top rail is probably this project's most difficult aspect. The angle for the four outermost holes (those that fit into the rails that seat into the frame of the barrow) should be 25 degrees. The outermost two of these holes are pitched toward the rear of the barrow; the two inside are pitched toward the front wheel. The three center holes are set on only a 15-degree angle and are, again, pitched toward the rear of the barrow. Although it seemed that attaching the support posts to the top rail first and then mounting them onto the frame might be easier, this turned out not to be the case. If you wrongly place the holes in the top rail, simply replace the rail; if, however, you drill incorrectly into the frame of the wheelbarrow itself, your problems are many.

For the final assembly of the dashboard, fit the top rail onto the five rear support posts; pull the entire assembly backward far enough to insert the forward support posts into the top rail; then push the assembly again into position. If looseness is unavoidable, it is better that the posts fit loosely into the top rail. After the dashboard assembly is finally in position, nail the support posts into place through the side frame and the top rail.

## Finish

As a purely utilitarian piece of equipment, it is unlikely that any medieval wheelbarrow saw even an occasional coat of oil to keep the wood moist. To be truly period, let the unfinished wood weather naturally.

## SIDE VIEW

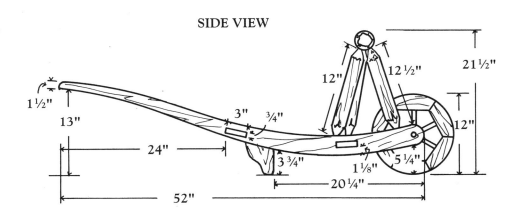

## TOP VIEW WITH DASHBOARD REMOVED

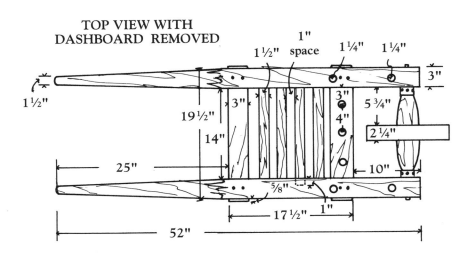

## SIDE, CUTAWAY VIEW

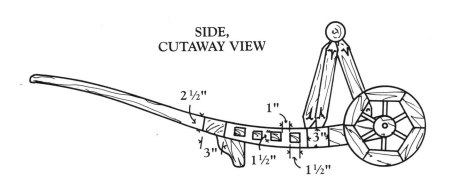

## FRONT VIEW

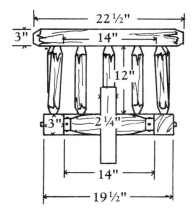

22 ½"
3"
14"
12"
3"
2 ¼"
14"
19 ½"

## WHEEL FRONT, CUTAWAY VIEW

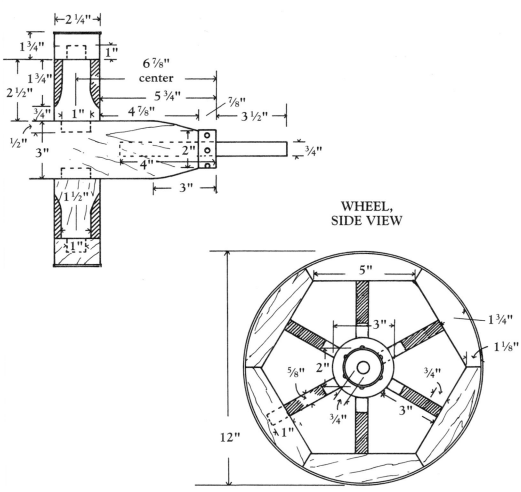

2 ¼"
1 ¾"
1"
1 ¾"
6 ⅞" center
2 ½"
5 ¾"
⅞"
¾"
1"
4 ⅞"
3 ½"
½"
3"
2"
¾"
4"
3"
1 ½"
1"

## WHEEL, SIDE VIEW

5"
1 ¾"
1 ⅛"
3"
⅝"
2"
¾"
¾"
3"
12"
1"

## DASHBOARD, TOP VIEW

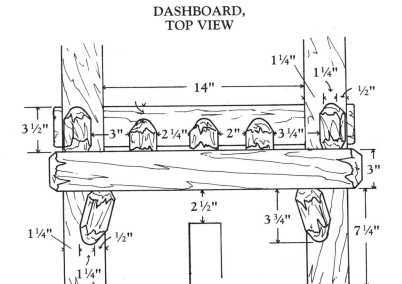

14"

1¼"

1¼"

½"

3½"

3"

2¼"

2"

3¼"

3"

2½"

3¾"

7¼"

1¼"

½"

1¼"

Rear edge

18½"

1¼"

## DASHBOARD TOP RAIL, BOTTOM VIEW

2"

3"

13¾"

22½"

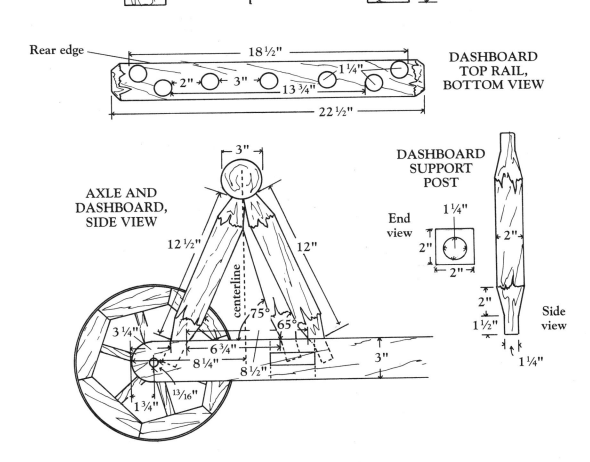

## AXLE AND DASHBOARD, SIDE VIEW

3"

12½"

12"

centerline

75°

65°

3¼"

6¾"

8¼"

8½"

3"

13/16"

1¾"

## DASHBOARD SUPPORT POST

End view

1¼"

2"

2"

2"

2"

2"

1½"

1¼"

Side view

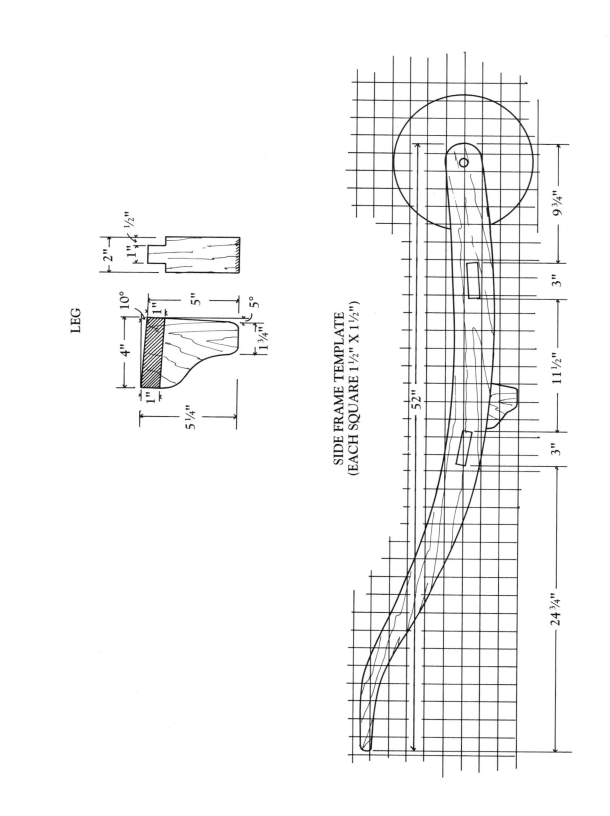

LEG

SIDE FRAME TEMPLATE
(EACH SQUARE 1½" X 1½")

# Project 10

# PANELED COFFER

This marvelous little oak chest probably dates from the middle of the sixteenth century. It is not as magnificent as the grand examples of Tudor furniture, but the finely worked linenfold panels on the front, as well as the overall care that went into its construction, mark it as the property of someone of importance and means. Neither large enough to have been a clothing chest, nor small enough to have held jewelry, this type of chest would typically have been used to carry the personal possessions of a nobleman, lady, or rich merchant on his or her frequent journeys. Medieval travel was an arduous, and often extended, undertaking, and wealthy travelers contrived to take as many attractive creature comforts with them as possible. That the lid doubles as a surprisingly comfortable seat is an indication that this coffer was intended as a multipurpose piece of travel furniture.

The small trough, or tray, built into the top left-hand corner of the box suggests a storage place for quill pens to keep them apart from the chest's other contents. If this is an accurate guess, it is quite possible that this was the traveling office of a merchant or the steward of a great estate, such as Haddon Hall, where it currently resides. The portable coffer is certainly attractive enough to have served equally well as a handsome piece of furniture in the home or place of business. Although no records of its original owner exist, Haddon Hall has housed it for several centuries.

## CONSTRUCTION NOTES

There is nothing complex about the chest's actual construction, but be aware that all of the framing members are connected with mortise and tenon joints and all the panels, as well as the bottom, are held in place with rabbet joints—a plethora of hidden joints. If you

carefully mark the location of each piece of the chest and follow the instructions step-by-step, you should have no trouble producing a rather extraordinary little piece of furniture that will fit comfortably in any modern or period home.

## Materials

The entire coffer is made of fine English oak. For those in the United States, we suggest using good white oak; it may cost more than red oak, but this charming chest deserves the best materials. The small size of this piece requires neither oversized timbers nor special millwork. The framing members can all be made from standard-dimension oak, and the panels planed down from standard 1-inch stock. The raised panels will require full 1-inch stock, which is available from any good lumber-mill.

All of the dowels used in this chest are ⅜ inch in diameter. We recommend using standard birch or maple doweling—both available at any lumberyard.

## Top Construction

To accustom yourself to the frame and panel type construction used throughout the chest, it is probably easiest to begin by making the top of the chest. Cut the two long rails and three stiles to length. Allow an extra 2 inches in length on each stile for the tenons. Cut the tenons to the same size as shown in the front detail drawing. Each tenon should be 1 inch long, 2 inches wide, and ½ inch thick.

To accurately cut the mortises, mark the location of each tenon in its proper location on the corresponding rail. If you have cut the tenons by hand, measure each of them individually, as there might be slight variations in their location. If, however, you have cut

# MATERIALS

## WOOD
All wood is oak.

| PART | NUMBER OF PIECES | THICKNESS | | WIDTH | | LENGTH |
|---|---|---|---|---|---|---|
| lid rails | 2 | 1½" | × | 3¼" | × | 28¾" |
| lid stiles | 2 | 1½" | × | 3¼" | × | 10¼" |
| lid stile | 1 | 1½" | × | 2¾" | × | 10¼" |
| lid panels | 2 | ½" | × | 9¾" | × | 11¼" |
| corner stiles, legs | 4 | 1½" | × | 3¾" | × | 16¾" |
| front and back center stiles | 2 | 1½" | × | 3¾" | × | 10½" |
| front and back top rails | 2 | 1½" | × | 4" | × | 21¾" |
| front and back bottom rails | 2 | 1½" | × | 2½" | × | 21¾" |

them on a table saw, they should be identical. Drill a small hole at each corner of the mortise to a depth of 1 inch. With chisels, remove the bulk of the material from the mortise. Be careful not to cut the mortise too large, or the tenon will be too loose. After removing the bulk of the material, clean up the sides and corners of the mortise with a small, sharp chisel. During this last phase of work, fit the tenon frequently to prevent overcutting the mortise. Gently tap the tenon into the mortise with a wooden mallet or softly smack it with the palm of your hand.

Now cut the chamfering around the edges of the panels with a router, a drawknife, or a spokeshave. If you are using a router, you can wait until the top is complete; if you are using hand tools, you must do this before the top is assembled. Chamfering dimensions are given in the section A drawing, but note that, as shown in the top view drawing, they stop ¼ inch short of the corners of the panel frame. If you cut the chamfers with a router, clean up these corners with a chisel

or sharp knife to be sure that they are crisp and clean. Now you are ready to install the panels.

Cut the panels to size, allowing ¾ inch of additional stock on each of the four sides so that they can be mounted into the frame.

For a cross-sectional view of the top panels, see the section A drawing. It is obvious that the panels are simple, flat pieces of ½-inch-thick wood that have been rabbeted into the surrounding frame. Disassemble the frame, being sure to mark the edge of each rail and each stile that will need to be rabbeted to receive a panel. Set up your table saw to cut a ½-inch-wide groove in the center of the 1½-inch-thick framing members. The grooves may run the entire length of the stiles, but be sure that they do not run through the ends of the long rails. If they do, the saw cuts will be visible on the lid ends. After cutting the rabbet grooves and checking the panels for a snug fit into the rabbets, assemble the entire frame of the top, with the panels in place. If the joints were well cut, the top should need

| PART | NUMBER OF PIECES | THICKNESS | | WIDTH | | LENGTH |
|---|---|---|---|---|---|---|
| front panels | 2 | 1" | × | 9¼" | × | 8¾" |
| back panels | 2 | ¾" | × | 8¾" | × | 9¼" |
| side top rails | 2 | 1½" | × | 3½" | × | 13⅛" |
| side bottom rails | 2 | 1½" | × | 2½" | × | 13⅛" |
| side panels | 2 | ¾" | × | 10½" | × | 12⅛" |
| interior tray bottom | 1 | ½" | × | 3¾" | × | 11⅝" |
| interior tray side | 1 | ½" | × | 1½" | × | 11⅝" |
| bottom boards | 2 | 1" | × | 6³⁄₁₆" | × | 20¼" |
| dowels | 2 | ¼" diameter | | | × | 36" |

## Metal

| PART | NUMBER OF PIECES | THICKNESS | | WIDTH | | LENGTH |
|---|---|---|---|---|---|---|
| hinge stock | 4 | ⅛" | × | 1⅛" | × | 3" |
| hinge pins and attachment pins | 6 | ³⁄₁₆" diameter | | | × | 2" |

very little adjustment to be pulled into square. If you are satisfied with the fit, disassemble the piece. If you wish, put a light coat of glue on the inside of the frame's mortises.

Reassemble the lid, pull it into square with cabinet clamps, and drill and dowel the mortise and tenon joints as explained in the chapter on general woodworking. Remove the clamps after the glue has dried thoroughly.

If you were waiting to chamfer around the panels with a router, do so now. Clean up the corners of the chamfers before laying the top aside.

**Framing the Case**
Now that you have a general feel for how to construct the chest, building the coffer should be simply an extension of the work that has been done on the lid.

Be careful to mark the proper location of each piece, and be aware that the dimensions of the rails and the panels are slightly different on the chest's front than they are on the sides.

Lay out the rails and stiles for the front of the chest in the same way that you did for the lid. Note that the top and bottom rails sit inside the end stiles, which also serve as the chest's legs. Allow extra length for the tenons on both rails and on the center stile. Cut the mortises and tenons as described above; use your palm or a wooden mallet to tap them together gently but firmly.

When you have successfully assembled the front, repeat the process for the chest's back. You can, of course, simultaneously make the component parts for the front and back, but unless you are confident that your pieces are fully interchangeable, it is best to construct one frame at a time. When the frames are complete, cut the rabbets for the panels. Note that the size and location of the grooves for the panels differ from those in the lid. These panels require a ⅜-inch-wide rabbet located ⅜ inch from the chest's inside face; these rabbets are only ⅝ inch in depth. The rabbets are the same size and depth on both the front and back panels of the chest. Also cut the rabbets to receive the panels on the ends of the chest. Although they are the same width and depth as the rabbets for the front panels, note that the side panels are ½ inch taller than those on the front and the back; this additional length is at the top of the panel.

### Decorative Molding

After the panel rabbets have been cut, reassemble the front frame, making sure it is square and plumb. The bottom rail is ornamented with a simple chamfer of the same dimension used around the panels on the lid. This chamfer also stops ¼ inch short of the panel's corners. The sides and top of the panel frame are decorated with an incised bead. In the case of the center stile, there are both a chamfer and a bead. The front detail and panel section drawings show how the beading and chamfering are configured. Cut both the chamfers before you begin to work the beading.

Cut the beading with a molding plane, a molding cutter attachment for a saw, a router, or carving gouges. If you use a router, be careful not to select a bit that will round over the edge of the wood along the bead's outside edge. Note that the beading on the top rail and the outside stiles stops ¼ inch short of the panel frame's corner, but the double bead and chamfer both run the entire length of the center stile.

### Bottom

Now you may want to cut the rabbets to receive the bottom panels. If you wait until the front and back are assembled, you will have to cut them with a router. At this time you can still use a table saw.

On the bottom rails of the front and back panels, mark out the location of the ½-inch-wide rabbets as shown in the section B drawing. Note that they are located 1 inch above the bottom edge of the rails. Cut the rabbets along the entire length of the bottom rails. The rabbet's top will probably open into the bottom of the mortise into which the center stile will fit, but this will not affect the strength of the finished piece.

Also run the rabbet into the end stiles; this is best done with chisels or a router, to prevent their cutting through the stile's outer edge. Temporarily reassemble the frames of the front and the back, and mark the locations of the rabbets across the backs of both end stiles. The rabbeting on the stiles should be 3⅛ inches in length, bringing them ⅞ inch from the stile's outside edge. If you use a router for this part of the work, square off the edges of the rabbet with a small chisel.

### Panels

The panels in the chest's back are simple ¾-inch-thick flat panels. They are fitted into the frame of the back with an offset lip. Cut the lip as shown in the panel section drawing. Be sure to install each panel so that its rear lies flush with the frame's interior surface. Be aware that the grain in the back panels runs horizontally, rather than vertically, as it does on the front panels. After these panels have been cut, fit the back together and dowel the mortise and tenon joints in the same manner as described above for the lid assembly.

### Carving the Linenfold Panels

The linenfold panels are cut from a 1-inch-thick board. Begin by cutting the lip around the edges of the panel. You will have to cut away excess wood around the edges of both the front and the back of the panel. As was true of the back panels, the lip is ⅜ inch wide and ⅝ inch deep. After you cut away extra wood around the face, remove a ⅝-inch width, as you did on the back. This leaves a raised face that is ¼ inch high, 8½ inches long, and 8 inches wide. Be certain that the wood grain runs vertically along the 8½-inch length of the face. Now carve the panel, following the instructions for carving a linenfold panel as outlined in the woodcarving chapter. When it is finished, the panel should fit snugly into the frame, the linenfolds just touching the stiles on either side. Assemble the front of the chest in the same way that you assembled the back and the top. After the glue has dried, remove the clamps.

### Interior Tray

Before you lay aside the front and back panels, you need to allow for the small interior tray, shown in cross section at the top of the section B drawing. On the back of each panel, mark the location where the rails on the end of the chest will be situated. Now mark the location of the two boards that form the trough. The bottom of the trough should just touch the inside face of the side rail. With a router or small chisels, plow out rabbets to receive the ½-inch-wide boards of the trough. These rabbets should be only ½ inch deep. Neatly square up the corners of the rabbets with a small, sharp chisel.

## Sides

Cut the top and bottom rails for the coffer's sides, noting that the top rails are only 3½ inches in width, ½ inch narrower than the top rails on the chest's front and back. After cutting the rails to length, as well as the tenons, cut the rabbets that will receive the panels. These rabbets will run the entire length of the rails. Mark and cut the mortises in the interior face of the front and back panels to receive the side rails. The exact locations of the mortises are shown in the section C drawing. Next, cut the beading along the bottom edge of the top rail and the chamfered edge along the top edge of the bottom rail, as shown in the end view drawing. Note that although the beading on the top rail runs the full length of the rail, the chamfer stops ¼ inch short of the ends of the bottom rail.

The lips around the edges of the end panels are similar to those on the coffer's front and back, being cut so that the interior of the panel lies flush with the interior surfaces of the top and bottom rails. Note that the grain on the end panels runs horizontally, as it does on the back panels.

After the panels have been cut to fit snugly into the top and bottom rails, temporarily assemble the chest. Mark the location of the rabbeting that will hold the bottom of the chest onto the side rails, disassemble the chest, and cut the rabbets along the full length of the rail.

## Bottom

The original chest bottom is made of two separate boards. These boards are not doweled together; they simply butt against each other near the chest's center. Cut a lip around the outer edges of the bottom boards to fit into the rabbets as shown in the section B drawing.

## Final Assembly

Lay the back of the coffer faceup on a worktable, and insert both top and bottom side rails into position. Set the end panels, the bottom panels, and the two boards of the interior tray in their appointed rabbets, and tap

the front of the chest into place. If the box fits square and plumb, disassemble it and coat the interior of the mortises lightly with glue before clamping the chest together and doweling the mortise joints into the end rails. After the glue is dry, remove the clamps. It is time to apply the hardware to the coffer.

## Lock Plate and Hinges

Following the instructions in the metalworking chapter, make two hinges from ⅛-inch-thick strap metal according to the dimensions shown in the hinge and hinge detail drawings.

The hinges are located 15 inches apart on the chest's back. They are 5 inches from either end of the chest. After determining the proper positions for the hinges, file a ¼-inch-wide flat spot (called a shoulder) on the top outside edge of the back. File a corresponding shoulder on the bottom rear edge of the lid. Note that the lid is slightly longer than the chest; be certain that it is positioned properly on the chest before you mark the shoulder's location.

Cutting the narrow slots into which the hinges seat may be this project's most challenging aspect. Begin by drilling away as much of the wood as possible with a ³⁄₃₂-inch-diameter drill. Being sure that the drill is on a 45-degree angle, bore a series of holes next to each other along the shoulder's width. The holes should be slightly more than 1 inch deep. With a sharp chisel or carving knife, remove the remaining wood from between the holes.

Square up the corners of the slot with a small, fine chisel. Working in this small hole will be time-consuming and frustrating.

Be sure the hinges fit snugly into the holes in the lid and the case, and that the spines of the hinges rest low enough in the shoulder so that the lid lies flush on the chest's back edge. After the lid rests flush on the case, insert the hinges into their slots, and with a ³⁄₁₆-inch drill bit, pierce through the case and the lid as shown in the hinge detail drawing. Press the drill gently against the hinge to mark the position of the pin. Remove the hinges from the coffer, and drill ⁷⁄₃₂-inch holes through the hinge, preserving the angle of the holes.

With the hinges still out of the case, replace the drill into the holes in the lid and chest, and continue drilling until the holes are slightly more than 1 inch deep. Replace the hinges in the lid and chest, and tap ³⁄₁₆-inch steel pins into the holes to secure the hinges.

The front detail and lock plate cross section drawings show this simple plate's dimensions. The wedge-shaped keyhole and the surrounding metal ornament form an almost floral-looking design on the plate's face.

The raised metal ornament is cut from the same $\frac{1}{16}$-inch sheet metal as the lock plate itself. Cut the ornament from a strip of metal that is $\frac{1}{4}$ inch wide. It is probably easier to form this small piece before tapering the top edge, as shown in the lock plate cross section drawing. After heating and shaping the metal, use a grinding wheel to taper and shape the top edge. Then weld it into place on the lock plate's face and clear away any excess weld. Drill four small holes in the corners of the plate, and attach it to face of the chest with four small nails.

### Finish

After the coffer is completely assembled, sand it lightly. A deep oil finish, enhanced by the addition of a little wood stain, will give you a lovely period-looking chest—almost indistinguishable from the original except for the lack of wear.

MEDIEVAL DECORATING. Interiors in homes of the Middle Ages, at least for the wealthy, were anything but dark and harsh, despite what is presented in today's popular culture. To the contrary, they were bright and colorful, even gaudy by modern standards. Wall hangings created by Tony Barton. *Photo by Daniel Diehl.*

HADDON HALL, BAKEWELL,
ENGLAND. *Photo by Daniel
Diehl.*

TAX BOX, ENGLAND, c. 1300 to
c. 1600. Oak and metal; H. 16⅞",
W. 10¾", D. 11". Collection of
Haddon Hall. *Photo by Daniel Diehl.*

PANELED COFFER, ENGLAND, c. 1550. Oak and metal; H. 18¼",
W. 28¾", D. 14¾". Collection of Haddon Hall. *Photo by Daniel
Diehl.*

MERRILLS BOARD, ENGLAND, c. 1545. Oak; H. 17¼",
W. 16", D. 1". Collection of *Mary Rose. Courtesy of Mary Rose Trust.*

WINCHESTER CATHEDRAL,
WINCHESTER, ENGLAND.
*Photo by Daniel Diehl.*

CHURCH PEW, ENGLAND, THIRTEENTH CENTURY. Oak; H. 52", W. 12¾", D. 20¾". Collection of Winchester Cathedral. *Photo by Daniel Diehl.*

HEWN-TIMBER CHEST, ENGLAND, FIFTEENTH CENTURY. Pine and metal; H. 27¼", W. 52½", D. 24". Collection of Hereford Cathedral. *Photo by Daniel Diehl.*

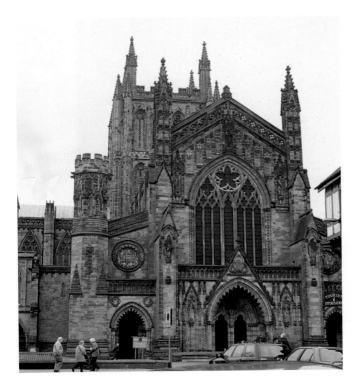

HEREFORD CATHEDRAL,
HEREFORD, ENGLAND.
*Photo by Daniel Diehl.*

LIBRARY SHELVES, ENGLAND, 1623. Oak; H. 78½", W. 90½", D. 18". Private Collection. *Photo by Daniel Diehl.*

WARWICK CASTLE, WARWICK, ENGLAND. *Photo by Daniel Diehl.*

REPLICA OF A WHEELBARROW, ENGLAND, FIFTEENTH CENTURY. Ash, birch, maple, and metal; H. 21½", W. 19½ ", L. 55¾". Collection of Warwick Castle. *Photo by Daniel Diehl.*

REPLICA OF A HALF-TESTER BED, ENGLAND, FOURTEENTH CENTURY. Pine and iron; H. 100", W. 54½", L. 78". Collection of Carlisle Castle. *Photo by Daniel Diehl*.

YORK MINSTER CATHEDRAL, YORK, ENGLAND. *Photo courtesy of the Dean and Chapter of York Minster.*

CATHEDRAL CABON, ENGLAND, c. 1530. Oak and metal; H. 78½", W. 64¼", D. 29⅝". Collection of York Minster Cathedral. *Photo courtesy of the Dean and Chapter of York Minster.*

BOLTON CASTLE, NORTH YORKSHIRE, ENGLAND. *Photo by Daniel Diehl.*

WRITING SLOPE, ENGLAND, 1670. Oak and metal; H. 12⅜", W. 29¼", D. 19". Collection of Bolton Castle. *Photo by Daniel Diehl.*

AMBRY CUPBOARD, ENGLAND, c. 1500. Oak; H. 44⅜", W. 42", D. 12⅜". Collection of Bolton Castle. *Photo by Daniel Diehl.*

SETTLE, c. 1550. Oak and metal; H. 54", W. 74½", D. 23".
Cloisters Collection, Metropolitan Museum of Art. *Photo by
Jay Grayson.*

DETAILS OF SETTLE.
*Photos by Jay Grayson.*

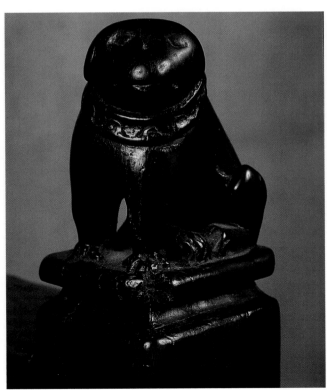
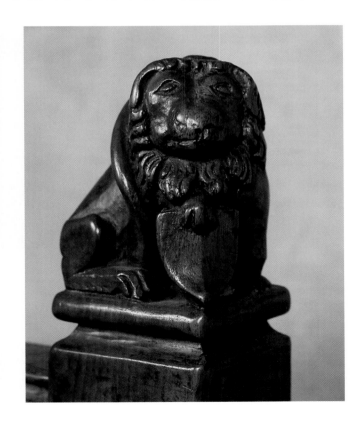

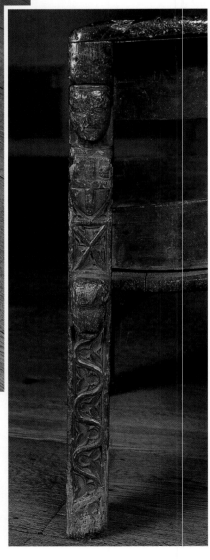

BARREL CHAIR, ITALY,
FIFTEENTH CENTURY.
Pine, walnut, and lime;
H. 27", W. 25", D. 19½".
Cloisters Collection,
Metropolitan Museum of Art.
*Photo by Jay Grayson.*

DETAILS OF BARREL
CHAIR. *Photos by Jay
Grayson.*

WORKTABLE, FRANCE, FIFTEENTH CENTURY. Oak and walnut; H. 27¼", W. 54½", D. 26½". Cloisters Collection, Metropolitan Museum of Art. *Photo by Daniel Diehl*

FRONT VIEW

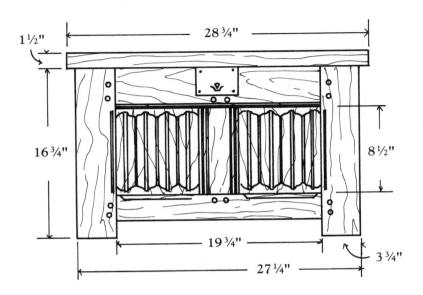

1½"

28¾"

16¾"

8½"

19¾"

27¼"

3¾"

Hinge
detail

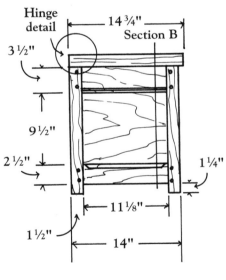

14¾"

Section B

3½"

9½"

2½"

1¼"

11⅛"

1½"

14"

END VIEW

TOP VIEW

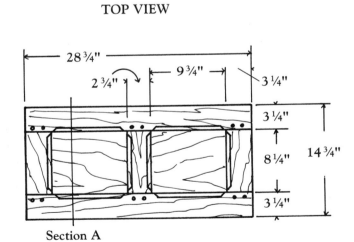

28¾"

2¾"

9¾"

3¼"

3¼"

8¼"

14¾"

3¼"

Section A

117

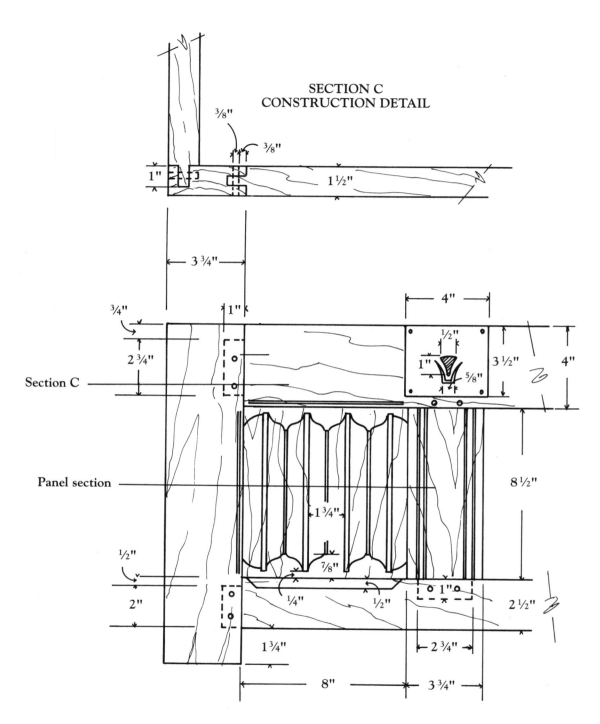

**SECTION C
CONSTRUCTION DETAIL**

**FRONT DETAIL**

**SECTION A**

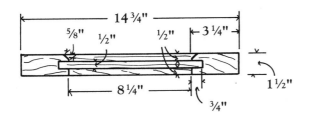

**LOCK PLATE, CROSS SECTION**

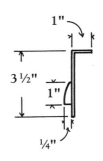

**HINGE DETAIL**

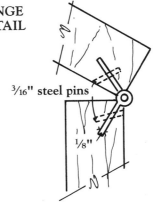

³⁄₁₆" steel pins

**SECTION B**

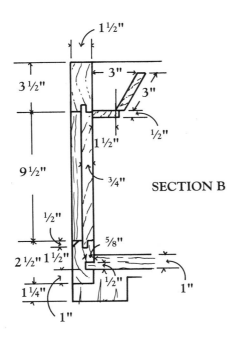

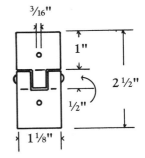

**HINGE**

**PANEL SECTION**

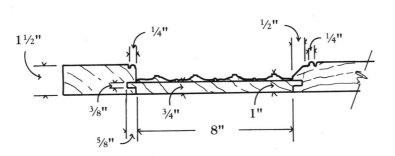

# Project 11

# WORKTABLE

This sturdy-looking table of oak and walnut, probably made in France, skillfully blends utilitarian efficiency and attractive detail work. Tongue-and-groove joints, turned legs, and several styles of ornamented panels remove any hint of the ordinary from this table.

Still, it was intended to be a functional worktable. It originally had a large drawer, now lost, in one end and another small drawer, which is also missing, in one of the long sides. Although the table probably dates from the fifteenth century, little more is known about it; what we can tell from looking at the piece raises more questions than it answers.

It is unlikely that it began life as a table, or even as a single article of furniture. The top and decorative panels appear to have been taken from doors; the linenfold carvings in the main panel should run vertically, not horizontally. The bottom rails on the long sides may have once been shallow drawer fronts. A carpenter in the distant past may have recycled existing materials from a pile of discarded furniture to cobble together a practical piece of furniture for the kitchen or pantry of some great estate. What is certain is that all the structural elements of the table date from the fifteenth century. It is also possible that they were reassembled in the nineteenth century from a pile of medieval remnants to cater to American nouveaux riches who were trying to buy up European culture by the shipload.

This piece now resides in the Campin room of the Cloisters Museum, where it has been kept since it was purchased at a private sale in 1949 for the astounding price of one hundred twenty-five dollars.

## CONSTRUCTION NOTES

Since this piece is a bit of a mongrel, we have taken a few liberties in planning its reproduction. Some of the internal structure in the existing table, which serves no functional purpose, has been eliminated from the plans. The resultant table will not differ appreciably in appearance from the original.

The rear view of the table, not shown in the photograph, is divided into a horizontal panel and a compartment once occupied by a drawer. The horizontal panel on this side of the table is decorated with linenfold carving—unfortunately the carving runs horizontally, and accurate linenfold panels always run vertically. The panel on the opposite side of the table (shown in the photograph) is peculiarly devoid of ornamentation. If you wish, adapt the table to a more cohesive design. All the panels can be left uncarved, or all of them can be carved with linenfold decoration. If they are carved, the carving should run vertically.

### Legs

The partly turned legs are made from 2¾-by-2¾-inch oak stock. The turning work was probably executed on a pole lathe that was not technologically sophisticated enough to provide a consistent cut along the length of a turning. As a result, these legs vary slightly in diameter, all of them being slightly larger toward the bottom.

After the legs have been turned, they can be grooved and mortised to receive the side panels and bottom rails. The panels are held in position by rabbets cut into the bottom and top rails. The panels and the bottom rails are then mortised into the legs. Take care to mark the position of each leg prior to cutting the panel and the rail mortises, and note that the bottom rail on the drawer end of the table is different from those on the other three sides. No mortise is required for the narrow top rails because they simply rest on top of the legs (see the detail F drawing).

## Bottom Rails

Cut to length the three large bottom rails, which can be milled from 2-by-4-inch oak, and work the tenons into the ends. Also cut and tenon the bottom rail on the drawer end of the table, shown in detail E.

Work the rounded corner onto the bottom edge of the three rails, which will hold paneling, with a molding plane or a router fitted with a ½-inch quarter-round bit. Do not yet work the chamfer into the edge of the rails that will face the inset panel. The decorative double bead can now be cut into the drawer end rail with a router or carving knives, as described in the chapter on the thirteenth-century Church Pew.

Work the tenons on the rails so that they fit into the mortises in the legs with a firm push or a light tap from a mallet. After the mortise and tenon joints fit together snugly, temporarily reassemble the table, and mark out the location of the slot (or rabbet) into which the panels will be mounted. Also mark the locations of the mortises that hold the vertical stiles separating the decorative panels on the table's short end, and the drawer opening on one of the table's long sides. Disassemble the legs and the rails, and cut the rabbets and the mortises. The rabbets may need to be widened slightly with a sharp chisel to accommodate the slightly wedge-shaped face of the panels.

## Top Rails

Temporarily assemble the bottom rails and legs; then stand the table in an upright position on a level surface. After making sure that the table is level and that all of the joints are fitted squarely, cut the narrow walnut top rails to length, and cut lap joints into the ends as shown in the detail F drawing. Set the top rails into place to assure a proper fit. Now cut rabbets into the underside of the top rails to accommodate the panels, and cut corresponding mortises in the bottom rails.

## Interior Frame

While the legs and the bottom rails of the table are temporarily assembled, measure and cut both the rail support and the drawer runner as indicated in the drawing of the top view with tabletop removed. The divider rail is mortised into the front and rear bottom rails, and the drawer runner is mortised into the drawer-end bottom rail and the divider rail. The exact location and direction of the mortise and tenon joints vary here from piece to piece; proceed carefully with these steps. Note that the rail support, obviously a later addition, is simply nailed to the bottom of the front

and rear bottom rails. It is clearly visible beneath the edge of the table in the front and rear view drawings.

After the mortises and tenons are worked to a snug fit, cut a ⅜-inch-wide panel groove into the divider rail's top face.

## Stiles

Cut the two stiles to length, then work the tenons into only their bottom ends. Now cut rabbets into these stiles to receive the panels as shown in the top view with tabletop removed. Note that there is a rabbet on only one side of the stile separating the linenfold panel and the drawer opening. This same rail receives a ⅜-inch rabbet in its rear surface to accommodate the interior divider panel. Carefully align this panel slot with the corresponding slot on the interior bottom rail.

Both stiles have tenons extending 1¼ inches into the bottom rails as well as tenons that run completely through the narrow, ⅞-inch thick top rail.

## Chamfering the Rails

Temporarily assemble one side of the table, consisting of a top and a bottom rail and two legs. Holding the structure in square with cabinet clamps, chamfer around the bottom and ends of the frame with a router or a sharp chisel. The dimensions and angle of the chamfer are shown in detail A. The chamfer curves around the corner rather than meeting at a 90-degree angle. After the chamfer is complete, disassemble the unit. Repeat the procedure for the two remaining sides of the table that receive decorative panels.

## Panels

Cut the four raised panels to the sizes indicated. If linenfold carving is to be worked into the panels, do it at this time. Follow the instructions for carving linenfold panels in the woodcarving chapter.

Also cut the flat panel separating the interior compartments. Finding a single panel of ⅜-inch-thick wood in this size will be difficult. Eliminate this panel altogether if a suitable alternative cannot be found. Be aware that this panel is held into position along only two edges: the divider rail and one stile. The other two edges float free, simply resting against the underside of the top and the rear surface of the panel.

## Frame Assembly

After the panels are finished, reassemble the table, including the drawer rail and the rail support; then fit all four panels into place. Brace and clamp the struc-

# MATERIALS

## WOOD
All wood is oak, except the top, which is walnut.

| PART | NUMBER OF PIECES | THICKNESS | | WIDTH | | LENGTH |
|---|---|---|---|---|---|---|
| legs | 4 | 2¾" | × | 2¾" | × | 26¼" |
| long bottom rails | 3 | 2" | × | 3⅝" | × | 44" |
| large end bottom rail | 1 | 2" | × | 3⅝" | × | 21½" |
| narrow end bottom rail | 1 | 1½" | × | 2¼" | × | 21½" |
| long top rails | 2 | ⅞" | × | 2¾" | × | 46½" |
| short top rails | 2 | ⅞" | × | 2¾" | × | 22" |
| rail support | 1 | 1" | × | 3" | × | 22" |
| drawer runner | 1 | 1" | × | 3" | × | 28½" |
| divider rail | 1 | 1" | × | 2" | × | 21½" |
| divider panel | 1 | ⅜" | × | 11" | × | 20¼" |
| raised panel | 1 | 1" | × | 7¾" | × | 41¾" |

ture together, making certain it is level, square, and plumb. With the table braced together, begin final assembly. The top rails are nailed directly into the top of the legs with one nail in each end of each lap joint.

Peg together the bottom rails, legs, stiles, and interior frame members. After drilling the pilot holes, dowel according to the instructions in the chapter on general woodworking techniques. Dowel each joint as it is drilled before drilling the next hole. This procedure prevents the possibility of the holes shifting before the dowels have been driven into place. After the doweling is completed, cut the dowels flush with the surface of the surrounding wood.

**Top**
Five boards form the top, three running the table's length, and the other two serving as end caps. The three center boards are tongue-and-groove jointed, but both tongues are on the middle board. The end caps, tongue-and-groove jointed to the main top boards, are irregular, with one end cap having the tongue and the other the groove (see the front and rear view drawings).

Although there is now no glue in this table, it is not unreasonable to assume that the top pieces were originally glued together. The three main boards would have been held in place by the nails holding the top to the table's frame. In the absence of other forms of fastening, however, the end caps could never have remained in place without glue. We recommend, therefore, that when the tongue-and-groove joints fit well enough to be lightly tapped together with the palm or with a mallet, they be glued and clamped together until dry.

| PART | NUMBER OF PIECES | THICKNESS | | WIDTH | | LENGTH |
|------|------------------|-----------|---|-------|---|--------|
| large linenfold panel | 1 | 1" | × | 7¾" | × | 26⅝" |
| large linenfold panel stile | 1 | 2" | × | 3¼" | × | 9⅛" |
| small linenfold panels | 2 | ¾" | × | 7½" | × | 7¾" |
| linenfold panel stile | 1 | 2" | × | 3½" | × | 9⅛" |
| top board | 1 | 1" | × | 9¼" | × | 47½" |
| top board | 1 | 1" | × | 9½" | × | 47½" |
| top board | 1 | 1" | × | 8¾" | × | 47½" |
| top end caps | 2 | 1" | × | 4" | × | 26½" |
| dowels | 2 | ⅜" diameter | | | × | 36" |

## METAL

| PART | NUMBER OF PIECES | LENGTH |
|------|------------------|--------|
| forged nails | 12 | 1¾" |
| square-headed forged nails to secure top | 4 | 4" |

## Top Installation

After the top is dry, set it into position and drill it for fastening to the top. The four main nails extend through the top and the top rail, fastening directly into the top of the legs. Nothing else seems to hold the top in place.

Fashioning the four large square-cut nails that hold the top in place could make an interesting experiment in nail construction. Be certain that their heads are large enough to hold the top in place.

## Options

If you decide to reproduce the missing drawers, make the drawer in the end of the table match the opposite end—it should look as though its face were divided into two panels separated by a stile. The drawer on the long side should probably be a smaller version of the linenfold panel adjacent to it.

Install drawer glides inside the bottom rails of the table where appropriate. The glides will wear best if they are made from maple rather than oak. Since there is already a variety of woods in this table, one additional species will scarcely seem anachronistic.

## Finish

Coat the entire table with a medium walnut stain followed by at least one coat of boiled linseed oil. To make your reproduction look as much like the original as possible, sparingly stain the tabletop—perhaps thin the stain with spirits of turpentine. Centuries of constant, heavy use have kept the top lighter and shinier than the rest of the table.

## FRONT VIEW

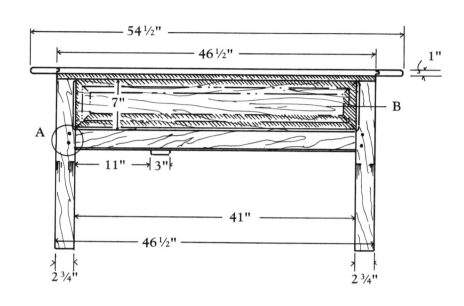

## REAR VIEW

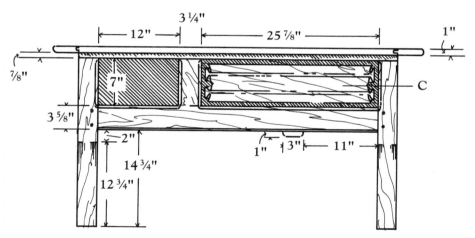

## RIGHT END

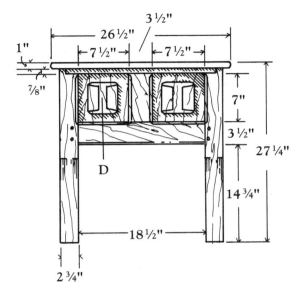

## TOP, CROSS SECTION

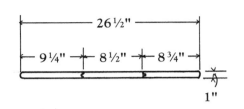

## LEFT END
## (DRAWER END)

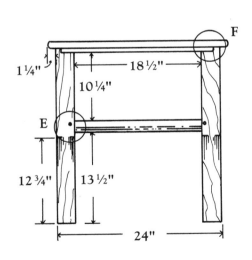

## TOP VIEW WITH
## TABLETOP REMOVED

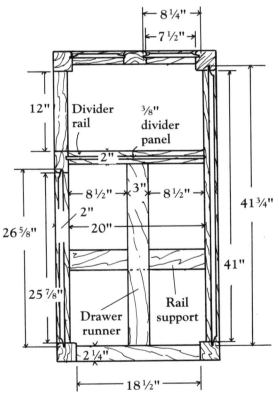

# TABLETOP

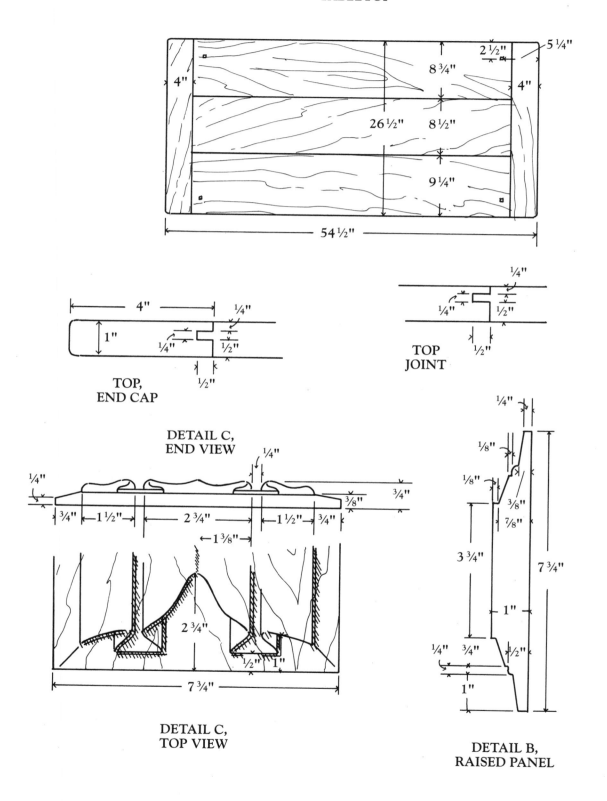

TOP,
END CAP

TOP
JOINT

DETAIL C,
END VIEW

DETAIL C,
TOP VIEW

DETAIL B,
RAISED PANEL

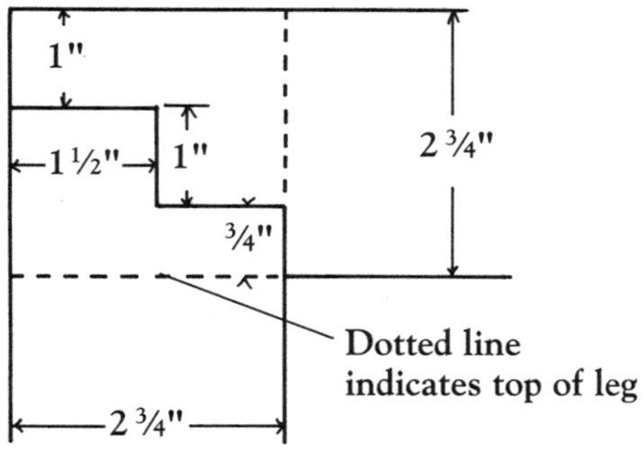
1"
1 1/2"
1"
2 3/4"
3/4"
Dotted line indicates top of leg
2 3/4"

DETAIL F,
TOP VIEW WITH
TABLETOP REMOVED

DETAIL A,
BOTTTOM RAIL,
TOP VIEW

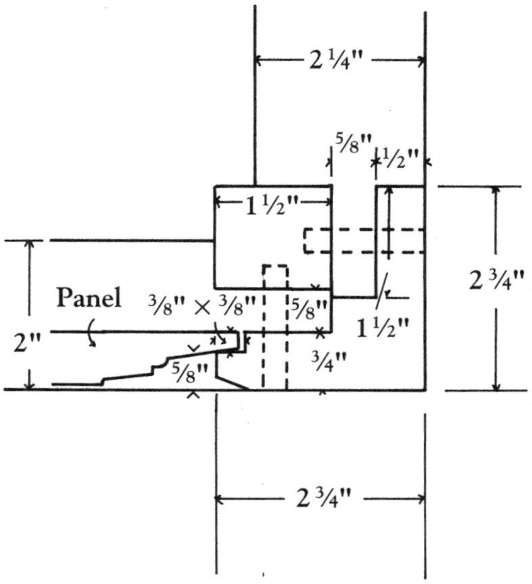
2 1/4"
5/8"
1/2"
1 1/2"
2 3/4"
Panel
3/8" × 3/8"
5/8"
1 1/2"
2"
3/4"
5/8"
2 3/4"

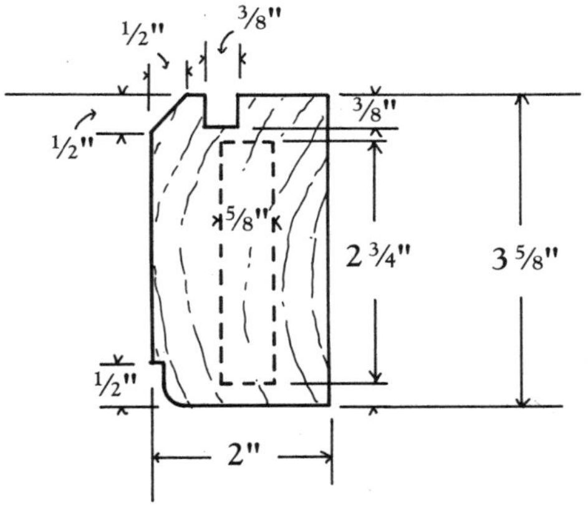
1/2"
3/8"
1/2"
3/8"
5/8"
2 3/4"
3 5/8"
1/2"
2"

DETAIL A,
CROSS SECTION

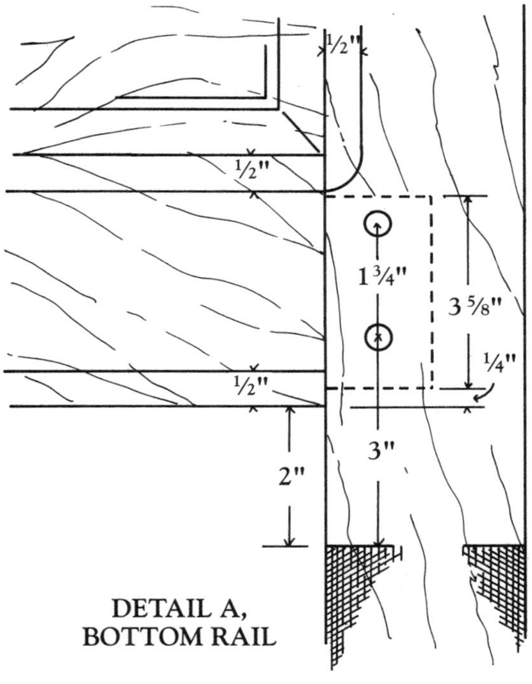
1/2"
1/2"
1 3/4"
3 5/8"
1/4"
1/2"
3"
2"

DETAIL A,
BOTTOM RAIL

## DETAIL E

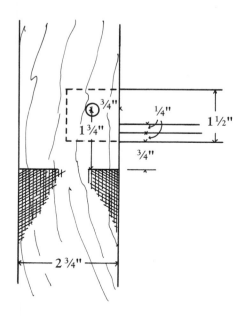

3/4"

1 3/4"

1/4"

1 1/2"

3/4"

2 3/4"

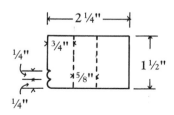

2 1/4"

3/4"

1/4"

5/8"

1 1/2"

1/4"

## DETAIL F,
## CROSS SECTION

## DETAIL D,
## END VIEW

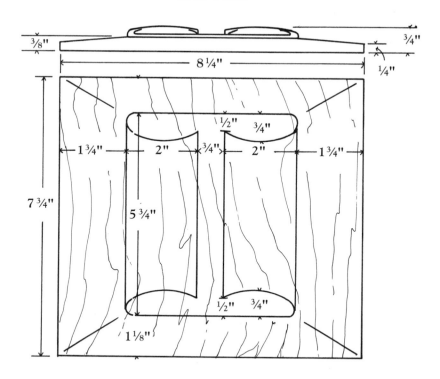

3/8"

3/4"

8 1/4"

1/4"

1/2"

3/4"

1 3/4"

2"

3/4"

2"

1 3/4"

7 3/4"

5 3/4"

1/2"

3/4"

1 1/8"

## DETAIL D,
## TOP VIEW

# Project 12

♦

# Cathedral Cabon

♦

Cabon was the medieval word for closet. If a cabon was large enough to serve as a private meeting room, it was referred to as a cabonette, which has come down to us as cabinet, meaning a ruling council (as in a cabinet ministry). More commonly, cabons were simply cupboards set into a wall. Like many early cabinets, this cabon was built directly into the stone wall of a building to keep its contents as secure as possible. During the Middle Ages cabons and ambries were designed to hold the treasures of both churches and noble households. At the time, treasures included not only gold and silver plate, but also richly worked clothes and ecclesiastical vestments. The poor had little need of closets and cabinets.

The magnificent oak cabon pictured here is located in the Zouche Chapel in York Minster Cathedral in York, England. Begun in 1350, the chapel was intended to be used as the tomb of Archbishop William de la Zouche, but when he died two years later, it was only partly built. From its completion in 1394 until the dissolution of the monasteries in the 1530s, the chapel was used as a chantry house where monks prayed for the souls of the dead. After the Reformation, the chapel was turned into a vestry, or sacristy, a church's storage area for ecclesiastical vestments and sacramental silver and gold plate. Closets were built here during this period.

This cabon is one of five similar cabinets that line two walls of the chapel. The cabinets, all of the same height and design, are made of English oak, but two are slightly narrower than the one shown here, and the other two are considerably wider, extending just over 11 feet.

These larger cabinets have only two ranks of doors, rather than the three seen here. By examining the door at the far right-hand side of the middle row, we can very closely date the construction of these cabinets. Here we find that a crown above a pair of crossed keys has been burned into the door's wooden panel. This symbol, the "new" arms of York Minster, was designed in the 1530s by Cardinal Wolsey, Henry VIII's chief minister of state and the papal legate in England, shortly before his own downfall and the final dissolution of the monasteries.

Although it has been repaired and slightly altered over the centuries, this closet looks much as it did when it was built in the early sixteenth century.

## CONSTRUCTION NOTES

This handsome cabinet was built as two separate units, the face and the interior case. We will approach the construction in the same way. First, we will construct the interior case, which is no more than a simple crate with two shelves and one divider; then we will build the elaborate facade. The construction of the interior case, the doors, and even the facade's frame are extremely simple, but carving the elaborate columns will challenge even the most experienced woodworker.

Adapting the cabinet's front to an existing cabinet or closet will handsomely alter it without the need to retrofit the interior case into an existing wall.

### Materials

The cabon is constructed entirely of oak, but the interior case could easily be made of a lesser wood such as pine or fir. The original case is constructed of 1-inch-thick material; standard ¾-inch wood would serve just as well.

# MATERIALS

## WOOD
Most wood is oak, but the interior case can be pine or fir.

| PART | NUMBER OF PIECES | THICKNESS | | WIDTH | | LENGTH |
|---|---|---|---|---|---|---|
| case, back boards | 3 | 1" | × | 11½" | × | 71½" |
| case, back board | 1 | 1" | × | 11¾" | × | 71½" |
| case, back board | 1 | 1" | × | 12" | × | 71½" |
| case, back battens | 2 | 1" | × | 5" | × | 58¼" |
| case, back battens | 2 | 1" | × | 5" | × | 64½" |
| case, end boards | 4 | 1" | × | 12½" | × | 71½" |
| case, end splats | 4 | 1" | × | 5" | × | 21" |
| case, end battens | 2 | 1" | × | 5" | × | 74½" |
| case, end battens | 2 | 1" | × | 5" | × | 64½" |
| case, top boards | 2 | 1" | × | 12½" | × | 58¼" |
| case, top battens | 2 | 1" | × | 5" | × | 26" |
| case, top battens | 2 | 1" | × | 5" | × | 48¼" |
| case, bottom boards | 2 | 1" | × | 12½" | × | 58¼" |
| case, skids | 5 | 2¼" | × | 4" | × | 26" |
| shelves | 4 | 1" | × | 12¼" | × | 56¾" |
| divider panel boards | 2 | 1" | × | 12" | × | 24⅝" |
| top left door | 1 | ¾" | × | 10" | × | 22¼" |
| top left door | 1 | ¾" | × | 7¾" | × | 22¼" |
| top left door splats | 2 | ⅝" | × | 2" | × | 16¼" |
| top center door | 1 | ¾" | × | 10" | × | 22¼" |
| top center door | 1 | ¾" | × | 8½" | × | 22¼" |
| top center door splats | 2 | ⅝" | × | 2" | × | 17" |

| PART | NUMBER OF PIECES | THICKNESS | | WIDTH | | LENGTH |
|---|---|---|---|---|---|---|
| top right door | 1 | ¾" | × | 12" | × | 22¼" |
| top right door | 1 | ¾" | × | 10" | × | 22¼" |
| top right door splats | 2 | ⅝" | × | 2" | × | 18½" |
| center left door | 1 | ¾" | × | 12" | × | 22⅛" |
| center left door | 1 | ¾" | × | 6¼" | × | 22⅛" |
| center left door splats | 2 | ⅝" | × | 2" | × | 16¾" |
| center center door | 1 | ¾" | × | 12" | × | 22⅛" |
| center center door | 1 | ¾" | × | 6" | × | 22⅛" |
| center center door splats | 2 | ⅝" | × | 2" | × | 16½" |
| center right door | 1 | ¾" | × | 12" | × | 22⅛" |
| center right door | 1 | ¾" | × | 8" | × | 22⅛" |
| center right door splats | 2 | ⅝" | × | 2" | × | 18½" |
| bottom left door | 1 | ¾" | × | 16" | × | 22⅛" |
| bottom left door | 1 | ¾" | × | 10" | × | 22⅛" |
| bottom left door | 1 | ¾" | × | 3" | × | 22⅛" |
| bottom left door splats | 2 | ⅝" | × | 2" | × | 27½" |
| bottom right door | 1 | ¾" | × | 12" | × | 22⅛" |
| bottom right door | 1 | ¾" | × | 7¾" | × | 22⅛" |
| bottom right door | 1 | ¾" | × | 6" | × | 22⅛" |
| bottom right door splats | 2 | ⅝" | × | 2" | × | 24¼" |
| stiles | 2 | 2" | × | 4" | × | 77⅛" |
| top rail | 1 | 2" | × | 6⅝" | × | 59¼" |
| bottom rail | 1 | 2" | × | 3¼" | × | 59¼" |

| PART | NUMBER OF PIECES | THICKNESS | | WIDTH | | LENGTH |
|------|------------------|-----------|---|-------|---|--------|
| shelf dividers | 2 | 1½" | × | 2½" | × | 59¼" |
| divider stile | 1 | 1½" | × | 2" | × | 25⅛" |
| columns | 2 | 2⅞" | × | 3¾" | × | 76" |
| top column, no base block | 1 | 2⅞" | × | 3¾" | × | 64" |
| cornice molding | 1 | 1" | × | 3⅝" | × | 64¼" |
| cornice spacer | 1 | 1" | × | 2⅜" | × | 64¼" |
| carved cornice blocks | 12 | 1⅛" | × | 1⅝" | × | 1⅝" |
| dowels | 3 | ½" diameter | | | × | 36" |

## METAL

| PART | NUMBER OF PIECES | THICKNESS | | WIDTH | | LENGTH |
|------|------------------|-----------|---|-------|---|--------|
| hinge butts | 12 | ³⁄₃₂" | × | 2¼" | × | 3½" |
| short hinges, front end | 8 | ³⁄₃₂" | × | 2¼" | × | 16" |
| double hinges, butt end | 4 | ³⁄₃₂" | × | 2¼" | × | 22¹¹⁄₁₆" |
| double hinges, front end | 4 | ³⁄₃₂" | × | 1⅝" | × | 19³⁄₁₆" |
| lock plates | 4 | ³⁄₃₂" | × | 5" | × | 5" |
| door pull back plates | 4 | ³⁄₃₂" | × | 4" | × | 4" |
| door pull rings | 4 | ⅛" diameter | | | × | 6" |
| door pull handles | 4 | ⅜" round or square stock | | | × | 12" |
| forged clinch nails | 156 | | | | | 2" |
| forged nails for lock plates and pulls | 40 | | | | | ¾" |
| forged nails for nailing battens to case | 250 | | | | | 2" |
| forged nails for assembling case | 150 | | | | | 2½" |

## Interior Case

The interior of the case is 56¼ inches wide, 71½ inches high, and 24 inches deep. To begin construction, separate the boards listed on the materials list according to their location—back, sides, top, and bottom.

Arrange the five back boards next to each other (the exact order makes no difference), and mark the locations where the two shelves will be rabbeted into the back, as indicated in the interior of case, cabinet section, and detail A drawings. Cut the rabbets 1 inch wide and ½ inch deep. Repeat the rabbeting process on the side panels.

After the rabbets for the shelves have been cut, locate the rabbets for the divider panel that sits on the lowest shelf. Note: This panel is rabbeted only into the cabinet's floor and the bottom face of the lowest shelf. It is not rabbeted into the cabinet's back wall. Lay the back boards facedown on your work surface after all the rabbets have been cut. To ensure proper alignment of the panels, cut two ½-by-1-by-60-inch strips of wood, and insert them into the shelf rabbets. Properly align and square the back panel. Place one of the 58¼-inch-long batten boards across the bottom of the back, allowing 2 inches of the board to extend below the bottom edge of the back boards. Place the other long batten across the top of the boards, allowing 2 inches to extend above the top of the back panels. Nail these two boards in place with 1¾-inch nails.

Next, set the bottom boards on the 2¼-by-4-inch skids as shown in the interior of case drawing. Allow the two outermost skids to extend 1 inch beyond the edges of the bottom, as shown in the detail B drawing. Place another of the skids directly beneath the rabbet that will hold the divider panel. The final two skids should be centered between the first three. Nail the bottom boards to the skids with 2-inch nails.

Now assemble the left and right sides. Lay the side boards facedown on the work surface, using the wooden strips to ensure that the rabbets are aligned. Position the battens on top of the side panels, making sure that the panels are properly aligned and square. The lower batten should extend 1 inch below the bottom of the side boards, and the top batten should extend 2 inches above the top of the sides. Nail the sides together using 1¾-inch nails. After the top and bottom battens have been nailed in place, nail the battens along the front and the rear edges of the sides. Note: The rear batten extends 2 inches beyond the side panel's back edge, but the front batten is flush

with the panel's front edge. Be certain to make one left and one right side panel.

Lay out and assemble the top panel. Keep all four of the battens flush with the panel's edges. Move the component parts to the room in which the cabinet will be installed; it will prove nearly impossible to move the case once it is assembled.

Final assembly requires the aid of several helpers. Stand one side on the bottom of the cabinet as shown in detail B, and nail it to the bottom. While someone holds this side upright, nail the second side in place. Set the top panel onto the sides and nail it securely. While gently supporting the structure of the cabinet, slide the shelves and the divider panels into place. Be sure that the shelves and the divider are flush with the front of the case before nailing them. The back panel should set easily in place, and the shelves should slide into the appropriate rabbets. After checking to ensure that the case is square, nail the back into place.

## Framing the Cabinet

Cut the rails and stiles to the sizes listed in the materials list. Lay the seven pieces (left and right stiles, top and bottom stiles, two shelf divider rails, and the divider stile) on a work surface in their proper arrangement. The top and bottom rails and the two shelf divider rails all sit between the stiles; in other words, when you look at the edge of the cabinet face, it is only the edge of the left or right stile that you will see. Note that the stiles and the top rail are no more than flat boards that serve as a backing on which the columns and the cornice are mounted. Mark the face and the interior edges of each board so that you can relocate them in their proper position as necessary.

Mark out the rabbets around the face of the door openings, into which the doors will be recessed. Front views of these rabbets are shown in the construction detail of the left side of the cabinet front. Front and side views of these rabbets are shown in the cornice and cornice profile drawings. Be aware that the rabbets are interrupted at the points at which the divider rails join the left and right stiles. These locations are shown in the cabinet front drawing.

The rabbets in the top and bottom rails stop 4 inches short of the ends of the board, as shown in the construction detail of the left side of the cabinet front. This drawing also shows that only the top edges of the shelf rails are rabbeted. The divider stile that separates the bottom row of doors must have rabbets on both front edges to support the locking edges of both the left and right doors. All of these rabbets are 1 inch wide across the face and ¾ inch in depth. After all the rabbets have been marked and cut, set the pieces back in their proper order to verify the positions of the rabbets.

Now cut the mortise and tenon joints that hold the face of the cabinet together. These are open mortise and tenon joints, which are no more than interlocking rabbets. Study the construction detail of the left side of the cabinet front to see how the finished joint should appear. If you remove the left stile from this drawing, and look down onto the top edge of the bottom rail, as shown in the top view of the bottom rail, you will see how the pieces fit together. The drawing labeled left stile, interior edge with rails removed illustrates the opposite member of this particular joint. All four main corner joints are constructed in the same way. After these have been marked and cut, the four main framing members should fit together so that the cabinet's frame appears the way it will be when the cabinet is complete.

Lay the frame on a level work surface, making sure it is square. Identify the position of the shelf rails. Their location should be clear because of the interruptions in the rabbet around the cabinet's face. Looking at the drawing labeled left stile, interior edge with rails removed, you can see that the shelf rails fit into the frame with simple mortise and tenon joints. It is not shown on the drawings, but the tenons on the divider rails are 1½ inches in length and the mortises are of a corresponding depth. After locating and marking the positions of the shelf rails, cut the mortises and tenons to fit snugly. Repeat the process with the stile separating the bottom row of doors.

After all the joints have been cut and fit, lay out the face of the cabinet on a level work surface and completely assemble it, fitting the joints snugly and squaring the face. Then drill and dowel the face together according to the doweling instructions in the chapter on general woodworking. The locations of the ½-inch-diameter dowels are shown in the construction detail of the left side of the cabinet front. Move the cabinet face to the room in which it is to be installed before final assembly, because the size of the unit will make it almost impossible to move through doorways once it is assembled.

## Mounting the Case and Frame
The completed frame can now be mounted on the cabinet's front, but first the cabinet itself must be recessed into a properly prepared alcove.

First, select an appropriate location for the cabon. With its 78½-inch height, it can appropriately be set at floor level, but the cabinet in our picture actually sits on a stone ledge 22 inches above the chapel's floor. Raising your own cabon 8 to 10 inches above the floor may make it more convenient. If it is raised above floor level, however, a platform will have to be built to support the cabinet. In either case, to mount the cabinet in the wall, an opening will have to be cut into which the case can be fitted. When cutting an opening in an existing wall, make sure that the opening is as near the size of the cabinet as possible. The frame is only 3 inches wider than the exterior dimensions of the cabinet; care in cutting will avoid the need for excessive plasterwork.

After the opening has been cut, build a sturdy frame around the interior edge of the hole—a surface on which to anchor the cabinet. The frame should be plumb and square, 1 to 2 inches wider than the cabinet, and ½ to 1 inch taller. Also make sure the floor, or supporting platform, is level; shimming the cabinet to level will be almost impossible once it has been eased into place. Once you are satisfied that the appropriately dimensioned opening is well framed, plumb, square, and level, slide the cabinet into place. Make sure that the cabinet's front edge is flush with the surrounding wall, and nail the cabinet to the frame. You will undoubtedly have to fill gaps between the cabinet and the frame; use scraps of wood or shims.

The face can be mounted on the front of the cabinet after it has been secured to the wall. Nail through the front of the face into the front edge of the case. Drive a few nails directly into the frame surrounding the cabinet to ensure a snug fit against the surrounding wall. Position the nails so that they will be hidden by the decorative columns.

## Constructing the Doors
Each door is made from several ¾-inch-thick oak boards. The height and width of the doors are shown on the cabinet front drawing. Construct the face of each door by doweling two or more boards together according to the instructions in the chapters on woodworking and on the Merrills Board. The grain on all the doors should run vertically.

Splats that run horizontally across the back support the doors and prevent them from warping. These splats, shown in the rear and edge views of the door, are all ⅝ inch thick and 2 inches wide and stop 1½ inches short of the edge of the door that will be fitted with a latch plate. On those four doors that are hinged to other doors, the splats at the hinge joints between the doors touch. The splats are located so that the hinges are nailed through both the door and the splats. This provides additional support for door and hinge alike. Take into account the positions of the hinges, shown in the hardware location A and B drawings, when you mount the splats to the back of the door.

## Hardware

You now need to shift your focus from the woodwork to the construction of the hardware, as the doors must be mounted on the cabinet before the columns and the crown molding can be installed. You may continue to execute the woodwork, but do not install the columns or the crown molding until the doors are mounted on the cabinet.

Before constructing the decorative hinge straps, decide whether to cut the entire design out of a piece of flat stock or to shape the decorative fleur-de-lis ends on the hinges. The materials list specifies 2¼-inch-wide stock, which is sufficient to forge the decorative ends. Cutting them out of a single piece of flat stock requires 3-inch-wide stock.

In either case, lay out and cut the general shape of the hinges as shown on the drawings of the butt end and front end of the hinge. Adjust the length of the hinges to fit the specific doors, according to the hardware location A and B drawings. Cut around both the floret designs and the decorative ornamentation at the butt end of the straps. Leave 1½ inches on the outermost ends of the hinge straps to form the spines of the hinges that connect the doors to the cabinet frame. Those hinges that connect one door to another will require 1³⁄₁₆-inch-long hinge tangs. Note on the butt end of the hinge drawing that the spines of these hinges are of a smaller diameter than those on the door-to-frame hinge.

There is no illustration for the end of the hinge buried beneath the decorative columns. We can assume that this hidden hinge is a simple rectangle that is 2¼ inches wide and no more than 3 inches long. Allow an extra 1½ inches on the 3-inch-wide stock for the tangs that form the spine. To be sure that the hinge supports the weight of the doors, drill holes for four mounting nails.

Refer to the chapter on metalworking for information on how to form the spine of a hinge. In this instance, not only are there twelve 12 hinges connecting the doors to the frame of the cabinet, but there are also four hinges that connect the center doors to the right-hand doors.

Next, form the decorative fleur-de-lis ends on the hinges. First, cut the ears of the fleur-de-lis design loose from the strap's center. The ears can either be sawn free of the center of the design or heated and split loose with a chisel. If the end of the strap is sawn, rather than split, roughly form the tapering ends on the decorative ears, which can then be bent and shaped.

After cutting the ears of the fleur-de-lis design loose from the center of the strap, bend them laterally (outward). Be careful when bending metal laterally; it may break if not heated enough. As the metal ears are stretched and pulled outward, and then bent around the mandrel, they should become slightly narrower toward the point. Execute a few sample pieces prior to working on the finished straps. Do not be concerned if your pieces lack perfect symmetry; neither do the originals executed by medieval craftsmen.

To give the edges of the hinge straps a truly hand-forged look, heat the metal until it is glowing and slightly distress the edges with a hammer. Similarly, to incise the strike lines in the flower petals, create the crosshatched pattern at the rear of the fleur-de-lis, heat the metal, set a cold chisel in the appropriate position, and strike it with a hammer. Do not hit it hard enough to cut the metal in half, just hard enough to score the surface of the metal to a depth of ¹⁄₃₂ inch.

After the hinges have been shaped, drill holes for the mounting nails at the positions indicated on the drawings.

Cut the basic shapes of the back plates for the door pulls and the lock plate as shown in the drawings. Drill ³⁄₁₆-inch-diameter holes for nails at the proper locations. Drill the hole for the door pull ring, located at the center of the door pull back plate, to a diameter of ⅜ inch.

A skilled metalsmith has obviously chiseled the handle on the door pull. You can either commission a reproduction casting or bend a simple ring out of round or square stock. If you decide to bend your own ring, heat the stock (specified in the materials list) and wrap it around a 1¾-inch-diameter pipe. Cut the ends of the stock to form a complete circle. Finally, weld the ends together.

The ring that holds the door pull to the back plate is shaped out of ⅛-inch round stock bent around a ⅝-inch-diameter pipe. Heat and bend the round stock to form one complete loop (or circle). Straighten the ends of the loop into the shape shown in the side view of the door pull ring. Cut the ears to a length of ½ inch. The ring should pass fairly easily through the hole in the center of the door pull plate. Place the handle on the ring, insert it through the back plate, and splay the ends attached to the ring outward. Cut away a small amount of wood on the door, directly behind the ears of the door pull ring, to allow the door pull plate to lie flat against the door.

Nail the door pulls and the lock plates to the door with ¾-inch-long forged nails. The original lock mechanisms on the cabon have been replaced with modern locksets positioned so that the original keyholes can still be used.

## Hanging the Doors

Attach the hinges to the doors in the positions shown in the hardware location A and B drawings, paying special attention to the two sets of doors that are hinged together. Position the hinges so that the splats on the door's back are directly behind the hinge nails. All the hardware is held in place with 2-inch clinch nails, which are bent over on the back of the door to prevent the nails from working loose over time. (See the detail on the rear view of the door.) Make sure the doors fit squarely and swing freely so that they will not bind when installed on the cabinet frame. Next, attach the door pulls and lock plates.

After the hardware has been mounted on the doors, place the doors in their proper positions. Shim the bottoms with slips of thin cardboard to prevent the doors from dragging against the lower rails when they are opened and closed. Also be certain that the doors do not bind against each other.

Drill pilot holes, then nail the butt ends of the hinges to the face of the cabinet frame.

## Carving the Columns

There is no secret shortcut to carving these columns. Because the base shown in section A is the largest point on the column, the entire length of the column can be cut to these dimensions. The area between the base and section line D is certainly the most difficult to deal with. Although it is hard to see in the drawings or photograph, each facet of this complex pattern is actually slightly concave. Rough out the shape with chisels, and finish it with carving knives and spoon-shaped gouges.

If the challenge of carving columns to surround the entire cabinet is too daunting, consider carving the two bases by hand and having the columns run off at a mill yard. In either case, note in the cornice profile drawing that the base of the cornice is the same shape

as the side columns and is joined to the columns with a miter joint, which ensures an unbroken line of columns across the cabinet's top.

After you have the bases and sufficient carved column stock to surround the face of the cabinet, nail them to the cabinet frame with headless nails. Because headless hand-forged nails are almost impossible to find, it is acceptable to use modern finishing nails in this instance. Drill pilot holes to prevent splitting the oak. You will undoubtedly have to rout out depressions on the back side of the columns to allow them to fit over the butt ends of the hinges.

Mount the two side columns in place on the frame, and then cut the top horizontal section to length. After it has been mitered to fit between the side columns, rip it to the proper width as shown in the cornice profile drawing. Nail it to the face of the cabinet frame. Trim the tips of the side columns to length with a small saw or a chisel.

## Carving the Rosettes

The rosette designs shown in the drawings of the carved cornice blocks represent the only six designs on the cabinet. To fill the thirteen spaces in the cornice molding, each design will need to be executed twice. Since the rosettes on the extreme left and right ends of the cornice are only partial blocks, one block can be split to fill both of these spaces, eliminating the need for a thirteenth rosette.

All the rosettes are carved from oak blocks that are $1\frac{5}{8}$ inches wide, $1\frac{5}{8}$ inches long, and $1\frac{1}{8}$ inches thick. Gouge the carvings to a depth of no more than ¼ inch, as shown by the dotted line in the side view of the cornice block. It is undoubtedly easier to carve the designs into a large piece of wood and then trim the blocks to size later. This approach also eliminates the dangers inherent in carving onto a small block of wood. The designs are shown here at half their actual size. You can enlarge them on a copying machine and transfer them directly to the wood.

## Crown Molding

The crown molding shown in the cornice and cornice profile drawings is simple enough that it can be executed with molding planes or a molding cutter. The real challenge is mounting the carved rosettes on the face of the molding.

When the molding has been cut to length, lay out the locations of the thirteen rosettes, all of which are visible in the photograph and the cabinet front drawing. Again, note that the rosettes on the left and right ends of the crown molding are incomplete. The rosettes fit snugly into the face of the crown mold; cut the sockets carefully. Note that the sockets pierce entirely through the 1-inch-thick crown mold. This makes cutting the sockets slightly easier than if they were simply hollows in the face of the molding. Remove the bulk of the excess wood with a jigsaw, and clean up the edges of the socket with a sharp chisel.

Once the rosettes fit snugly into the sockets, cut the 1-by-2⅜-inch filler strip, shown in the cornice profile drawing, to length. Position the filler strip behind the cornice molding, and mark the position of each of the rosette blocks. Notch out the positions of the rosettes to a depth of ⅛ inch. These notches can be cut on a table saw, because they can extend across the entire width of the filler strip.

After ascertaining that all of the component parts fit, glue together the cornice assembly. Glue and clamp the filler strip to the back of the cornice molding, and then insert the rosettes into place, making certain that the designs repeat in the intended order.

## Arms of York

The armorial device on the center right door was originally burned into the wood. Short of constructing a branding iron specifically to this design, the easiest way to reproduce the emblem is with a woodburning set. The design is shown here near its actual size of 1 inch in height.

## Finish

A rich, dark oak finish will replicate the look of the original. We recommend using a combination of boiled linseed (or olive) oil, dark oak wood stain, and a little turpentine, as described in the chapter on finishes.

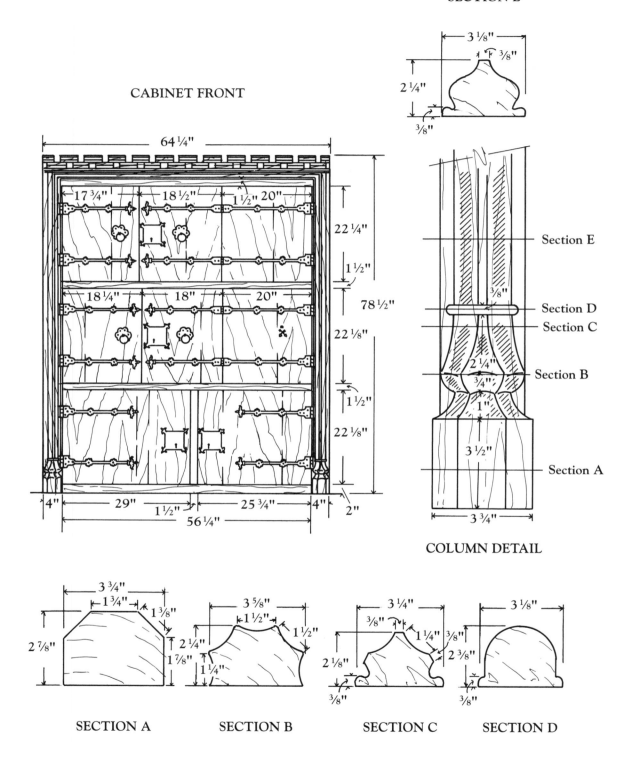

**CABINET FRONT**

**SECTION E**

**COLUMN DETAIL**

**SECTION A**

**SECTION B**

**SECTION C**

**SECTION D**

138

REAR OF CASE

INTERIOR OF CASE

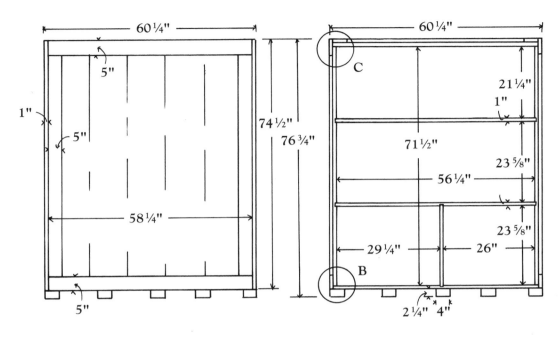

60¼"

5"

1"

5"

74½"
76¾"

58¼"

5"

60¼"

C

21¼"
1"

71½"

23⅝"

56¼"

23⅝"

29¼"

26"

B

2¼"  4"

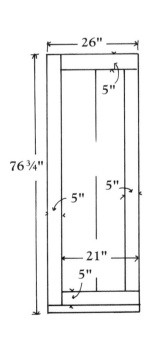

26"

5"

76¾"

5"

5"

21"

5"

LEFT END OF CASE

1"

5"

5"

5"

DETAIL C

1"

1"

1"

DETAIL B

5"

4"

2¼"

1"

1"

1"

½"

1"

DETAIL A

139

## CABINET SECTION

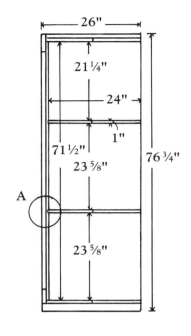

26"

21¼"

24"

1"

71½"

23⅝"

76¾"

A

23⅝"

## HARDWARE LOCATION A

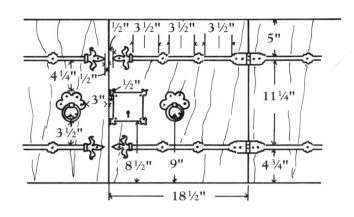

½" 3½" 3½" 3½"

5"

4¼" ½"

½"

3"

11¼"

3½"

3½"

8½" 9"

4¾"

18½"

## HARDWARE LOCATION B

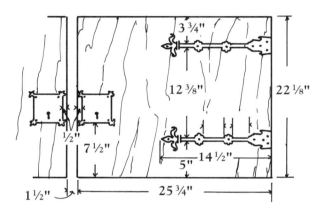

3¾"

12⅜"

22⅛"

½"

7½"

5"

14½"

1½"

25¾"

1"

## ARMS OF YORK

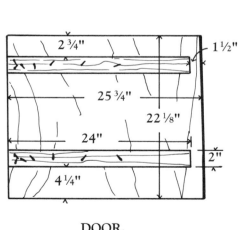

2¾"

1½"

25¾"

22⅛"

24"

2"

4¼"

### DOOR,
### REAR VIEW

¾"

⅝"

### DOOR,
### EDGE VIEW

## LEFT STILE, INTERIOR EDGE WITH RAILS IN PLACE

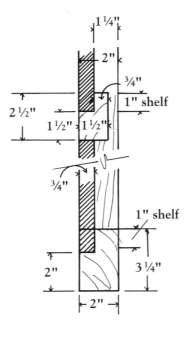

1¼"

2"

¾"

1" shelf

2½"

1½" 1½"

¾"

1" shelf

2"

3¼"

2"

## LEFT STILE, INTERIOR EDGE WITH RAILS REMOVED

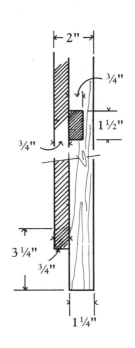

2"

¾"

1½"

¾"

3¼"

¾"

1¼"

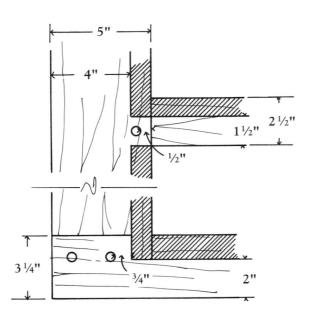

5"

4"

2½"

1½"

½"

3¼"

¾"

2"

**CABINET FRONT CONSTRUCTION DETAIL, LEFT SIDE**

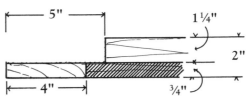

5"

1¼"

2"

4"

¾"

**BOTTOM RAIL, TOP VIEW**

DOOR PULL RING,
SIDE VIEW

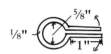

5/8"
1/8"
1"

HINGE,
BUTT END

2 1/4"
1/2"
1 1/2"
3"
1 3/4"
3"

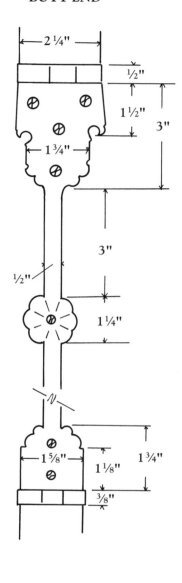

1/2"
1 1/4"

1 5/8"
1 1/8"
1 3/4"
3/8"

3 3/4"
1 3/8"
1/2"
3/8"
2 1/2"

DOOR PULL

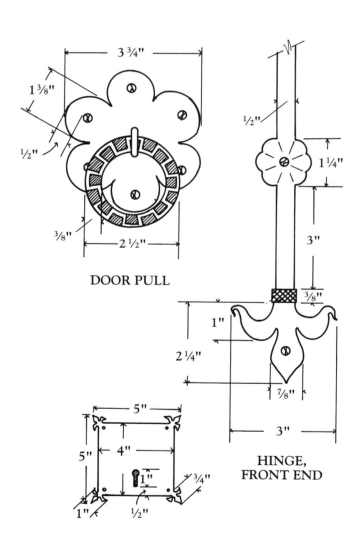

1/2"
1 1/4"
3"
3/8"

1"
2 1/4"
7/8"
3"

HINGE,
FRONT END

5"
4"
5"
1"
3/4"
1"
1/2"

LOCK PLATE

## CORNICE PROFILE

## CORNICE

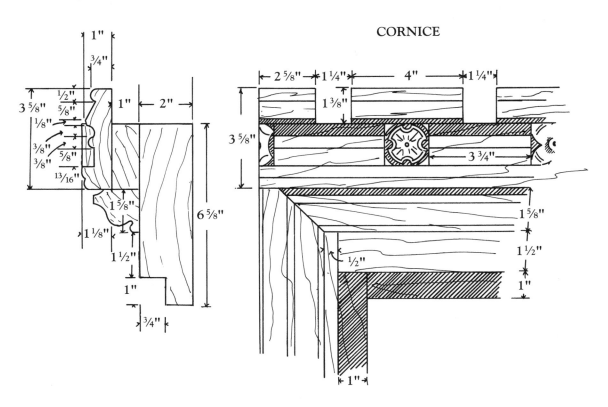

## CARVED CORNICE BLOCKS

1⅝"

  1⅝"

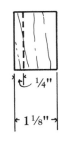

CORNICE
BLOCK,
SIDE VIEW

143

# Project 13

## SETTLE

Throughout the Middle Ages and well into the eighteenth century, settles were the most common form of public seating. By definition a settle is a long bench fitted with a back and arms. More elaborate than a simple bench, a settle—like the furniture found in the waiting rooms of modern banks and law firms—was intended to impress visitors with its owner's power and status.

This settle was constructed in the southern part of the Low Countries during the mid-sixteenth century, probably for the convent of San Benito, located near the town of Valladolid, Spain. As a fine piece of imported furniture, it may have been placed in a waiting room outside the abbess's office, as a convenient, but not too comfortable, place for visitors to sit while they contemplated God's power and the impermanence of temporal life.

As is typical of much medieval furniture, this piece is constructed of oak and decorated with linenfold paneling, but it has a few unusual features, as well. Surmounting the support columns for the arms and the back are carvings of dogs and lions, representations most frequently found on tomb effigies. The lions, at the highest points of the back, represent bravery and the power of the church and the king; the dogs, located on the lower level of the arms, represent obedience. On the inside face of each arm are two panels with curious circular holes. Since the space between these openings and the outside panel is not large enough to be used as storage compartments, we assume that they were simply handles to aid in moving the settle from one place to another. Finally, to make the best possible use of the space occupied by this large piece of furniture, the base does double duty as both seat and storage chest. The chest may have held important objects, such as books or vestments, because a small plate now covers the scar where a lockset once existed.

Now a part of the collection of the Cloisters in New York City, this magnificent settle testifies to the grandeur that was once a routine part of medieval monastic life.

### CONSTRUCTION NOTES
Although this is a large unit of furniture, its general construction does not significantly differ from that of the small paneled chest found earlier in this book. Carving the fourteen linenfold panels on the settle's front, back, and sides is time-consuming and is the project's biggest challenge.

### Materials
Made entirely of oak, this settle does not contain any of the massively oversized timbers found in many of the articles of furniture featured in this book; the only metalwork is the two hinges on the storage compartment lid. Obtaining the material should, therefore, not require any special millwork or blacksmithing, but purchasing the lumber is likely to amass a hefty bill.

### Setting Up
Since many of this settle's components are repeated, the construction will go more quickly if you first prepare the framing members and the linenfold paneling.

Cut to size the five small front panels, the five long panels on the face of the back, and the four panels for the outside of the arms. All of these panels are ¾ inch thick. As noted in the materials list, the front panels measure 12½ by 13½ inches. Note that the grain runs with the 12½-inch dimension of these panels. The back panels are 12½ by 24½ inches; the arm panels are 8½ inches by 28½ inches. Also cut the panels for the settle's rear. Like the carved panels, these are all ¾ inch thick. The five upper panels are 12½ by 27½ inches; there are also two lower panels that are 15¾ by 21½ inches and a single panel that is 15¾ by 23½ inches. Chalk the locations of the panels and lay them aside. If you wish, also cut the two panels for the interior of the arms. These panels, shown in the interior arm panel drawing, are 11¼ inches wide, 18½ inches long, and ½ inch thick. You may also cut the circular holes in these panels and chamfer the edges with a rasp or router. With so many panels to keep track of, it is best if like panels are stacked together.

## Carving the Linenfold Panels

Now lay out and carve the linenfold panels. Although the same design appears on all the panels, note that the four arm panels contain only the central section of the design; the extreme left and right folds have been eliminated to adapt the design to the panel's narrow width.

Transfer the design of the panels from the front view of the typical panel to each panel's face, allotting a 1-inch border around the design. Following the instructions in the woodcarving chapter, execute the linenfold pattern on all fourteen panels.

## Decorative Panel Molding

Cut the decorative molding around the edges of all the panel frames at once to most efficiently use shop time. The majority of the framing members are 3½ by 2¼ inches, but there are exceptions, and all four sides of the panel frames are not molded with the same decorative pattern.

The panel frames on the settle's front and back have a consistent molding pattern around the top and sides, but only a simple chamfer details the bottom of the frames. These moldings and their arrangement around the panels are shown in the detail A and B drawings.

The vertical stiles separating the panels on the front and the back of the settle are all 3½ by 2¼ inches and have the same molding pattern cut along both front edges. These stiles are shown in the typical back stile drawings. Here you will find top, front, and side views that provide a clear pattern for cutting the molding. The top view of detail B can serve as a template for the molding.

The top rail on the back and the support rail at the front of the seat are both 3½ by 2¼ inches. Both of these rails have the panel mold cut along only one edge. The top edge of the seat support rail is left square; the molding along the top edge of the top rail is shown in the cutaway view of the top rail. Notice that this last molding differs only slightly from the panel molding.

The divider stiles that separate the panels on the ends of the settle are shown in the side view and the arm section 2 drawings. These stiles are only 2½ by 2¾ inches but, like the larger stiles on the settle's front, display the panel mold design along both front edges (across one of the 2½-inch-wide faces). Note in the side view drawing that there is no other decorative molding around the end panels.

Whether you are using a molding cutter, molding planes, or another method to cut the panel molding, do not hesitate to cut the molding pattern along the entire length of a framing member. The intersections of rail and stiles need not interrupt the pattern.

## Cutting the Framing Members to Length

If you have cut the panel mold on long lengths of stock, now cut the stock to the proper length for individual framing members as indicated in the materials list. The lengths given allow enough stock to cut tenons as necessary. Again, since there are so many framing members, chalk the location of each piece as it is cut, and stack like pieces together for easy identification. While you are cutting framing members, cut the stiles that separate the lower panels on the rear of the settle, the central support rail running across the middle of the rear, and the front and back lower rails that support the bottom edge of the front and back panels. Also cut the rail at the back of the seat—the rail supporting the linenfold panels in the back. This rail is only ¾ inch thick. Do not cut the tenons on the ends of the rails or stiles at this time.

## Rabbeting the Panels

With the framing members cut to length, next rabbet out the grooves into which the panels will be set. All these rabbets will be cut ¾ inch deep, but the width will vary from one location to another. Notice on the typical back stile drawings and the cutaway view of the top rail that the rabbet in these members is 1⅛ inches wide. The rails and the stiles on the front of the settle, as well as the rail at the back of the seat and the stiles separating the end panels, are rabbeted to a width of only ⅜ inch. In the case of the rail at the back of the seat, this is an open rabbet (see the detail D drawing).

# MATERIALS

## WOOD
### All wood is oak.

| PART | NUMBER OF PIECES | THICKNESS | | WIDTH | | LENGTH |
|------|------------------|-----------|---|-------|---|--------|
| front panels | 5 | ¾" | × | 12½" | × | 13½" |
| back panels | 5 | ¾" | × | 12½" | × | 24½" |
| arm panels | 4 | ¾" | × | 8½" | × | 28½" |
| rear top panels | 5 | ¾" | × | 12½" | × | 12½" |
| rear bottom panels | 2 | ¾" | × | 15¾" | × | 21½" |
| rear bottom panel | 1 | ¾" | × | 15¾" | × | 23½" |
| interior arm panels | 2 | ½" | × | 11¼" | × | 18½" |
| top rail | 1 | 2¼" | × | 3½" | × | 71½" |
| seat support rail | 1 | 2¼" | × | 3½" | × | 71½" |
| lower front rail | 1 | 2¼" | × | 2¼" | × | 71½" |
| central support rail | 1 | 3½" | × | 3½" | × | 71½" |
| lower back rail | 1 | 2¼" | × | 2¼" | × | 71½" |
| arm supports | 2 | 2¼" | × | 2¾" | × | 33" |
| front stiles | 4 | 2¼" | × | 3½" | × | 14½" |
| back stiles | 4 | 2¼" | × | 3½" | × | 25½" |

The difference in the width of the rabbets is caused by the addition of secondary panels on the rear of the settle. This second set of panels can be seen in section A; how they relate to the framing members is shown in the typical back stile drawings and the cutaway view of the top rail. Keep the narrow, ⅜-inch rabbets toward the front edge of the rails and stiles to maintain a constant relationship of the panels to the rails and stiles throughout. When you are cutting the rabbets that hold the lower panels on the rear of the settle, cut the rabbets ¾ inch wide. The rabbet in the top edge of the central support rail, shown in detail D, must be 1½ inches wide. Do not worry that the rabbets in the long rails run across the future location of mortise and tenon joints. The mortises are designed to utilize the rabbets.

## Corner Posts, Armrests, and Feet

After the rails and the stiles have been molded, cut to length, and rabbeted, cut the four corner posts, which

146

| PART | NUMBER OF PIECES | THICKNESS | | WIDTH | | LENGTH |
|---|---|---|---|---|---|---|
| lower back stiles | 2 | 2¼" | × | 3½" | × | 16¾" |
| armrests | 2 | 2¼" | × | 2¼" | × | 19½" |
| back support posts | 2 | 2¼" | × | 2¾" | × | 48¾" |
| feet | 2 | 2¾" | × | 4½" | × | 23" |
| seat and lid | 1 | 1" | × | 19¾" | × | 71½" |
| floorboard | 1 | 1" | × | 8¾' | × | 71½" |
| floorboard | 1 | 1" | × | 9" | × | 71½" |
| floor end support rails | 2 | 1½" | × | 1½" | × | 14¾" |
| floor back support rail | 1 | 1½" | × | 1½" | × | 71½" |
| figural carvings | 4 | 2¼" | × | 2¾" | × | 4" |
| dowels | 5 | ⅜" diameter | | | × | 36" |

## Metal

| PART | NUMBER OF PIECES | THICKNESS | | WIDTH | | LENGTH |
|---|---|---|---|---|---|---|
| hinge fronts | 2 | ⅛" | × | 1½" | × | 12" |
| hinge rears | 2 | ⅛" | × | 2½" | × | 3" |
| forged nails | 12 | | | | | 2" |

include two back support posts and two arm support posts. The lengths given for these posts in the materials list do not provide enough length for the carvings. To ease execution, the carvings will be made from separate pieces and pegged into place later. With a router or carving knives and files, mold the tops of the arm supports and back supports according to the diagrams beneath the drawings of the animals. Locate the center of the top of each of the four corner posts, and drill a ⅜-inch hole that is 1 inch deep. This

hole will allow the carved figures to be doweled to the posts.

Also cut the armrests and feet, as shown in the exterior and bottom views of the arm construction and the side, top, and front views of the foot. After the feet have been cut to length, rough out the quarter-round shape of the front of the feet. As the side view of the foot indicates, the 2-inch quarter-round shape of the foot begins 1 inch ahead of the front end of the tenon.

## Tenons

Cut the tenons on the stiles as shown in the various drawings after the stiles, rails, armrests, and feet have all been cut to length. The drawing labeled back stile, bottom tenon provides an example. The only tenons that vary from this model are those on the stiles separating the arm panels. These tenons are the full 2½-inch width of the stile but only ⅝ inch thick, and they are set 1 inch behind the face of the stile. See the bottom view of the arm construction.

There are no drawings of the tenons on the ends of the rails; however, the tenons on the top rail, the seat support rail, and the central support rail (the rail in the middle of the settle's back) are all 2 inches wide, 1¼ inches long, and ¾ inch thick. The tenons on the lower front and lower back rails will be the same thickness and length as those mentioned above but only 1½ inches wide. Keeping the front face of the tenons level with the front edge of the rabbeted panel grooves is essential for the proper alignment of the panel frames with the carved panels.

The tenon on the rail at the back of the seat is 2 inches wide and 1¼ inches long, but because the rail is only ¾ inch thick, the tenon can be only ½ inch thick. This tenon lies flush with the back of the rail, recessed ¼ inch behind the front.

## Assembling the Front and Back of the Settle

After all the tenons have been cut, separate the framing members integral to the front of the settle. These include four stiles, the seat support rail, and the arm support posts. Arrange the pieces facedown on a level work surface, in their proper locations. Measure and mark the locations of the mortises that will connect the stiles to the rails. For proper spacing, refer to the front view drawing. Bear in mind that the front of the mortises should be on the same plane as the front of the rabbeted panel grooves. Chisel out the mortises to a depth of 1¼ inches. Insert the tenons as deep as possible into the proper mortises, ensuring that the fit is square and snug.

Referring to detail A and the front view of the typical back stile, mark the panel molds at a 45-degree angle at the point where they intersect. Remove the excess wedge-shaped pieces of panel mold from each side of the stiles and the corresponding sections of molding from the rails. Trim the molding carefully; if too much is cut away, the joints will appear loose and sloppy even if the mortises fit snugly.

After the entire front assembly has been joined together, insert the linenfold panels to check for fit. It may be necessary to sand or file the edges of the panels to allow them to fit easily into the panel frames.

After ensuring that the entire front assembly is plumb and square, again lay the assembled front facedown on a level work surface. Position and mark the mortises on one of the 2¼-inch-wide faces of the arm support posts. The bottom edge of the arm support should be level with the bottom edge of the lower front rail. The 2¼-inch gap beneath the lower front rail, shown in the front view drawing, is created when the feet are attached to the settle. After the mortises have been marked and opened, assemble the entire front of the settle to ensure it is plumb and square. Now cut the chamfers along the bottom edge of each panel frame as shown in the detail B drawing.

Repeat this process for the back assembly. Be sure to lay the pieces of the back facedown on your work surface when you are laying out the location of the mortise joints so that the face of the top rail and the rail beneath the back panel lie on the same plane. The tenons on the stiles should fit precisely inside the rabbeted panel groove on the top rail, making precise location of the mortises quite easy. The mortises on the rail beneath the back panels are slightly unusual. As shown in the detail D drawing, this rail is only ¾ inch thick; consequently, the mortise must be cut ⅜ inch deep across the rail's entire width. The oddly shaped tenon on the bottom of the stiles should lock easily into place on this rail and on the central support rail.

After the back has been mortised and fitted together, attach the frame to the back corner support posts in the same manner that you attached the front frame to the arm support posts. Determine the proper location of the corner posts by aligning the top rail 1½ inches beneath the top edge of the corner post. When the entire assembly fits square and plumb, rout or cut the chamfers along the bottom edge of the panel frames.

Next, lay out and cut the mortises for the lower rear panels. Now assemble the entire back, including both layers of paneling. Do note, however, that the lower back rail does not intersect the corner posts. They will both be joined to the foot unit during final assembly.

## Arm Assembly

Remove the arm support posts and back corner posts from the front and back assemblies. Lay aside the remaining pieces of the front and back.

Mark the feet, and rabbet out the groove for the linenfold panel as shown in the top view of the foot. After completing the rabbet, lay out and cut the front and rear tenons as shown in the side and top views of the foot. Positioning the corner posts so that the mortises for the front and back assemblies are properly aligned in relationship to the feet, mark and cut the mortises on the bottom ends of the corner posts. These mortises will, obviously, be open on two sides to allow them to slide over the tenon. Now lay out and cut the mortises to receive the armrest. With the foot and armrest fitted into place, mark and cut the mortises to receive the central stile. The face of the stile should lie flush with the face of the frame, so it is best to lay the end assembly facedown on your work surface to mark the location of the mortises. After the stile has been fitted into the foot and the armrest, assemble the side frame, and with a pencil, connect the panel groove in the foot with the one in the armrest, along the inside faces of the front and rear corner posts. Disassemble the unit, rabbet out the penciled line to a ¾-inch depth, and reassemble the frame.

On the bottom of the armrest there should be a second rabbeted groove. Extend the line of this rabbet 11¼ inches down the front and back corner posts. This rabbet will receive the interior arm panel. To insert the panel, however, you need to cut away a ¾-inch-wide strip from the central back of the stile. This notch should be 11½ inches long (1 inch longer than the height of the interior arm panel). The extra inch allows the bottom edge of the notch to serve as a seat support.

The final step in the assembly of the arm unit is to cut a mortise in the foot to receive the lower back rail, as shown in the top view of the foot. Now temporarily assemble the entire frame, including all the panels, making certain the entire structure fits square, plumb, and snug.

Make any necessary adjustments, then remove the front and end panels, and peg together the back assembly, following the doweling marks on the front and rear view drawings. Similarly, assemble and dowel together the front. Do not dowel together the ends at this time.

### Interior Floor
There is a floor in the interior of the settle that serves as the bottom of the storage compartment. This is shown in cutaway in the section A drawing. Notice that the front edge of the floor assembly rests on the interior edge of the lower front rail. The rear edge (also

shown in section A) and the ends of the floor rest on 1½-by-1½-inch rails that are attached to the back assembly and the end panels. Cut to length and install the rail for the rear edge, making sure it is level with the lower front rail. When measuring the height of the lower front rail, allow 2¼ inches for the height of the feet.

The floor itself is made from random-width boards simply laid on the rails. The materials list suggests appropriately wide boards, but you may use any width you wish, the wider the better. They need not be pegged together, but do attach them to the support rails with either pegs or small, hand-forged nails. Fit the floorboards into place before permanently attaching the ends of the settle, because a notch will have to be cut to allow the central floorboard or floorboards to fit around the stile in the middle of the end panel. Attaching the floor to the support rails should be the last step in construction.

### Seat
Now that the settle is temporarily assembled, measure for the seat. Bear in mind that the left and right edges of the seat slide beneath the interior arm panels as shown in the interior arm panel drawing; this allows them to rest on the shoulder of the divider stile in the arm assembly. See the top view of section B and the arm section 1 drawings.

The original seat was cut from a single plank, the lid having been cut out and reattached with hinges. Since it is unlikely that you will find a 19¾-inch-wide oak plank, you will probably have to peg and glue several boards together. (Instructions for doweling boards together is given in the chapters on woodworking and on constructing the Merrills Board.) This allows you to make the lid and the surrounding seat separately. Extra support for the left and right ends of the lid is provided by a lap joint, visible in the front view drawing. Note that the front corners of the seat will have to be notched to fit around the front arm supports.

### Final Assembly
After the seat has been set in place on the assembled frame, check the structure of the settle to ensure that it is square and level. Now peg the end assemblies together, and attach them to the arm supports and the rear corner posts.

Roll the settle onto its back to give full access to the interior of the storage compartment. Lay the floorboards inside the settle, and attach the 1½-by-1½-inch support rails to the stiles and the corner posts on the ends of the settle. Stand the settle upright and arrange the floorboards on the support rails; then nail them in place.

## Hinges
Following the pattern for the hinges shown in the top view of section B drawing, make a pair of hinges according to the instructions in the metalworking chapter. Set the lid in place on the chest's seat, position the hinges, and attach them to the seat and the lid with hand-forged nails. Be sure to drill pilot holes for the nails to avoid splitting the wood. Clinch the back of the nails to prevent the hinges from shifting or working loose.

## Carved Figures
Cut blocks of wood to size, according to the animal figure drawings. In the center of one end of each block of wood, drill a ⅜-inch hole to a depth of 1 inch. This will allow you to dowel the finished figures to the top of the arm supports and the corner posts.

The drawings of the lion and the dog shown here are reproduced at 50 percent of their actual size; enlarge them on a photocopier and transfer them directly to the wood. Remember that there are left and right sides to each figure. Following the instructions for sculptural carvings in the woodcarving chapter, execute the figures as shown in the drawings.

Cut four 1⅞-inch lengths of ⅜-inch doweling, and gently insert them into the base of the carved animals. Tap the animals into place on the arms and the corner posts.

## Finish
A mixture of three parts dark oak stain and one part red mahogany stain, combined in equal parts with boiled linseed oil, and a touch of turpentine, will give the settle a finish comparable with that of the original.

## FRONT VIEW

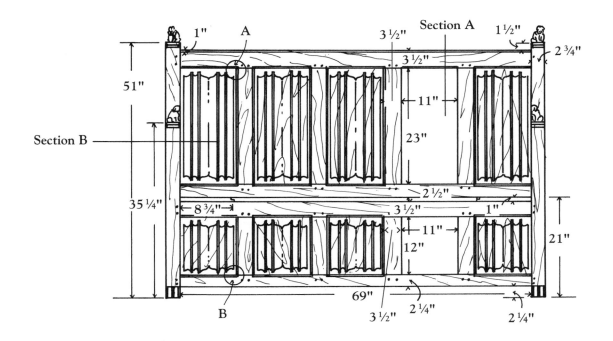

1"  A  Section A  3½"  1½"  2¾"
3½"
51"  11"
23"
Section B
2½"
35¼"  8¾"  3½"  1"
11"
12"  21"
69"
B  2¼"
3½"  2¼"

## REAR VIEW

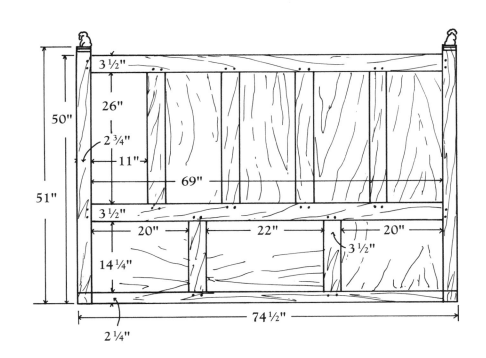

3½"
26"
2¾"
50"  11"
69"
51"  3½"
20"  22"  20"
14¼"  3½"
74½"
2¼"

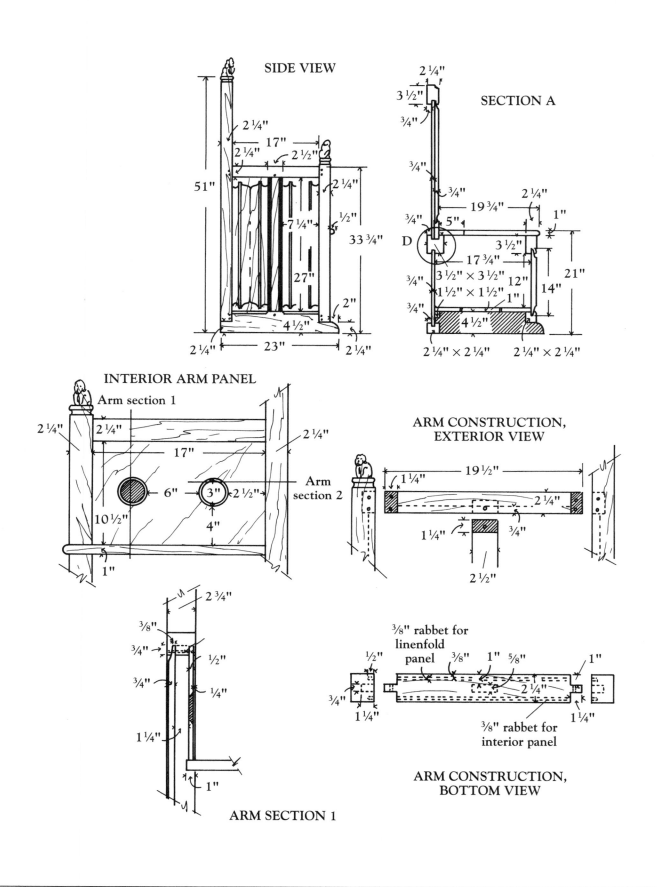

SIDE VIEW

SECTION A

INTERIOR ARM PANEL

Arm section 1

Arm section 2

ARM CONSTRUCTION,
EXTERIOR VIEW

ARM SECTION 1

⅜" rabbet for
linenfold
panel

⅜" rabbet for
interior panel

ARM CONSTRUCTION,
BOTTOM VIEW

152

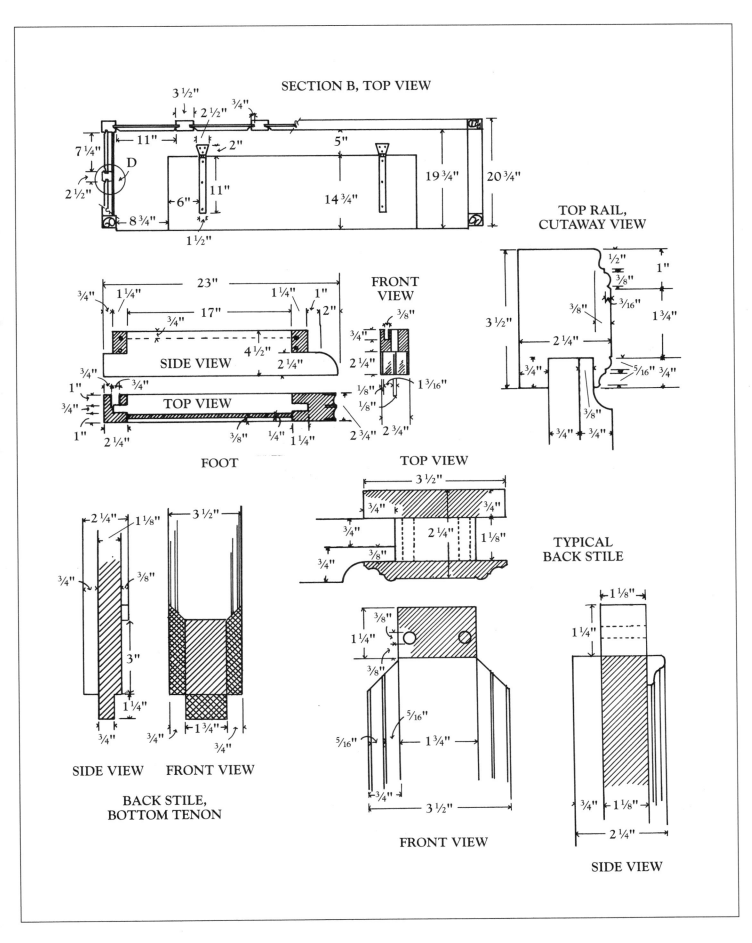

SECTION B, TOP VIEW

TOP RAIL, CUTAWAY VIEW

FRONT VIEW

SIDE VIEW

TOP VIEW

FOOT

TOP VIEW

TYPICAL BACK STILE

SIDE VIEW      FRONT VIEW

BACK STILE, BOTTOM TENON

FRONT VIEW

SIDE VIEW

DETAIL A

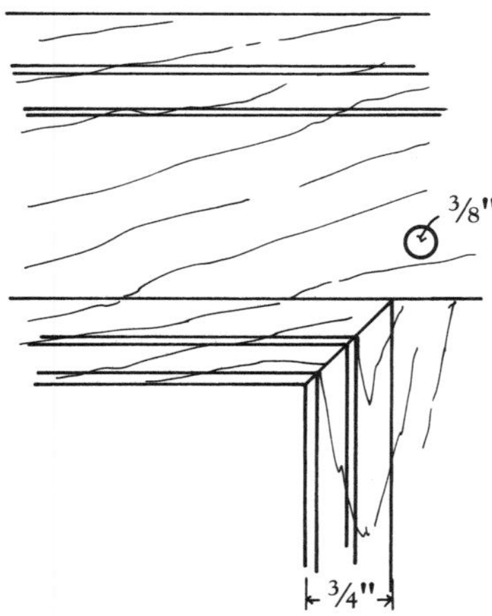

DETAIL B

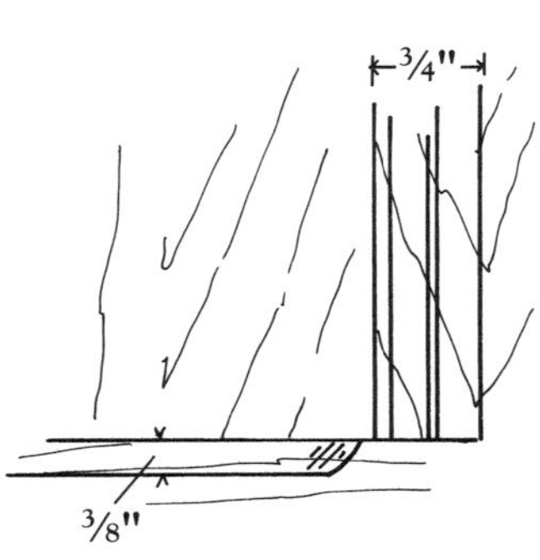

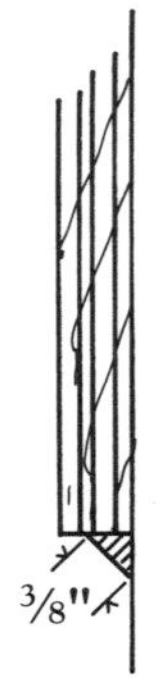

$\frac{3}{4}$"

$\frac{3}{8}$"

$\frac{3}{8}$"

DETAIL B,
SIDE VIEW

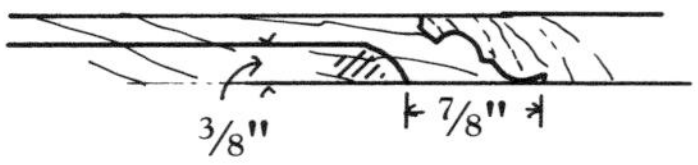

$\frac{3}{8}$"

$\frac{3}{8}$" $\frac{7}{8}$"

$\frac{3}{4}$"

DETAIL B,
TOP VIEW

TYPICAL PANEL,
FRONT VIEW

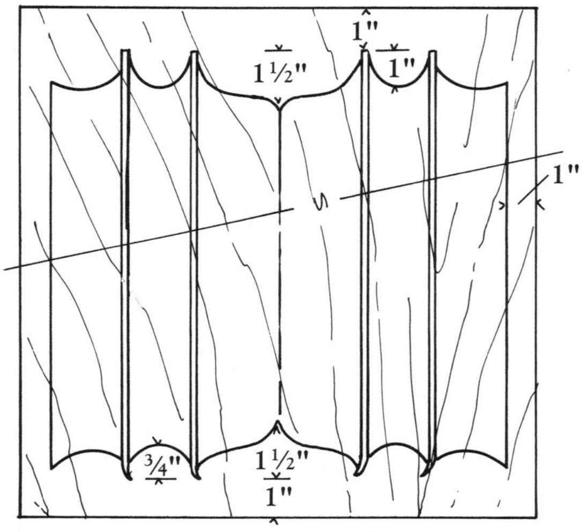

1"

$1\frac{1}{2}$" 1"

1"

$\frac{3}{4}$" $1\frac{1}{2}$"
1"

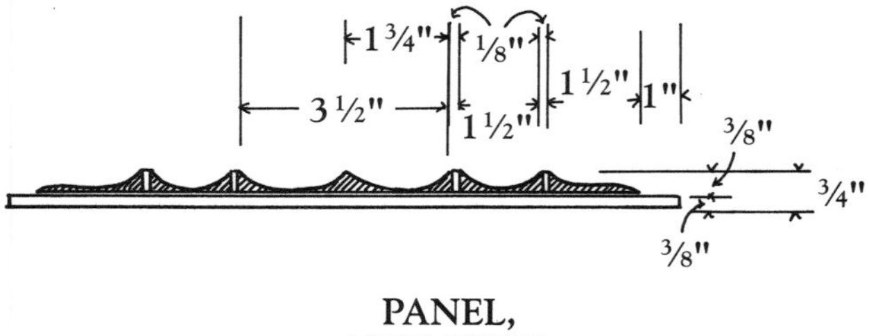

$\frac{3}{4}$"
$\frac{3}{4}$"
$\frac{3}{4}$"
$\frac{3}{4}$"

$\frac{3}{4}$"

$\frac{3}{4}$"

$4\frac{1}{2}$" 1"

$3\frac{1}{2}$" × $3\frac{1}{2}$"

DETAIL D

$1\frac{3}{4}$" $\frac{1}{8}$"
$3\frac{1}{2}$" $1\frac{1}{2}$" 1"
$1\frac{1}{2}$"

$\frac{3}{8}$"
$\frac{3}{4}$"
$\frac{3}{8}$"

PANEL,
END VIEW

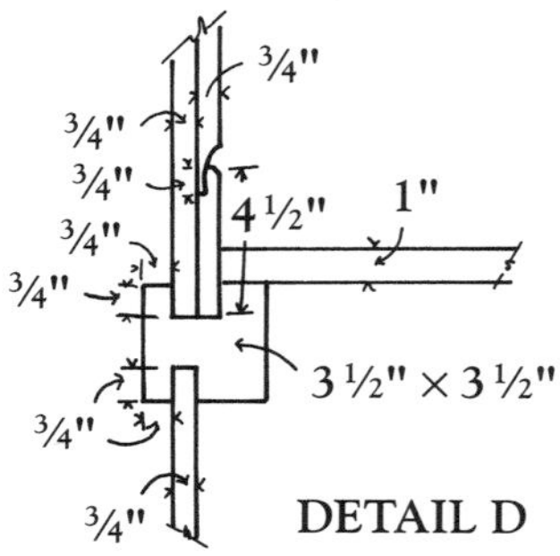

$\frac{3}{4}$" $\frac{1}{2}$"
$\frac{3}{8}$" $1\frac{1}{4}$"
$2\frac{1}{2}$" 2"
$\frac{3}{4}$"
$2\frac{3}{4}$"

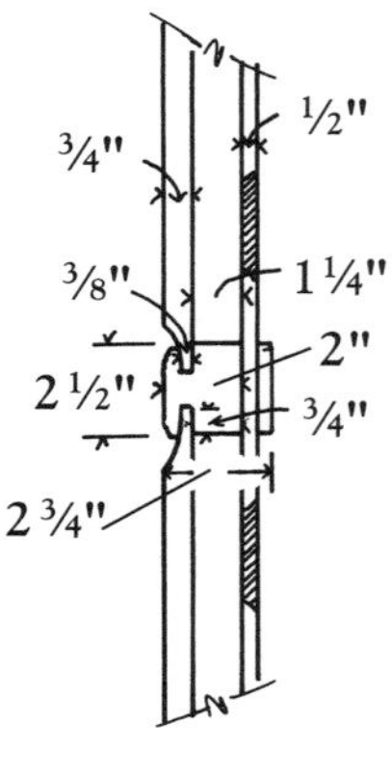

ARM SECTION 2

154

BACK FINIAL, RIGHT SIDE

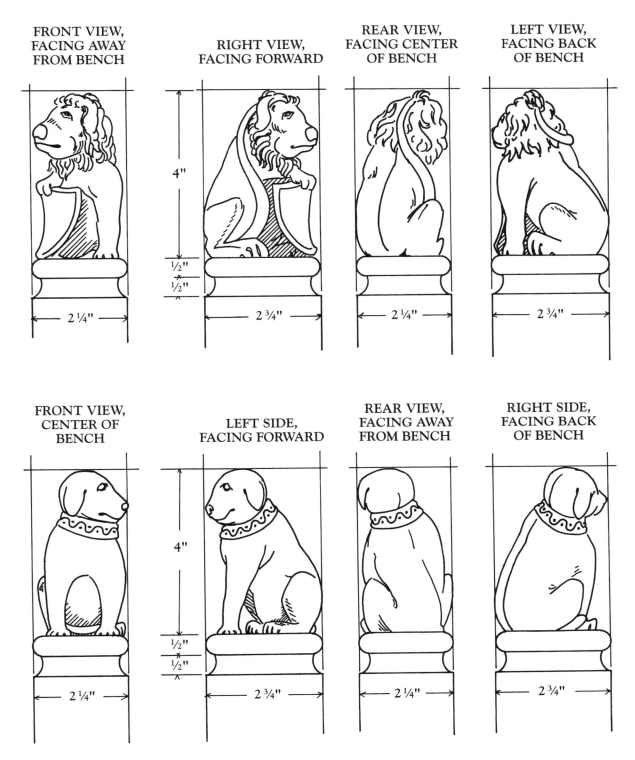

FRONT VIEW, FACING AWAY FROM BENCH

RIGHT VIEW, FACING FORWARD

REAR VIEW, FACING CENTER OF BENCH

LEFT VIEW, FACING BACK OF BENCH

FRONT VIEW, CENTER OF BENCH

LEFT SIDE, FACING FORWARD

REAR VIEW, FACING AWAY FROM BENCH

RIGHT SIDE, FACING BACK OF BENCH

ARM FINIAL, RIGHT SIDE

# Project 14

# Barrel Chair

Throughout the Middle Ages, and well into the Renaissance, chairs symbolized social status. The larger and more ornate the seat, the wealthier and more powerful its owner. Although peasants and villagers seldom owned anything more elaborate than a stool, merchants usually owned at least one or two chairs with both backs and arms. Petit nobles and abbots sat on armchairs with carvings suitable to their station, while kings and popes sat on magnificent thrones surmounted by upholstered canopies. Now located in the Campin room of the Metropolitan Museum's Cloisters, this ornately carved chair was long the property of the Church of San Orsto, located in the Val d'Aosta of the Italian Piedmont. Constructed during the latter half of the fifteenth century, this chair was probably commissioned for an abbot of a local monastery or one of the Church of San Orsto's canons.

More than one craftsman may have worked on this piece that combines pine, walnut, and limewood. It is possible that both a furniture builder and a carver worked on the chair. Curiously, the chair's decorative work lacks the sophistication of the Renaissance art that was flowering across Italy at the time. The shop that produced this chair may have been so provincial that it remained unaffected by the sweeping changes affecting Italian urban artists and craftsmen. Despite its artistic limitations, this chair wonderfully exemplifies provincial craftsmanship from the late Middle Ages.

## CONSTRUCTION NOTES

Despite this barrel chair's intimidating appearance, its basic construction is amazingly simple. The carving details and bentwood slats provide an opportunity for the craftsperson to sharpen his or her existing carving skills and to learn the art of bending wood with steam. The completed chair will instantly become the focal point of any room it occupies.

## Materials

The seat, the horseshoe-shaped arm unit, and the kick panel in the chair's front are pine, while the two curved splats encircling the back are bent from limewood. The rest of the chair is walnut. European walnut is normally much lighter in color, and rather softer, than the notably hard black walnut familiar to Americans. If carving black walnut seems too daunting, you can substitute mahogany with very little change to the chair's finished appearance. The nails, with their impressively large heads, will have to be specially forged.

## Frame

Begin constructing the chair frame by roughing out the legs. Cut the three legs to size according to the materials list. Next, notch the inside faces of the legs to receive the back splats, and cut the general outline of the leg as shown in the drawings. Note: There is one long notch along the inside of the left and right legs, but two separate notches in the rear leg. The notches on the left and right legs begin $14\frac{3}{8}$ inches from the bottom, whereas those on the rear leg begin only $13\frac{3}{8}$ inches from the bottom. Within the notches on the left and right legs are secondary notches into which the back splats are rabbeted. Cut these notches, shown in the drawing of the inside face of the right leg, to a depth of $\frac{3}{8}$ inch. Incise mirror-image notches into the left leg. The shape of the feet also differs between the front and rear legs. The heels on the left and right legs are notched out, while the bottom of the rear leg is

# MATERIALS

## WOOD
The woods are pine, walnut, and lime.
Mahogany may be substituted for walnut; ash, pine, fir, or poplar may be substituted for lime.

| PART | NUMBER OF PIECES | THICKNESS | | WIDTH | | LENGTH |
|------|------------------|-----------|---|-------|---|--------|
| left and right legs | 2 | 2¼" | × | 4" | × | 26⅜" |
| rear leg | 1 | 2¼" | × | 4¼" | × | 26⅜" |
| seat support | 1 | 2" | × | 2" | × | 15¾" |
| angle brace | 1 | 1" | × | 1" | × | 4" |
| kick panel | 1 | ¾" | × | 10¾" | × | 19½" |
| skirt board | 1 | ¾" | × | 4½" | × | 17" |
| seat boards | 2 | 1" | × | 8¼" | × | 19¼" |
| back supports | 2 | 1¼" | × | 3½" | × | 12½" |
| arm segments | 2 | ⅝" | × | 12" | × | 19½" |
| back splats | 2 | ⅜" | × | 3½" | × | 42" |

## METAL

| PART | NUMBER OF PIECES | THICKNESS | | WIDTH | | LENGTH |
|------|------------------|-----------|---|-------|---|--------|
| large-headed nails | 22 | | | | | 2½" |
| large-headed nails | 24 | | | | | 1½" |
| small-headed nails | 2 | | | | | 2" |
| clinch | 1 | ⅛" | × | ¼" | × | 4½" |

curved. This curve begins approximately 8 inches from the leg's bottom.

The outside faces of all three legs are slightly concave. This curve is more pronounced on the left and right legs than it is on the rear leg. To cut the general shape of the legs, enlarge the drawings to full size on a photocopier and trace them directly onto the wood. If you lay out and cut the rough shape of the leg without the aid of a pattern, allow for the small head at each leg's center.

After the legs have been cut to shape, lay them aside and cut the seat support and its accompanying angle brace as shown in the side view of the seat and support. Be aware that the seat support has a tenon on only one end. Mark and cut the tenon as shown in the same drawing, as well as in the end view of the seat support tenon. Then cut the corresponding mortise on the inside face of the rear leg. Next, cut the tenons on the ends of the angle brace as shown in the small detail drawing beneath the side view of the seat and support. Aligning the front face of the angle brace with the front edge of the seat support, locate and cut the mortise for the angle brace into the bottom of the seat support.

Cut out the large pine kick panel that connects the front legs and supports the front of the seat. This panel is shown in the front view drawing and in profile in the side view of the seat and support. Allow for the 1¼-inch tenons on each end of the kick. The tenons, shown in the front view, are ½ inch thick. Simply remove ¼ inch from the face of the kick panel to create a tenon of the proper thickness and at the proper location.

Lay the seat support on a workbench with the top of the support facedown on the work surface. Insert the angle brace into the mortise. Standing the kick panel in front of the seat support, with the seat support at the center of the kick panel, locate the position for the mortise. After you have cut the mortise into the kick panel, fit the three pieces together, checking for snugness and alignment.

Mark and cut mortises on the inside of the left and right legs to receive the tenons on the kick panel. These ½-inch-wide mortises should be located 1 inch behind the leg's front surface as shown in the drawing of the inside face of the right leg. Locate the kick panel so that its top edge is 1 inch below the long notch on the inside of the left and right legs. The location of the kick panel is clearly shown in the front view drawing. Be sure that the mortise and tenon joints fit snugly. Now temporarily fit together the frame of the chair, consisting of the legs, seat support, angle bracket, and kick panel.

## Seat

With the assembled chair before you, make a template for the seat. The front-to-back depth of the seat should be 16⅜ inches. The width between the front legs should be 17 inches, and the width behind the legs should be 19¼ inches. The seat's dimensions can be found in the side and front views of the seat and support and in the top view with arm removed. Be certain that the seat is deep enough to extend from the rear of the notch in the back leg to the front edge of the front legs.

The seat is made from two 1-inch-thick boards pegged together with three dowels that are ¼ inch in diameter. See the instructions for doweling in the chapters on woodworking and the Merrills Board. After the seat has been doweled together and cut to shape, it should lie easily on the chair frame. The side view of the seat and support shows the seat resting on the seat support, the notch in the rear leg, and the top edge of the kick panel. The seat should now extend ¾ inch beyond the front of the kick panel.

## Carvings

Disassemble the chair, and execute the carvings on the legs as shown in the drawings. Note that the depth of the carving is indicated on the drawings by the hatched lines. Areas with cross-hatch lines running in two directions (forming a checked pattern) are carved to a greater depth than surfaces with lines running in only one direction. The different depths of carved work are particularly noticeable in the interlocking vine and trefoil pattern on the sides of the left and right legs.

Getting multidepth patterns right can be a little tricky; practice on a wood scrap before beginning the actual work on the legs. Since both faces of the leg have identical carvings, we show only one side of each leg. Techniques for executing the flat, incised carvings are detailed in the chapter on woodcarving; details for sculpting the more fully rounded figures are covered in the chapter on the settle.

On the right leg of the original, the small head near the center of the leg has been carved from a separate piece of wood and attached to the leg, presumably with a dowel. Did the woodcarver change his mind about the design halfway through the project, or did he simply replace a ruined head? We will never know. This head, like most of the heads on the chair, has unfortunately been nearly worn away over the centuries. Although we often attempt to rectify in our blueprints the degradation of time, we have no idea what the heads originally looked like.

After you have completed all three legs, next cut out and carve the skirt board shown in the front view and skirt board drawings. A profile of this carving is shown in the section A drawing. The skirt board does not have tenons to hold it in place—it is simply nailed to the front of the kick panel. The skirt board drawing is printed here at 50 percent scale and can easily be enlarged to full size on a photocopier.

## Arm

Reassemble the frame after the carvings have all been executed. Using the tops of the legs as a guide, make a template for the arm sections as shown in the top view with arm and the side view. The arm is made of two pieces of ⅜-inch-thick pine that form a horseshoe. The pieces meet on the top of the rear leg.

After the arm has been cut to size and shape, round the edges with a file or a ½-inch round-over router bit. Then cut the two back supports as shown in the back support drawing.

## Frame Assembly

Since the structure of this chair is not too well engineered, you should glue all the joints. Note in the side view of the seat and support that the angle bracket is held in place with two large-headed nails that are 1½ inches in length. A similar nail holds the seat support tenon into the mortise in the rear leg; four more hold the kick panel to the front legs. The nails in the front legs are driven through the rear face of the legs as well as through the tenon in the kick panel; two nails are used on each end of the kick panel.

The front of the seat support is fastened to the kick panel and the skirt board with another nail. There are a total of seven nails attaching the skirt board to the kick panel, six of them simply extending through the panel to be clinched over on the back. The nail at the top center, however, continues straight into the seat support. Judging from the amount of clinch on the other nails, this nail must extend into the support an inch or more.

Set the seat in place after the frame has been assembled. It is not attached to the frame; the curved splat just above it holds it in place.

Immediately attach the horseshoe-shaped arm sections to the chair. The arm will keep the legs in their proper position and help hold the frame square while the glue dries. The arm sections are fastened to the legs by the large-headed nails shown in the top view with arm. In addition to the fourteen nails holding the arm in place, an iron clinch, like a giant staple, keeps the arm sections from pulling apart. This clinch is not detailed in the drawings but is described in the metalwork section below. It can be added after the glue on the frame is dry. Be sure to drill pilot holes for the clinch. Since the clinch is made from ¼-by-⅛-inch stock, it will be best to drill two pilot holes, ³⁄₃₂ inch in diameter, next to each other. This gives ³⁄₃₂-by-³⁄₁₆-inch pilot holes that will accommodate the clinch's rectangular shape. This seemingly confusing procedure will become clear when you hold the clinch in position in the arm.

## Back Supports

Install the two back supports after the arm has been secured to the legs. Their location is indicated in the top view with arm removed and the side view. The supports are nailed through the top of the arm as shown in the top view with arm. The bottom edge of the supports, shown in the back support drawing, only rests on the edge of the seat. Although they are not evident, there must be small nails driven through the seat bottom and into the supports. Since these nails go into the end grain of the back support, it is essential that you drill pilot holes to prevent the wood from splitting.

## Back Splats

The two horizontal splats that form the back and sides of the chair are made from ⅜-inch-thick limewood that is 3½ inches wide and 42 inches long. It is necessary to bend these splats into a horseshoe shape that nearly conforms to the curve of the seat and arm.

Bending wood is a challenge that most amateur woodworkers never encounter and, as such, requires some explaining. Although modern, commercial wood bending requires sophisticated machinery, duplicating traditional medieval methods can reproduce the technique with simple materials and a little patience.

Medieval craftsmen bent wood by several methods for a variety of uses. The simplest, but most time-consuming, technique was to train a live sapling to the desired shape as it grew by slowly bending it around a series of forms, each bringing the growing tree closer to the desired shape. This method was most often used to produce scythe and ax handles. After the sapling reached the desired length and diameter, it was harvested, allowed to cure, and shaped as necessary. This was an interesting approach to the problem, no doubt, but one requiring several years. More practical for our purpose is bending a board to shape by the application of wet heat combined with slow, steady pressure.

The best candidates for bending are lime and ash, but pine, fir, and poplar can also be bent without too much danger of splitting. To make the bending as easy as possible, obtain green wood that has not been cured either by prolonged exposure to air or by the heat-treating process used on most commercially available wood. Although thin wood can be bent over several weeks by the steady application of pressure alone, it will adapt to a shape much more quickly, and with less chance of breaking, if the wood fibers are softened by being exposed to wet heat for a few hours. We recommend steaming, but first a forming jig must be constructed against which the wood can be shaped after it has been softened.

The jig is no more than a framework cut to the desired shape and the width of the board being bent around it; in this case, the shape is the hatched area on the top view with arm removed, and the width is 3½ inches. The forming jig can be made from two pieces of ¾-inch plywood cut to shape and separated with a series of 2-inch-thick spacers nailed between them. Check the forming jig for proper shape by laying it in position on the chair seat. It should sit neatly between the legs. Now you need a means by which to attach the steamed board to the framework. Mark a line along the curved edge of both faces of the forming jig. This line should be located 1 inch from the edge. Drive nails along this line at 2-inch intervals, allowing the nails to protrude 1 inch from the jig. Set the forming jig aside while you steam the wood.

To steam wood, it is necessary to build a case to hold the wood while the steam is channeled around it. Build a long, narrow, open-ended wooden box with interior dimensions of 8 by 4 inches and a length of 50 inches. Do not use plywood, which would fall apart when exposed to the steam. After the box is built, cover one end of it with a layer of finely woven cotton or linen, such as a strip of an old bedsheet or pillowcase. On top of the cloth, nail a layer of coarse mesh screen (such as ¼-inch hardware cloth) to support the weight of the box's contents. Since this box will have to be suspended over a large pot or a kettle of boiling water for 4 or 5 hours, decide whether the work is going to be done indoors or outdoors, and construct a framework to hold the box accordingly. Over an outdoor fire, a simple tripod of iron pipe can be used. Working over the kitchen stove may require a more elaborate apparatus. In either case, the bottom of the box (the end covered with cloth and mesh) will have to be suspended 20 to 24 inches above the flame. Next, insert two screw eyes in opposite sides of the box near the top end, and attach to them 6 to 8 inches of chain. Attach the chain to the tripod or other apparatus, allowing the box to hang beneath it, directly over the fire.

You will also need a large kettle in which to boil water. An old restaurant spaghetti pot is ideal, but any large pot or even an old metal bucket will do, so long as it will hold 8 to 10 gallons of water. After finding a suitable kettle, fabricate a sheet metal funnel to fit loosely over the top. The funnel does not have to be a perfect fit, nor does the seam where it is joined together need to be airtight—its purpose is only to direct the steam from the kettle into the wooden box. Cut off the funnel's point to form a rectangular hole just large enough for the box's end to fit through. The closer the funnel fits around the box, the more steam will be directed onto the wood inside the box.

Stand the box on a relatively level surface, with the cloth-covered end pointing downward, and pour 1 to 2 inches of clean sand into it. Place one of the boards to be steamed inside the box so that it rests on the sand and is roughly centered in the box. Fill the box with sand until it just covers the board. Suspend the box on the tripod, slide the funnel over the bottom of the box, and set the kettle in place under the funnel. Adjust the chains so that the bottom of the box is approximately halfway between the top of the kettle and the top of the funnel.

Raise the funnel, and fill the kettle two-thirds full of water. Build a fire under the kettle, and bring the water to a steady boil. Keep the heat consistent to ensure a continuous boil. Check the water level every hour, replenishing the water as necessary. If possible, add boiling water to the kettle so that the flow of steam is not interrupted. Continue this process for four or five hours.

After lifting the steaming box from the tripod, remove the splat. Lash the board into place on the forming jig with strong twine that will not stretch. The lashing should run back and forth, across the face of the board, in a zigzag pattern. Allow the piece to dry in the sun for two days. Then remove the lashing; the board should be ready to be attached to the chair. Trim the ends to length to allow them to fit into the notches on the inside of the front legs. Repeat the process for the second board.

**Metalwork**

The heads on the iron nails are the same size throughout the chair, although the lengths vary according to location. All the nails have heads with a diameter of ½ inch. Most of the nails appear to be about 2½ inches in length, but those that hold the curved splats to the back supports have to be considerably shorter. The two nails that hold the angle bracket to the seat support and to the kick panel must also be shorter than average, probably no more than 1½ inches in length.

The clinch, or large staple, that holds the two halves of the arm unit together is bent from a length of flat stock that is ¼ inch wide, ⅛ inch thick, and 4½ inches long. Bend the stock so that it forms three sides of a square, 1½ inches to the side. The metal stock from which this clinch is made is small enough that it should not require much heat to become malleable. The finished clinch should look very much like a giant staple. After the clinch is bent to shape, sharpen the ends to points.

**Finish**

Long years of wear and accumulated oils have colored this barrel chair a rich amber-black. An initial coat of golden stain, made from equal parts of golden oak stain, mahogany stain, and turpentine, followed by a second coat of very dark oak, or Jacobin, stain that has been brushed into the corners and recesses of the carvings and then wiped off, should give the desired color. A final treatment of several coats of boiled linseed oil will give the chair a durable finish.

# FRONT VIEW

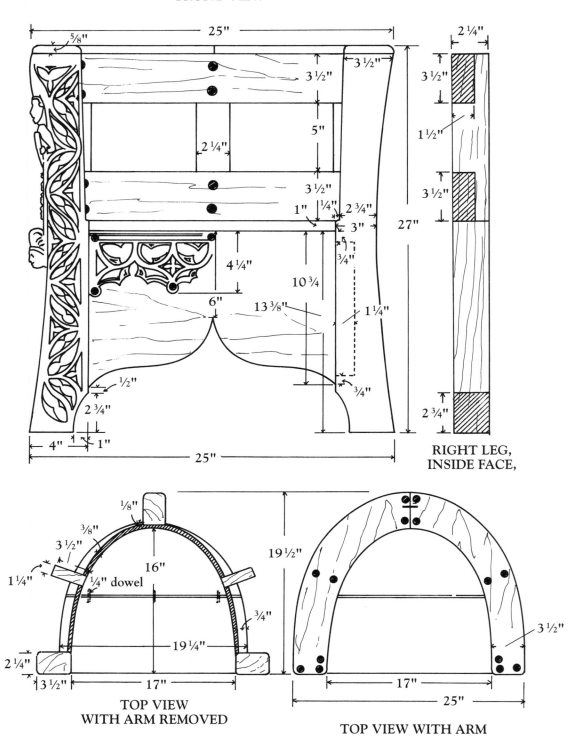

25"

5/8"

3½"     3½"

5"

2¼"

3½"

1"   ¼"   2¾"

3"

¾"

4¼"

10¾

6"     13⅜"     1¼"

27"

½"

2¾"

4"   1"

25"

2¼"

3½"

1½"

3½"

2¾"

**RIGHT LEG,
INSIDE FACE,**

⅛"

3/8"

3½"

1¼"     ¼" dowel     16"

¾"

2¼"     19¼"

3½"     17"

19½"

3½"

17"

25"

**TOP VIEW
WITH ARM REMOVED**

**TOP VIEW WITH ARM**

## BACK SUPPORT

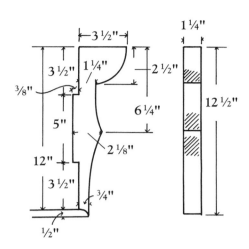

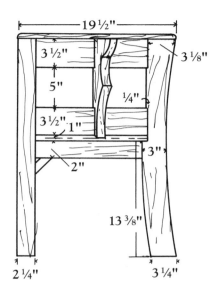

## SEAT AND SUPPORT, FRONT VIEW

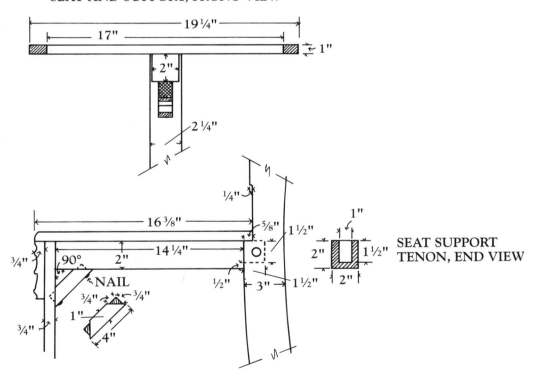

SEAT SUPPORT
TENON, END VIEW

NAIL

SEAT AND SUPPORT,
SIDE VIEW

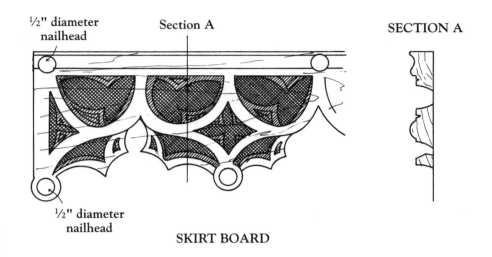

½" diameter nailhead

Section A

SECTION A

½" diameter nailhead

**SKIRT BOARD**

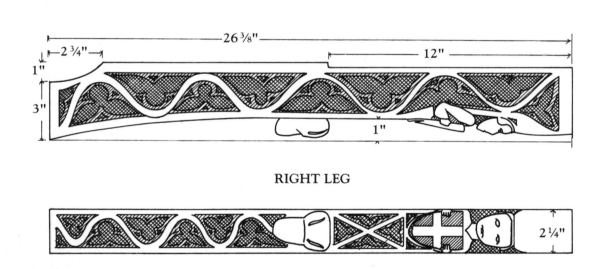

26 ³⁄₈"

2 ¾"

1"

3"

12"

1"

**RIGHT LEG**

2 ¼"

LEFT LEG

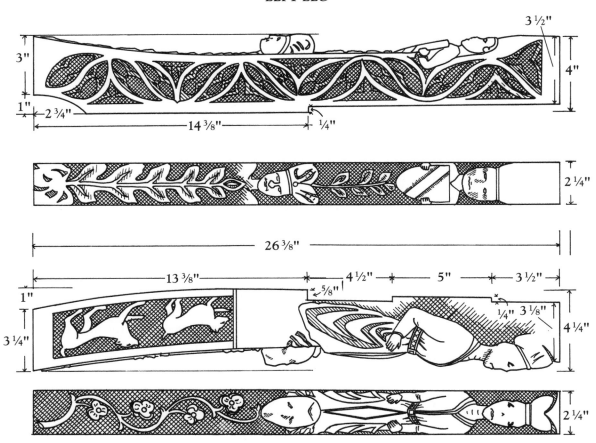

REAR LEG

# Furniture Locations

## BOLTON CASTLE
### (Writing Slope, Ambry Cupboard)

Bolton Castle has seen adventure and intrigue over the centuries. The powerful Scrope family, who once owned it, have produced both heroes and villains, including an outstanding archbishop of York and the traitorous Henry Lord Scope of Masham found in Shakespeare's play *Henry V*. First fortified in 1379, the castle has a checkered history. It served as a prison for Mary, Queen of Scots, for four months during her long years of imprisonment and had its roof burned off by Henry VIII's troops in retribution for its owner's part in resisting Henry's brutal suppression of the monasteries during the 1530s.

Bolton is one of the more complete medieval castles still in private hands. Although it is open to the public throughout the tourist season, Bolton has not been turned into a museum; it remains largely as it has been for centuries. Its location deep in the Yorkshire Dales undoubtedly makes Bolton one of the most picturesquely sited castles in all the British Isles.

For further information, write Bolton Castle, Leyburn, North Yorkshire DL8 4ET, England, or phone 1969-623-981 or fax 1969-623-332.

## CARLISLE CASTLE
### (Half-Tester Bed)

Originally constructed in the twelfth century to guard the border between England and Scotland, Carlisle Castle eventually grew to immense proportions. It looms over the northern edge of Carlisle like some red brick monster waiting to pounce on anyone foolish enough to challenge it.

Most of the rooms, which are furnished with fine reproductions of medieval furniture, are open to the public. Extensive displays provide a history of the turbulent life experienced by those on both sides of the border during the "great troubles" that plagued these countries from the time of the Norman conquest to the regime of the Stuarts.

## CLOISTERS COLLECTION, METROPOLITAN MUSEUM OF ART
### (Settle, Barrel Chair, and Worktable)

A trip to the Cloisters in New York City is an unparalleled experience. Housed in a collection of medieval ecclesiastical buildings transported from Europe at the end of the nineteenth century by John D. Rockefeller, the Cloisters boasts one of the most extensive collections of medieval religious objects in the world. After being mesmerized by art, furnishings, and architecture, do not miss the treasury where vestments, gold and silver plate, and a variety of reliquaries display the marvels of the medieval church.

Located at the northern tip of Manhattan Island in Fort Tryon Park. For more information, call (212) 923-3700.

## HADDON HALL
### (Paneled Coffer, Tax Box)

Located in the charming Derbyshire Peak countryside, Haddon is one of the most amazing medieval survivals in existence. Begun as a simple manor house in the twelfth century, it was licensed to construct its fortification walls, shortly after 1200, by the unhappy King John. Continuing life as a fortified manor, Haddon eventually evolved into the splendid Elizabethan country home that greets today's visitor. Now owned by the duke of Rutland, the lovingly restored Haddon is full of furnishings, tapestries (including one monumental piece presented by Queen Elizabeth), and the oddments of daily life in the Middle Ages and the Renaissance that are usually absent from a publicly owned museum. Haddon has been featured in such films as *The Princess Bride* and *Jane Eyre*.

For more information, write the Estate Office, Haddon Hall, Bakewell, Derbyshire DE45, 1LA, England, or phone 1629-812-855 or fax 1629-814-379.

## HEREFORD CATHEDRAL
### (Hewn-Timber Chest)
Located in the "marches," the borderlands between England and Wales, Hereford Cathedral is one of the architectural gems of western England. The main nave of the cathedral is still predominantly twelfth-century Norman in structure and design, with the side aisles being in the more highly decorated style of the fourteenth century.

As an added attraction, the cathedral has just completed construction of a new library building, which houses some of the most magnificent literary remnants to survive the dissolution of the monasteries and the Reformation. In addition to a number of medieval chests and coffers, there is one of the few remaining reliquaries built to hold relics of the murdered Thomas Becket. Additionally, there is a chained library considered to be the finest such collection in the British Isles. With over two hundred medieval manuscripts making up part of a much larger collection, the chained library is still in situ in its seventeenth-century shelves. Best of all, the room is open daily to the public.

Hereford also boasts the Mappa Mundi, the only complete surviving medieval map of the world. At 5 feet in height and over 3 feet in width, this is a most impressive example of how medieval man conceived his universe.

For more information, write Hereford Cathedral Library, 5 College Cloisters, Cathedral Close, Hereford HR1 2NG, England, or call 1432-359-880.

## MARY ROSE
### (Merrills Board)
When the *Mary Rose*, flagship of Henry VIII's navy, sank suddenly in a storm in 1545, she took to the bottom of Portsmouth harbor her entire crew of 415 with their belongings and equipment. Raised from the bottom of the harbor in the 1980s, with the support of Prince Charles, the great ship revealed over 13,000 artifacts of everyday life in Tudor England. Containing everything from leather shoes to great bronze cannons and a complete ship's kitchen, the *Mary Rose* exhibit provides greater insight into Tudor life than all the other museum displays of the period combined—an absolute "must see" on any trip to the south of England.

For more information, write the *Mary Rose* Trust, College Road, HM Naval Base, Portsmouth PO1 3LX, England, or phone 1705-705-521 or fax 1705-870-588.

## WARWICK CASTLE
### (Wheelbarrow)
Held as a castle since the Norman conquest, the present castle was built predominantly in the fourteenth century. Last having seen action during the English Civil War, Warwick somehow escaped being destroyed by Cromwell's cannons and was later converted into a stately home. Warwick wonderfully displays the variety of changes and adaptations that many castles underwent during their long history. Currently owned and operated by Madame Tussaud's Museums, Warwick is peopled by both costumed guides and frighteningly lifelike waxworks. The display showing the life and career of the conniving, manipulative earl of Warwick, known as "the Kingmaker," is particularly impressive.

For more information, write Warwick Castle, Warwick CV34 4EU, England, or telephone 1926-495-421.

## WINCHESTER CATHEDRAL
### (Church Pew)
Deceptively simple on the exterior, Winchester Cathedral has a rich and splendid history. Begun in 1079 as a humble Benedictine abbey church, Winchester boasts the longest central nave in Europe. With over a half-dozen distinct architectural styles, Winchester clearly shows the changing tastes of medieval England, as well as the church's ability to adapt to a changing world. Surviving the brutal destruction of the monasteries at the hands of Henry VIII in the 1530s, Winchester adapted to a new life as a secular church.

Of particular interest are a reredos screen in the perpendicular style, a chair used by bloody Queen Mary Tudor, and wonderful tomb effigies and statues of such monarchs as James I, who authorized the first standardized English language translation of the Bible, and Charles I, who lost his kingdom and his head to Oliver Cromwell and the Roundheads.

For additional information, write Winchester

Cathedral Office, 5 The Close, Winchester YO2 6LB, England, or telephone 1962-853-137.

## YORK MINSTER CATHEDRAL
### (Cathedral Cabon)

Magnificent York Minster Cathedral (properly, the Cathedral and Metropolitan Church of St. Peter in York) has been a site of worship for over 1300 years. There are records of a Christianized Roman bishop having a seat in York as early as A.D. 314, but the location of his church is unknown. A Norman cathedral was built on the site of the current minster in 1080 following the Normans' destruction of the wooden church that had stood there for over 450 years.

The present building was begun in 1253, and over the next 250 years the Norman cathedral was transformed into the soaring Gothic masterpiece that still dominates York's skyline. The minster is the largest Gothic cathedral north of Italy, with a seating capacity in the nave of 2,000 people. When the choir and transepts are used for additional seating during Christmas and Easter services, more than 4,000 people can be accommodated. With its soaring architecture, magnificent carvings, sumptuous treasury, and medieval and Renaissance tomb effigies, including St. William's shrine, York Minster attracts over 2.25 million visitors each year.

Situated in the heart of the medieval walled city of York, the minster is open daily from 7:00 A.M. until 8:30 P.M. in the summer and from 7:00 A.M. until 5:00 P.M. in the winter. For further information, telephone 1904-639-347 or fax 1904-613-049, or write to the Visitors Department, York Minster, York YO1 2JF, England.

168

# SOURCES OF SUPPLIES

## MEDIEVAL WOODWORKING SUPPLIES

### USA

**Tremont Nail**
P.O. Box 111
Wareham, MA 02571
(508) 295-0038
*Makes and supplies a variety of historical reproductions of hand-forged nails. Send for a catalog.*

**Jamestown Distributors**
28 Narragansett Ave.
P.O. Box 348
Jamestown, RI 02835
(401) 423-2520 or, in US only, (800) 423-0030
*Supplies traditional boat-building nails that look very much like hand-forged ones. Available in 50-pound lots only, but come in every size from 1 to 6 inches. Also good selection of tools. Catalog available.*

**T. W. Moran**
Livonia Smithery
3913 Clay St.
Livonia, NY 14487
(716) 367-2130 or e-mail TWM13@stellar1.com
*Good-quality smithery willing to quote prices on any of the hardware in either of our books.*

### UNITED KINGDOM

**Chris Blythman**
The Flat
Brook House Farm
Middleton, Ludlow
Shropshire SY8 2DZ
1584-878-591
*Chris produces some of the best-looking medieval metalwork we have found in England, and he is willing to undertake commissions for any of the hardware shown in our books. Just send him your request (including a photocopy of the hardware you want), and he will be glad to quote you a price.*

**Period House Shop**
141 Corve St.
Ludlow, Shropshire SY8 2PG
1584-877-276
*This marvelous store carries a wide variety of period nails, forged hinges, and other accoutrements for period furniture and houses. It has a charming period-looking catalog available on request and will ship anywhere.*

## SALVAGED LUMBER AND TIMBER

### USA

**North Fields Restoration**
Hampton Falls, NH 03884
(603) 926-5383

**Architectural Timber & Millwork**
35 Mount Warner Rd.
P.O. Box 719
Hadley, MA 01035
(413) 586-3045

### UNITED KINGDOM

**Fenby M. S. Timber**
Windhill Farm
Flyingdales, North Yorkshire YO22 4QL
1947-880-419

## CALLIGRAPHY AND ARTWORK

### USA

**Brendan's Banners**
c/o Bob Rich
1211 Logan Ave.
Tyrone, PA 16686
(814) 684-1232
*Bob Rich produces some of the finest reproduction painted wall hangings that we have found anywhere. Subjects and banner dimensions executed to your specifications.*

**Gabriel Guild**
c/o Karen Gorst
6 North Pearle St. (404E)
Port Chester, NY 10573
(914) 935-9362
*Gabriel Guild produces some of the finest available custom calligraphy and illumination and occasionally deals in original manuscript pages.*

### UNITED KINGDOM

**Tony Barton**
4 Ramsey Ave.
Bishopthorpe, York YO23 1SQ
1904-709-170
*Mr. Barton produced the wall hangings at Barley Hall, shown in the photo that accompanies our article on medieval decorating. He will undertake work by commission.*

## SCULPTURE

### USA

**Design Toscano**
17 E. Campbell St.
Arlington Heights, IL 60005
*Design Toscano manufactures and markets high-quality statuary, sculpture, and tapestries. Catalog $4.00.*

# BASKETS

## USA

**Mountain Trail Baskets**
631 Valencia Rd.
Mars, PA 16046
   *Mountain Trail weaves a wide variety of historically accurate baskets.*

## UNITED KINGDOM

**I. W. Taylor & Son**
Ings Road
Ulleskelf, Tadcaster
Yorkshire LS24 9SS
1937-832-138
   *Mr. Taylor is a fourth-generation basket maker and one of the finest in his trade in England.*

# ARMS AND ARMOR

The following companies produce their own high-quality medieval armor, blades, and battle regalia.

## USA

**Illusion Armory**
21618 N. 9th Ave.
Suite H
Phoenix AZ 85027
(602) 582-1355

**MacKenzie-Smith Medieval Arms & Armour**
c/o Robert MacKenzie
P.O. Box 3315
Truckee, CA 96160

## UNITED KINGDOM

**Dave Hewit**
White Rose Armoury
Unit 59
Stavely Workshop
Hollingwood, Chesterfield S43 2PE
1246-475-782

**Peter Leight**
The Old Barn
Thornton Le Fen
Lincoln LN4 4YN
1205-286-836
   *Mr. Leight not only does commercial work, but also executes museum-quality reproduction and restoration work for the Royal Armouries Collection.*

# METRIC CONVERSIONS

## INCHES TO MILLIMETERS

| in. | mm | in. | mm |
|---|---|---|---|
| 1 | 25.4 | 51 | 1295.4 |
| 2 | 50.8 | 52 | 1320.8 |
| 3 | 76.2 | 53 | 1346.2 |
| 4 | 101.6 | 54 | 1371.6 |
| 5 | 127.0 | 55 | 1397.0 |
| 6 | 152.4 | 56 | 1422.4 |
| 7 | 177.8 | 57 | 1447.8 |
| 8 | 203.2 | 58 | 1473.2 |
| 9 | 228.6 | 59 | 1498.6 |
| 10 | 254.0 | 60 | 1524.0 |
| 11 | 279.4 | 61 | 1549.4 |
| 12 | 304.8 | 62 | 1574.8 |
| 13 | 330.2 | 63 | 1600.2 |
| 14 | 355.6 | 64 | 1625.6 |
| 15 | 381.0 | 65 | 1651.0 |
| 16 | 406.4 | 66 | 1676.4 |
| 17 | 431.8 | 67 | 1701.8 |
| 18 | 457.2 | 68 | 1727.2 |
| 19 | 482.6 | 69 | 1752.6 |
| 20 | 508.0 | 70 | 1778.0 |
| 21 | 533.4 | 71 | 1803.4 |
| 22 | 558.8 | 72 | 1828.8 |
| 23 | 584.2 | 73 | 1854.2 |
| 24 | 609.6 | 74 | 1879.6 |
| 25 | 635.0 | 75 | 1905.0 |
| 26 | 660.4 | 76 | 1930.4 |
| 27 | 685.8 | 77 | 1955.8 |
| 28 | 711.2 | 78 | 1981.2 |
| 29 | 736.6 | 79 | 2006.6 |
| 30 | 762.0 | 80 | 2032.0 |
| 31 | 787.4 | 81 | 2057.4 |
| 32 | 812.8 | 82 | 2082.8 |
| 33 | 838.2 | 83 | 2108.2 |
| 34 | 863.6 | 84 | 2133.6 |
| 35 | 889.0 | 85 | 2159.0 |
| 36 | 914.4 | 86 | 2184.4 |
| 37 | 939.8 | 87 | 2209.8 |
| 38 | 965.2 | 88 | 2235.2 |
| 39 | 990.6 | 89 | 2260.6 |
| 40 | 1016.0 | 90 | 2286.0 |
| 41 | 1041.4 | 91 | 2311.4 |
| 42 | 1066.8 | 92 | 2336.8 |
| 43 | 1092.2 | 93 | 2362.2 |
| 44 | 1117.6 | 94 | 2387.6 |
| 45 | 1143.0 | 95 | 2413.0 |
| 46 | 1168.4 | 96 | 2438.4 |
| 47 | 1193.8 | 97 | 2463.8 |
| 48 | 1219.2 | 98 | 2489.2 |
| 49 | 1244.6 | 99 | 2514.6 |
| 50 | 1270.0 | 100 | 2540.0 |

The above table is exact on the basis: 1 in. = 25.4 mm

## U.S. TO METRIC

1 inch = 2.540 centimeters
1 foot = .305 meter
1 yard = .914 meter
1 mile = 1.609 kilometers

## METRIC TO U.S.

1 millimeter = .039 inch
1 centimeter = .394 inch
1 meter = 3.281 feet or 1.094 yards
1 kilometer = .621 mile

## INCH-METRIC EQUIVALENTS

| Fraction | Decimal Equivalent Customary (in.) | Metric (mm) | Fraction | Decimal Equivalent Customary (in.) | Metric (mm) |
|---|---|---|---|---|---|
| 1/64 | .015 | 0.3969 | 33/64 | .515 | 13.0969 |
| 1/32 | .031 | 0.7938 | 17/32 | .531 | 13.4938 |
| 3/64 | .046 | 1.1906 | 35/64 | .546 | 13.8906 |
| 1/16 | .062 | 1.5875 | 9/16 | .562 | 14.2875 |
| 5/64 | .078 | 1.9844 | 37/64 | .578 | 14.6844 |
| 3/32 | .093 | 2.3813 | 19/32 | .593 | 15.0813 |
| 7/64 | .109 | 2.7781 | 39/64 | .609 | 15.4781 |
| 1/8 | .125 | 3.1750 | 5/8 | .625 | 15.8750 |
| 9/64 | .140 | 3.5719 | 41/64 | .640 | 16.2719 |
| 5/32 | .156 | 3.9688 | 21/32 | .656 | 16.6688 |
| 11/64 | .171 | 4.3656 | 43/64 | .671 | 17.0656 |
| 3/16 | .187 | 4.7625 | 11/16 | .687 | 17.4625 |
| 13/64 | .203 | 5.1594 | 45/64 | .703 | 17.8594 |
| 7/32 | .218 | 5.5563 | 23/32 | .718 | 18.2563 |
| 15/64 | .234 | 5.9531 | 47/64 | .734 | 18.6531 |
| 1/4 | .250 | 6.3500 | 3/4 | .750 | 19.0500 |
| 17/64 | .265 | 6.7469 | 49/64 | .765 | 19.4469 |
| 9/32 | .281 | 7.1438 | 25/32 | .781 | 19.8438 |
| 19/64 | .296 | 7.5406 | 51/64 | .796 | 20.2406 |
| 5/16 | .312 | 7.9375 | 13/16 | .812 | 20.6375 |
| 21/64 | .328 | 8.3384 | 53/64 | .828 | 21.0344 |
| 11/32 | .343 | 8.7313 | 27/32 | .843 | 21.4313 |
| 23/64 | .359 | 9.1281 | 55/64 | .859 | 21.8281 |
| 3/8 | .375 | 9.5250 | 7/8 | .875 | 22.2250 |
| 25/64 | .390 | 9.9219 | 57/64 | .890 | 22.6219 |
| 13/32 | .406 | 10.3188 | 29/32 | .906 | 23.0188 |
| 27/64 | .421 | 10.7156 | 59/64 | .921 | 23.4156 |
| 7/16 | .437 | 11.1125 | 15/16 | .937 | 23.8125 |
| 29/64 | .453 | 11.5094 | 61/64 | .953 | 24.2094 |
| 15/32 | .468 | 11.9063 | 31/32 | .968 | 24.6063 |
| 31/64 | .484 | 12.3031 | 63/64 | .984 | 25.0031 |
| 1/2 | .500 | 12.7000 | 1 | 1.000 | 25.4000 |

# INDEX